O Freedom!

O Freedom!

*Afro-American
Emancipation
Celebrations*

William H. Wiggins, Jr.

THE UNIVERSITY OF

Tennessee Press

Publication of this book has been aided by a grant from the American Council of Learned Societies from funds provided by the Andrew W. Mellon Foundation.

The paper in this book meets the minimum requirements of the American National Standard for Permanence of Paper for Printed Library Materials. ∞ The binding materials have been chosen for strength and durability.

Library of Congress Cataloging-in-Publication Data

Wiggins, William H., 1934–
 O Freedom! : Afro-American Emancipation celebrations.
 Bibliography: p.
 Includes index.
 1. Emancipation proclamation—Centennial celebrations, etc. I. Title.
E453.W65 1987   973.7'14   86-14597
ISBN 0-87049-520-8 (alk. paper)

For my parents Mabel Leora Washington Wiggins
and William Hawthorne Wiggins, Sr.,
a.k.a. Mama Wig and Daddy Wig

Contents

Illustrations

Preface

When I began my research into Afro-American freedom celebrations, there were no scholarly books in print on the subject. Aside from a meager list of articles,[1] such freedom observances had generated little interest within America's intellectual community. John Hope Franklin's *The Emancipation Proclamation,*[2] which chronicled President Lincoln's moods, thoughts, and actions during his writing of that document, and J. Mason Brewer's *Juneteenth,*[3] a collection of jokes and folktales often told on this southwestern celebration of Emancipation, are two excellent examples of this scholarly lethargy toward the subject. Neither writer paid significant attention to Afro-Americans' reactions to freedom. Franklin and Brewer mention celebratory reactions to Emancipation only as afterthoughts. Their studies contain no hint of the existence of the dramatic proclamation readings, historical pageants, colorful parades, all-night barbecues, exciting ballgames, or the myriad other customs and rituals with which the masses of Afro-Americans have celebrated their freedom during the last century and a quarter. A Juneteenth celebrant, summing up this scholarly snub, wrote, "I grew up in the tradition, and I am surprised to know that scholars have ignored this event."[4]

The celebrants themselves entertain a wide range of attitudes toward these freedom observances. For a significant number of Afro-Americans, their particular local independence observance—whose date varied from region to region—was "the biggest day in the United States" and held more cultural significance for them than July 4th. In 1863 Frederick Douglass called January 1 "the most memorable day in American Annals" before concluding that: "The fourth of July was great, but the first of January, when we consider it in all its relations and bearings is incomparably greater."[5] Many celebrants whom I interviewed shared Douglass's point of view.

For Mrs. Lula Bass, "the 28th of May was far more exciting than the 4th of July."[6] Mrs. Mary Morris recalled the first time she realized August 4 was Emancipation Day: ". . . somebody told me. I said, 'Well, what's the big holiday?' And they said, 'Well, that's the Negroes' Independence Day,' you know. And, you know, 'we ain't got no business celebrating the 4th of July; we weren't freed. It wasn't our Independence.' This is their reasoning, you know, that August 4 was freedom day for them."[7] Dr. Jimmy Williams remembered that when he was growing up in Columbus, Mississippi: "We looked upon the 8th of May as our day. The 4th of July never really had any real significance for us."[8] Miss Sue Owings wrote: "The legend has it that a Negro got a mule in Washington and arrived in [each?] town on June 19th with the Emancipation Proclamation. So that July 4th is whites' Independence and June'teen [is] Negro Independence Day."[9] Mr. Jerry Wilson summed up this divided loyalty: "Well, as a patriot and a citizen I celebrate the 4th of July, but from a race standpoint I still like the 19th of June."[10]

Another large segment of Afro-American society does not ascribe as much social significance to freedom holidays, however. Many characterize them as "just a ballgame and a picnic," a day for "fun and frolic and red soda water and watermelon,"[11] "a second Christmas," or another "nigger day," a cultural term for good times. Senility is robbing a growing number of older celebrants of their remembrances of how these freedom events were observed in the past. One retired schoolteacher confessed that she was "bothered that none of the few remaining relatives and friends of my age could even remember the 8th of August."[12] A few younger "blacks have been ashamed of the 19th of June"[13] and other observances.

Somewhere, despite the scholars' neglect and the celebrants' mixed attitudes, I felt I would find answers to all the as yet unposed cultural, historical, social, and political questions regarding these freedom celebrations. From June 1972 to February 1973, supported by a Rockefeller Foundation Grant, I logged more than twenty thousand miles in the family Volkswagen, crisscrossing America's South, Southwest, Midwest, and Northeast to conduct interviews and to observe celebrations of June 19 in Rockdale, Texas, August 8 in Allensville and Crofton, Kentucky, January 1 in Columbus, Georgia, and February 1 in Philadelphia, in search of answers to these questions.

I used several methods of collecting field research data. Throughout the day I constantly entered valuable information into my daily log, a 98-cent spiral notebook. In this field-work diary I recorded interviews of celebrants who refused to be taped, the names, addresses, and telephone numbers of new informants, bibliographic references from area libraries and newspapers, spur-of-the-moment ideas, travel routes, and the costs of food and lodging. The next morning I would always review the last day's notes in order to get some sort of direction for the day.

I was governed by a collect-all-you-can philosophy at each celebration site. I took over three hundred black-and-white and color slide pictures. Baseball scorecards, raffle tickets, posters, programs, and flyers were some of the celebration memorabilia that I dutifully collected and labeled. I also used two different types of tape-recording technique during my observations of the four celebrations. The January 1st, February 1st, and June 19th services that I attended were recorded in their entirety with either a reel-to-reel tape or with several 90-minute cassette tapes. I also conducted a series of five-to-fifteen-minute interviews with a random cross section of celebrants. Transcriptions of the former enabled me to study the structure of these observances, while the interviews gave me a true reading of what the celebrants thought about the celebrations.

I also devised and used two questionnaires during my field work. The first model was a cumbersome six-page document that I distributed before morning worship at Miles Chapel Christian Methodist Episcopal (CME) Church in Little Rock, Arkansas, and during classes at Jarvis Christian College in Hawkins, Texas; Texas College in Tyler, Texas; and Houston-Tilloston College in Austin, Texas. I handed out a streamlined one-page questionnaire at the January 1st and February 1st celebrations I attended. Both of these instruments, especially the shorter version, gave me the addresses of several new interviewees, as well as some idea of the geographical regions for the various celebrations.

Between the four field trips, I telephoned or wrote to the new interviewees and contacts that I had collected during my last trip. I collected valuable oral and printed celebration data through my correspondence. Celebration sponsors, such as August first's Mr. Ted Powell and February first's Mr. Emanuel Wright, sent me numerous copies of old celebration programs, posters, and flyers. Mr. Wright's and Mr. Powell's letters also contained fascinating descriptions of the histories and activities of their celebrations. A telephone call to the Texas Legislative Council earned me a four-page memorandum on "Emancipation Day in Texas as a State Holiday," copies of the 1972 House Resolution 23 which honored "the Black people of Texas" and recognized "'Juneteenth' as an annual holiday of significance" and of the 1978 House Bill 1016 which made Juneteenth a legal state holiday in Texas, an address by Representative Al Edwards, the bill's sponsor, to the Texas House of Representatives, and three "related clippings" on Juneteenth from area newspapers.[14]

My most successful library research has been accomplished by sifting through microfilms of old Afro-American newspapers. Through trial and error, I finally devised a research methodology that was effective and simple: all I had to do was match the newspaper (*The Atlanta Daily World*) with the celebration common to that geographical region (January 1st) in order to reap reams of celebration data. A wealth of front page stories, editorials, political cartoons, photographs, and complete speech texts were recovered through this method. The titles of celebration speeches and pageants were collected by systematically reading the community news pages of these newspapers. National Afro-American weeklies, such as the *Chicago Defender* and the *Pittsburgh Courier,* devote several pages to local news from such small, southern black communities as Social Circle, Georgia. More often than not, these nameless local reporters included the speaker's name, sermon title, and celebration site of their local freedom celebration. And the systematic reading of all the letters to the editor during a particular celebration's observance month also turned up a few letters on the subject.

I also had some success retrieving celebration data from the *Congressional Record.* The National Freedom Day debate, personal remarks of Afro-American representatives on Negro History Week and Juneteenth, and the several years of congressional debates and hearings over the issue of making the birth date of Dr. Martin Luther King, Jr., a national holiday were among the subjects of interest. The King holiday materials were catalogued in the *Congressional Record Index.* However, I was able to retrieve my information on Juneteenth, National Freedom Day, and Negro History Week only by closely reading those issues of the *Congressional Record* that coincided with the anniversaries of these celebrations.

This intellectual quest has not been a lonely one. Henry Glassie, John F. Moe, Fred McElroy, Roger D. Abrahams, Gladys-Marie Fry, Cam Collins, Peter Wood, Jerry Davis, Marilyn White, Roby Cogswell, Judy McCulloh, John McGuigan, Anne Schockley, Phyllis May, Bess Lomax Hawes, Stanley Warren, Dan Ben-Amos, Adrienne Seward, Robert Chrisman, and Richard M. Dorson are just a few of the scholars who took the time either to write flattering letters of recommendation, to offer helpful suggestions and encouraging words when I needed them most, to read and edit my rough drafts, to send me seminal celebration sayings, articles, and interviews, or to just give me "that look" when we greeted one another at all the American Folklore Society meetings that have been held since I began writing this book.

My family has been most supportive. My parents, my in-laws, Mr. and Mrs. Dallas and Mary Slaughter, Auntie Leila Blakey, and Mr. and Mrs. Anthony and Effie Lewis, Sr., are just some of the relatives who either gave me food and lodging, provided me with fresh interview contacts, found old celebration memorabilia for me, or allowed their food to cool as I made yet another "important point" about my research. My children, Wesley and Mary Ellyn, handed out celebration questionnaires. And my wife, Janice, did it all. She packed my bags, made my travel reservations, prepared field-trip lunches, kept the house quiet when I was writing, traveled with me when she could, read my rough drafts, and always let me know that she believed in my ability to write this book.

The weaknesses and shortcomings of this study are mine, not theirs.

*And even if the American people in the United States didn't
really set that day aside for us, I believe they owe it to us
anyway. . . . [Because] they really did have slaves. They* did do
*that. And since they celebrate their day for they freedom, then
they ought to give the colored man a day for his freedom. It
should be a red spot on the calendar and really took aside for.*
                                        Mr. Paul Darby, November 1972.

Introduction

President Abraham Lincoln's issuance of the Emancipation Proclamation
initiated a series of celebrations among the newly freed slaves. An Afro-
American editorial provides the cultural outsider with an idea of the history, geographical scope, and civic evolution of these observances:

> Every year since the signing of that celebrated document, driving
> slavery from the shores of this country, there has been staged among our
> group some sort of an anniversary of grateful expression. Hardly any
> individual or specific organization can claim credit for the initiation of
> this practice, for it had its beginning among the early freedmen in every
> state involved in the slavery question.
> Ever since Uncle Ned perched upon a shuck-pile, strummed off from
> his fiddle the old air—"Befor' I'd be a slave, I'd be buried in my grave,"
> setting the black feet to pranching in this historic jubilation that started
> them off on the road to a fuller and more wholesome freedom, there have
> been annual celebrations.
> The movement started in country churches, old schoolhouses and
> lodge rooms and from the Carolina lagoons across to where the great west
> started, the leaders of that day have staged celebrations meant to give vim
> and spirit to the new freedom that had come to our people.
> Beginning at first as mere celebrations which rehearsed many incidents
> of torture and privations, these functions have taken on a new order.
> Turning from narrations of hard and bitter experiences in the memories of
> the slave, they have been those schools of citizenship and the training of a
> new group in the army of struggle for the realization of first-class
> citizenship for all people.[1]

Although this editorial concludes with the assertion that "January 1st is
the official day for these mass celebrations," an article from a program
celebrating February 1st underscores the fact that there is no such clear
consensus among Afro-Americans as to which should be "the official day."

Major Wright [founder of National Freedom Day], too, knew of the confusion among the colored people as to what they should celebrate for their Emancipation; he suggested that February 1, would be the answer. Many dates have been and are celebrated; some celebrate August 1; some in September, some January 1, and others think that they should celebrate March 5, the so-called Attucks Day; and some even think they should celebrate February 12, the birthday of Abraham Lincoln.[2]

Celebrants who grew up annually celebrating one of these days express a lifelong preference for their childhood observance date. An Oklahoma celebrant of June 19th wrote, "'My father was born in Arkansas and he preferred to celebrate Aug. 4th.' (I never learned why.)"[3] An Indiana celebrant of September 22nd noted that Afro-American immigrants to his state from Kentucky often carried "the custom of observing the 8th of August" with them.[4] And a January 1st celebration speaker compared the attitudes of northern and southern celebrants of this date: "It was a very enthusiastic thing, for indeed they had enough southerners there to recognize what was happening. But the original older Brooklynites didn't pay it too much attention. But the southern Brooklynites jumped in there and we had a great time."[5]

Some celebrants are genuinely surprised when they move into a region of the country where their celebration date is not observed: Dean William H. Ammons told me:

> The first time I remember not celebrating the Juneteenth—after I reached the age of twenty-one—it was after I was drafted into the army. And . . . I was in New York I believe. And they didn't celebrate it there and it began to wonder me. And I began to ask people, "Aren't you going to celebrate the Juneteenth? When is the Juneteenth celebration?" And everybody wanted to know what the Juneteenth was. And I had to sit down and explain it to them as to what it was.[6]

Similarly, Mr. Robert Lee Perry, who was born and raised in a North Carolina community that celebrated July 4th, was introduced to Juneteenth when he moved to Texas and married a Waco woman. He told me: "When I come into Texas I didn't know [about Juneteenth] and I asked my wife. She said 'I'll tell you. . . . The 19th of June, that's our Emancipation Day.'"[7] And Professor Joseph L. Grimes, who grew up celebrating July 4th in St. Louis, was introduced to Juneteenth in 1964 while teaching summer school at Prairie View A&M College. He recalled that on the "18th of June the students said they were not having classes on the . . . 19th of June. So I wanted to know why [*chuckles*]. So they said this was the black man's

Emancipation, and it was very funny to me. I laughed. . . . [But] I noticed everyone just didn't come to class."[8]

This loyalty to a particular celebration has produced a group of celebration regions. Rare indeed are the cases such as Burton, Texas, where Afro-Americans celebrate August 1st instead of June 19th—the preference in the rest of the state. These exceptions appear on the cultural maps that I constructed out of cardboard, oil company road maps, and colored straight pins much like a single stalk of corn in the midst of a wheat field. September 22nd is observed as the day of celebration in the northern border states of Illinois, Indiana, and Ohio. January 1st, which was initially celebrated in New York City and Boston and in all of the deep South slave-holding states of Alabama, Georgia, North Carolina, South Carolina, and Virginia, has spread into such neighboring southern states as Tennessee and Maryland; it was also carried north by Afro-Americans during the 1910 urban migration. June 19th, which was originally celebrated in east Texas, western Louisiana, southwestern Arkansas, and southern Oklahoma, has also been transplanted into California by Afro-Americans who moved west during World War II. August 4th and 8th are celebrated in northcentral Tennessee, southwestern Kentucky, northeastern Arkansas, central Oklahoma, southeastern Missouri, and southwestern Illinois. August 1st is annually observed in Windsor, Ontario, Canada. May 8th is celebrated in eastern Mississippi. May 20th is observed throughout the state of Florida. May 28th and 29th celebrations are annually held in numerous Alabama and Georgia towns that border the Chattahoochee River. And February 1st is celebrated in Philadelphia.

Historically speaking, the first of these celebrations was held on January 1, 1801, to commemorate the abolition of the foreign slave trade in America.[9] The most recently initiated observance was begun on February 1, 1940, to honor the ratification of the Thirteenth Amendment.[10] During this 132-year period, divergent historical circumstances have given rise to at least fifteen different Emancipation celebrations. In addition to the two above-mentioned events, five other edict-based celebrations and the legislation they commemorate are: July 4, 1827, the termination of slavery in the state of New York;[11] August 1, 1834, the abolition of English slavery in the West Indies;[12] April 16, 1862, the end of slavery in the District of Columbia;[13] and November 1, 1864, the date that Maryland issued a constitutional decree eliminating slavery.[14]

Four celebrations began with the issuance of various freedom proclamations. The May 9th celebration dates from 1862, when General David

Hunter, commander of the Department of the South from March 31 through August 22, 1862, issued an order on that day freeing all slaves in South Carolina, Georgia, and Florida.[15] September 22 is celebrated because on that date, in 1862, President Abraham Lincoln issued his "preliminary proclamation" which gave the seceding states one hundred days to abandon their pro-slavery position.[16] On January 1, 1863, Lincoln issued his historic Emancipation Proclamation and set in motion the hallowed "Day of Days celebration."[17] And on June 19, 1865, General Gordon Granger landed at Galveston, Texas, and read a governmental order freeing all of the slaves in east Texas and thereby initiating Juneteenth celebrations.[18]

Jerry Rescue Day in Syracuse, New York, began on October 1, 1851, when a group of white citizens freed and sent to Canada a slave named Jerry.[19]

The geneologies of the remaining seven celebrations are not easily traced. Like many of their slave celebrants, these celebrations have no recorded date of birth. And, just as the parentage of many slaves is undocumented, the historical circumstances which gave birth to these events are also not known. They cannot all trace their lineages back to a congressional act, a heroic feat of abolition, or a presidential proclamation. Their celebrants simply say that on some past May 5, 8, 20, 22, 28, 29, or on August 4 or 8, their ancestors were freed.

Almost a century and a quarter of annual celebration have fashioned these freedom jubilees into three distinguishable types of observances, whose structural and conceptual origins can be traced back historically to such earlier slave celebrations on Election Day, Pinkster, John Canoe, and Christmas. January 1st celebrations, which are traditionally held in a church, are primarily sacred celebrations that feature prayers, sermons, dramatic readings of the Emancipation Proclamation, and the singing of "Lift Every Voice and Sing," the Afro-American national anthem. August 8th celebrations, which are normally held in a community park or on church lawns are secular celebrations, characterized by baseball games, barbecues, excessive alcohol-drinking, and dancing. And some June 19th, August 1st, and September 22nd celebrations, whose multiple rituals are observed in community auditoriums and open fields, are a part of a third variety of celebration that combines elements from both the sacred and secular.

I have arranged my study of these celebrations into six chapters. Chapter 1, "Following the Freedom Trail," is a condensation of my June 19th,

August 8th, January 1st, and February 1st field trips into one continuous narrative. Each celebration is fully described, and celebrants are quoted liberally in order to give a vivid image of these respective celebrations. I also share the emotions I experienced during this year of field work.

Chapter 2, "The Roots and Fruits of Emancipation Celebrations," explores both the cultural parentage and progeny of these celebrations. Earlier slave holidays are analyzed to determine how they have influenced the structure of Emancipation celebrations. Contemporary celebrations such as Black History Month (née Negro History Week), Black Expo, and Black Music Month are also studied in order to assess how much they owe to these freedom celebrations.

Chapter 3, "The Afro-American Saga," studies *Up From Slavery, Out of the Darkness Into the Light,* and several other spiritual-based celebration pageants in order to demonstrate how they effectively convey each phase of the four-part Afro-American saga of a lost, glorious African past, a bitterly endured American slavery, a joyous Emancipation, and a never-ending struggle for ultimate freedom.

Chapter 4, "A Circus of Symbols," examines the celebrations' various rituals, customs, games, cuisine, and verbal expressions in order to demonstrate how these observances annually provide their celebrants with a barrage of tactile, visual, oral, and olfactory symbols that reaffirm their sense of "down home" and their ultimate worth as free human beings.

Chapter 5, "The Politics of Protest," explores the persistent political role played by these celebrations. Celebration resolutions, proclamations, petitions, voter-registration drives, and other political stratagems are analyzed to show the continuing major political impact that these celebrations have had upon the American body politic.

Chapter 6, "An Encore of Afro-American Freedom," concludes my study with an analysis of how the birth date of Dr. Martin Luther King, Jr., evolved from an informal post-civil-rights era observance to a formal, contemporary national holiday. This chapter will explore the cultural and ideological ties between the successful movement to make Dr. King's birthday a legal holiday and earlier efforts by celebrants of Emancipation to have one of their freedom celebrations declared a national holiday.

In terms of style, I address each informant as Mr., Mrs., or Miss. This bestowing of titles may be awkward at times, but I feel that it allows me to show my respect for these Americans who have been denied this simple social courtesy for so long.

O Freedom!

*I ain't telling you nothing. You're gonna
have to dig for your information like I did.*

Juneteenth celebrant (1972)

Following the Freedom Trail

My research began with four field trips. In June of 1972 I drove over twelve hundred Volkswagen-punishing miles to attend a Juneteenth celebration in Rockdale, Texas. In August of that same year I witnessed an August 8th Emancipation homecoming in Allensville, Kentucky. New Year's Day, 1973, found me and my family participating in the annual Emancipation Day service in Columbus, Georgia. And thirty days later I was in Philadelphia, Pennsylvania, observing a National Freedom Day celebration. Although they occurred more than a decade ago, I still find myself reliving some of the myriad personal experiences of these four freedom celebration journeys.

The road to Rockdale wound past numerous icons of southern life and culture. Tennessee cotton fields, their green bolls still closed like unopened rosebuds, were silent symbols of the region's economy. The Arkansas rice paddies, with their willowy, green shoots bowing in the wake of the highway's traffic, were gentle reminders of the impact of African slaves on the local agronomy. And Texas melon patches, endless acres of gnarled vines, broad leaves, and ripening fruit, conjured up images of the region's racial stereotypes.

There were other reminders of slavery and Jim Crow poverty. Crossing the churning, muddy Mississippi triggered thoughts of slavery and the horrors of being sold "down the river." In all of the southern states I passed abandoned shotgun shacks, whose warped gray walls and sagging russet-rusted roofs poignantly symbolized the region's gripping poverty and ruthless segregation.

I stopped in Houston long enough to rendezvous with my Juneteenth guides and family friends, Reverend and Mrs. J.L. Parks. After quickly shifting my suitcase, camera, and tape recorder into the trunk of their larger Chevrolet and parking my Volkswagen in their garage, we headed for Mrs. Parks's farm, which was located on the outskirts of Ennis, Texas.

Déjà vu rode with us on this leg of our trip. My parents had taught at nearby Prairie View A&M College in the late 1930s. Glimpses of my Texas childhood flashed back to me as I viewed the roadside melon stands on the outskirts of such area towns as Cypress and Hockley. Everything about them looked so familiar: purple stalks of sugarcane leaning against white-washed walls; bushel baskets of fresh tomatoes, green beans, okra, corn, greens, and other vegetables set on crude, handmade tables; and neatly stacked mounds of watermelons—both the oblong, two-toned green, jagged-striped, and the round, dark green variety—towered over all this produce. Propped against the bases of these fruit towers were "red ripe watermelon" signs, printed in uneven, whitewash brush-lettering on torn pieces of cardboard boxes; and evenly cut scarlet melon halves, glistening in the hot sun, were drawing both customers and flies.

As we passed a Hempstead produce stand, a boyhood incident burst forth from my subconsciousness like a clap of summer thunder. Thirty summers earlier, at another Hempstead farmer's roadside stand, I had

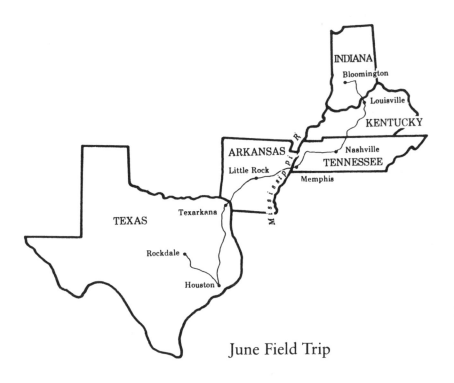

June Field Trip

bolted from my mother's side, scrambled over to the melon pile, thrown my body in a bear hug over one of the larger melons, and begged, "Momma, please buy me this watermelon. Please, Momma, please." My naive antics amused the white cronies of the stand manager, causing one of them to chuckle, "Sambo really loves that melon." Angered by the farmer's pejorative remark, my mother replied tartly, "His name is NOT Sambo!" She also derived some sense of personal satisfaction from ordering the manager to "Put that melon in the trunk of my car!" as she paid for the purchase with a flourish. The family still laughs about this childhood incident that initiated the family custom of marking my birthday with a watermelon instead of a cake. As we drove by, I smiled faintly and wondered if that stand was located on or near the same spot where my boyhood drama had been acted out.

This rich, black land, with its freshly plowed rows glistening in the hot afternoon sun like rolls of licorice in a candy store's lighted display case, also stirred bittersweet memories in Mrs. Parks. She recalled picking cotton in these same fields in 1925 and never earning more than forty cents a day, despite working nonstop from sunup to sundown. But forty-some years later—"Praise God!"—she was riding through the same fields in her own air-conditioned car. She concluded her reverie with a triumphant chuckle and the traditional saying that I was to hear often during the next few days, "Yeah, we've come a long way. From the pigpen to the palace!"

An hour later, we arrived at Mrs. Parks's "homeplace," a neat forty-acre farm just west of Ennis. A group of about ten, including relatives and friends who had driven down from Austin for the day, were just taking their seats around two long tables set under the front yard's two shady oak trees. The white-tablecloth-covered tables were loaded with platters of barbecued chicken, long link sausages and brisket-sized chunks of beef, bowls of steaming brown beans seasoned with hunks of jowl bacon, a cold apple, lettuce, and mayonnaise salad, trays of white "store-bought" bread, frosty pitchers of red lemonade, jugs of homemade blackberry wine, and a pan of peach cobbler. As we joined them, mention of my being born in Louisiana caused one of the diners to remark jokingly, "Oh! You from Lousyana. That's the place where this Negro got off the train and asked these white fellas, 'Where do the colored folks hang out in this town?' One of them said, 'The last one hung out in that tree over yonder.' [We all laughed.] Negro said, 'When is the next train due?' 'Ain't another due for four hours.' Negro said, 'That's all right, I'll catch the one that just left!' "[1]

This meal proved to be the first of several opportunities for me to enjoy black east Texans' food and fellowship. That night the Parkses reminisced over past Juneteenth celebrations, Aunt Polly served some delicious homemade ice cream, and I nursed numerous headaches from eating it too fast. Sunday was spent visiting churches in Lyons and Palestine. At the latter church, I had to convince some reluctant interviewees that I was neither a "professional football player" nor an "FBI agent" before I was finally able to spend the remainder of the day talking with them about Juneteenth and University of Texas football, and eating too much free barbecue, potato salad, cornbread, and lemon meringue pie.

Monday morning Mrs. Parks made a fire in the ranch's old black woodburning stove and cooked her husband and me a delicious "ranch style" breakfast of thick strips of bacon, scrambled eggs, grits, biscuits, and black coffee. After breakfast, Reverend Parks, who was my "chauffeur for the day," drove us to the all-black Griffin community, a rural, dirt-road, cul-de-sac village, centered around a general store and an African Methodist Episcopal (AME) church, located six miles outside of Milano just off State Highway 36. For more than an hour Reverend Parks joshed with old friends. "Lord, have mercy! What are you doing here?" "I'm like the devil walking to and fro on the earth seeing whom I might devour." After sharing gales of laughter and breath-stopping bear hugs, Reverend Parks introduced me to a portly friend and told her of my interest in Juneteenth, to which she replied laughingly, "Oh, you want to know about nigger day." I persisted, and she finally continued in a more serious vein, ". . . way back in the old folk's days, way back when I could remember, old folks used to have picnics, you know. . . . We'd walk from here, usually nothing but teenagers, you know, nothing but kids walking here. And they'd have it over in Minerva and we'd go over there and they'd have all kinds of amusements for the young people. . . . They'd have all kinds of little dresses, little umbrellas to match the dresses. You know and all just like that." And she concluded incredulously, "You don't know nothing about it?"[2]

I pondered my cultural ignorance as we drove under a wrought-iron archway sign proclaiming "Fair Park" in one-foot letters, into about sixty acres of flat, amber, sandy land, dotted with tufts of parched grass, with a few brownstone stands nestled under scattered clumps of scrub oak trees. The central recreational area was dominated by a baseball diamond, a quarter horse racetrack, and a covered dance pavillion, enclosed with a freshly painted, gray chain-link fence, which glistened in the hot sun like a cowboy's silver hatband.

The barbecue stand was the first of several booths that I visited prior to attending the afternoon worship services scheduled for the dance pavillion. As I chewed on my extra-hot barbecue sandwich, Mr. Artis Lovelady, the vendor and celebration sponsor, explained why he was having a Juneteenth observance: "I just wanted to do something, just wanted to kinda bring back old times and let the younger people see what we used to do to celebrate it on account of our Emancipation Proclamation."[3]

At the beer stand, a few men had gathered to swap jokes and bits of community gossip between absent-minded swigs from frosty brown bottles of Pearle Beer, which they fondled incessantly like performing comedians manipulating their microphones. Although they agreed with Mr. Lovelady's reasons for sponsoring the Juneteenth celebration, their strong disapproval of the upcoming afternoon sermon was aptly summarized by one of the men, who remarked, "I ain't never been to a 19th in my life where they had preaching . . . I ain't never heard tell of nothing like that."[4]

The beer drinker's claim that a sermon was not usual for a Juneteenth celebration seemed to be confirmed by the initial unsettled atmosphere at the pavillion where the services were scheduled. In fact, Reverend Marvin Smith, the worship-leader, was himself moved to make these critical observations on first seeing the worship site.

> I never been in anything like this. You come out to a open space, no people to give attention; children just running and playing and all this noise . . . I think we ought to be more concerned, serious, because this is a one hundred seven years since Emancipation, since our freedom. And we ought to recognize that this is a blessing coming from God that we were liberated and set free . . . I wouldn't have been here if I would have known that it was just going to be set up lightly, like nothing was going on.[5]

Expressing very low expectations for the scheduled service, he concluded, "However, we're here now and we'll go on with song, Scripture, and prayer . . . and get out of here."

No doubt because of these misgivings, Reverend Smith opened the service with less than Sunday morning fervor. He led us in a long-meter chanting of the hymn, "I Hasten to His Throne," read the "entire one-hundred-and-twenty number of Psalms," and intoned a traditional prayer that thanked God "for bringing us through the journey seas of life," warned the wicked "that the building is on fire," and "begged" spiritual power for the speaker.

Smith: Lord, bless this man of yours.
People: Yes!

> *Smith:* Give him the power to preach your word.
> *People:* Ooooooh, yes!
> *Smith:* May the gospel that fall from his lips.
> *People:* Yes!
> *Smith:* Be as sharp as a two-edged sword.
> *People:* Yes!
> *Smith:* May it cut sin to the right and to the left![6]

After the prayer, Reverend Smith led us in chanting another chorus of "I Hasten to His Throne." He concluded his perfunctory devotion with this somewhat uninspired introduction of the speaker: "The service is now in the hands of Dr. Williams from San Antonio."[7]

Before the service was over, Reverend Smith's half-hearted prayer that the speaker be given the power to preach was answered. Reverend Kelley Williams was somehow able to rise above his distracting setting and indifferent audience to deliver a powerful freedom sermon, steeped in the traditional images, cadences, and themes of earlier Emancipation Day addresses. By the time Reverend Williams reminded his congregation of Juneteenth's cultural significance, his black suit coat lay discarded, crumpled in a gray metal folding chair; and his sweat-soaked white shirt had been loosened at the collar to better allow his bulging vocal cords, which contracted and expanded under a glistening patina of sweat, to proclaim:

> *Williams:* God has made a way for us, Ooh Black man, you ought to turn to God.
> *People:* Yes!
> *Williams:* And tell Him take you and use you in Thy service.
> *People:* Amen.
> *Williams:* You have been good to me.
> *People:* Sure have!
> *Williams:* You opened doors for me.
> *People:* Yeah!
> *Williams:* You opened doors for me.
> *People:* Yeah!
> *Williams:* That's been closed in my face.
> *People:* Yes!
> *Williams:* Ooooooh Lord, almighty! You stood by my side.
> *People:* Yes.
> *Williams:* When doors were shut in my face.
> *People:* Yes.
> *Williams:* When I was beaten and whipped.
> *People:* Yes.
> *Williams:* You stood by my side.

Smith: Right, Elder!

Williams: Oooooooooh church, why don't you say amen today?

People: Amen!

Williams: God is on your side.

People: Yes.

Williams: You ought to turn to God.

People: Yes.

Williams: [*Glancing at the men gathered at the beer stand*] You ought to throw away your beer can.

Smith: Right, Elder!

Williams: You ought to throw away your whiskey bottles.

People: Amen.

Williams: And get down on your knees and say, "Lord, I thank ya."

People: Amen!

Williams: "That you brought me from a long ways."[8]

After the sermon, Reverend Smith helped the exhausted Reverend Williams back into his coat before striding to the pulpit and confessing, "I'm just happy! Look like I've been in church today now. At first it didn't register with me very much, but, you know, you have to get in touch with God. Wherever you stop at and call on His name you can have church. Under your own vine and fig tree. So you don't have to go back to yonder's mountain. But anywhere you kneel down, call on God. You can hear from heaven."[9] Yes, we had had church that day.

The next morning, as Reverend Parks and I loaded his car for our return trip to Houston, he complained about not hearing enough sermons in Houston that could match the emotion and eloquence of yesterday's Juneteenth sermon. However, he would not miss using the farm's outhouse. Nodding toward the backyard privy, Reverend Parks confessed, "I just can't take it. I tried to use that thing but that turd just went back up! Like that Negro who was falling and one of his friends told him he was about to fall on a white woman, so he curved back up!"[10] I often recalled this anecdote during the one-and-a-half-month research period between field trips.

A tip from my mother, who had overheard some friends making plans to attend the "8th of August homecoming" in Allensville, Kentucky, had me headed for this western Kentucky hamlet on August 5, 1972. West of Central City I entered a strip-mining region. Monstrous yellow coal shovels were scooping jagged black and brown gashes of coal and topsoil out of the green landscape. Growling bulldozers added to the ecological carnage by uprooting live trees and piling them on top of mounds of dead trees

August Field Trip

whose smoldering brown leaves and gasoline-doused trunks scented the air with wreaths of acrid blue smoke.

After checking into Hopkinsville's Holiday Inn, I headed east to Allensville. The pastoral vista seen through my front window conjured up a vision of slavery's agrarian age. The fields of beige feed corn—soon to be harvested—yellow burley tobacco, and green soybeans, alternating with the gently sloping pastures, dotted with herds of Black Angus cattle and an occasional chestnut horse, reminded me of a slave quilt.

The region's genteel past was faintly echoed by the massive front columns featured on many of the neat mass-produced tract homes. Occasionally, an authentic "Big House," complete with tall columns, wide porches, and large front gates would come into view. Of all the dwellings, these old and genteel mansions were the most vivid reminders of the region's past tradition of slavery. For local residents, memories of that era still ebb and flow in oral family histories. During an earlier interview, for example, Mrs. Bennie Mae Smith recalled a "slave story" that her grandmother had told her: ". . . the master didn't want Bill to go into the army because he was a good worker. He hid him up under a strawstack until February in the storm because he didn't want them to take him because he knew how to work and he'd do it."[11] I found myself wondering if one of these old plantations was the scene of this long-preserved family story.

My reverie was momentarily broken by the appearance up ahead of a rectangular black-lettered sign that read: "Allensville, Ky., Pop. 300." Within seconds I was driving slowly on the village's tree-lined main street. As I bumped across the L&N railroad tracks, the sight of the deserted, dingy gray depot called to mind another memory of Mrs. Smith's, a happy childhood remembrance of the pageantry and excitement surrounding the arrival of past 8th of August excursion trains:

> When I was a child it was really something. Really big. Reverend Wiggins, I have known express trains to run out of Louisville and pull in down there with two carloads and just unload there and celebrate. . . . And the brass band would meet the train eight o'clock in the morning, and they would start their celebration. And boy, I'd just go mad. Early in the morning I'd be dressed. I'd be jiggling soon as that band started playing, until my mother couldn't tie a ribbon on my head, when that band would start. It was wonderful.
>
> They would use those undertakers' horses—and those were the most prettiest prancing horses keeping time with that music—and they would ride those horses with those high hats [*laughter*]. It would be interesting to watch those horses walk with that band. . . .[12]

No bands or prancing horses welcomed me. Once over the railroad crossing I turned right at the first street and soon began to find cars parked on both sides of the street. At the next intersection I turned right again and drove two blocks to the Mt. Pleasant Baptist Church, the celebration site, where I parked my dusty Bug alongside the other sparkling clean Chevrolets, Buicks, Fords, Cadillacs, customized vans and motorcycles, bearing Indiana, Wisconsin, Illinois, Ohio, Michigan, New Jersey, Pennsylvania, Tennessee, and Kentucky license plates. The majority of the Kentucky plates were issued in Todd County, the home county for Allensville. License plates from Jefferson, Louisville's home county, and Christian, nearby Hopkinsville's home county, were also prevalent. Getting around in this mass of machinery brought to mind something else that Mrs. Smith had told me. "We just get there and meet. And there are so many cars coming in there. You can [see cars] for miles. Cars on top of cars."[13] How right she was.

The red-brick church's front yard was teeming with commercial and social activity. On either side of the front walk was a huge maple tree whose leaves provided cooling shade for the neatly dressed celebrants and busy concessionaires. The Methodists ran an open-air barbecue stand under the tree on the left, while the host Baptist committee had constructed a neatly screened-in barbecue booth under the tree on the right side of the yard. Round, galvanized tin washtubs, filled with ice and bottled and canned soft drinks, were visible at both booths. And over at the Methodist stand a young boy was busy cranking an ice-cream freezer. Women workers, their once spotless white aprons now soiled with orange smudges of barbecue sauce, used their similarly sullied towels to shoo flies away from the sweet-potato, pecan, apple, and transparent pies (the latter a regional favorite made with egg whites, sugar, and butter) and from the multi-layered chocolate, vanilla, coconut, and pound cakes. Tired celebrants rested on old church pews located throughout the yard, nibbled on spicy barbecue sandwiches, and swigged from cool bottles of pop, while conversing with old friends. As Mrs. Smith had said earlier, "They done told the boss man that they wanted off for that day. And the white people understand . . . that the Negroes celebrate that day."[14]

After mingling with celebrants in the churchyard for several hours, conducting interviews, taking pictures, and observing the various events, I gathered my equipment and walked up the gravel road leading from the church to Bradford Park, the local baseball diamond. The park, which was named after a deceased local baseball star, had a skinned red-clay infield, crooked lime foul lines, and an outfield of ankle-deep meadow grass. Several hundred fans had gathered to see the Allensville Hoppers play the Merrittown All-Stars. Most of the spectators were sitting in the three-row-high wooden grandstand, either dodging foul balls that penetrated the rust-weakened chicken-wire backstop, or stuffing themselves on soft drinks, hot dogs, potato chips, chewing gum, and candy purchased from a wooden concession stand located behind the home-plate screen. About ten male spectators were shooting craps at the end of the left-field foul line.

The four-hour contest had several interesting side shows. The left-field crapshooters scattered in comical pell-mell fashion each time a home run was hit into that section, and the fans engaged in good-natured, game-long "signifying," the traditional game of verbal insults, with the players and umpire. (One fan offered the umpire his glasses through a hole in the rusty foul-screen in an effort to improve the arbiter's calls.) Between innings a lone bootlegger strutted back and forth before the crowd with full bottles of whiskey crammed into both of his rear pants' pockets; and members of a Louisville motorcycle club, astride chrome-plated cycles and dressed in sequin-studded leather jackets that glistened in the bright afternoon sun, drew high-pitched squeals of admiration from the teenage girls in the stands every time they bounced slowly across the outfield grass to the accompaniment of roaring motors belching plumes of blue smoke into the hot summer air.

The sun had set behind Mt. Pleasant Baptist's steeple before the Hoppers had defeated the All-Stars 16 to 11, and I started the forty–five minute drive back to the sanctuary of my Hopkinsville motel room.

Before checking out of the motel the next morning, I reviewed my field notes while eating a delicious western Kentucky breakfast of the region's distinctively salty ham, grits, scrambled eggs, homemade biscuits, and several cups of coffee. On my way to observe Crofton's 8th of August celebration, I stopped to say hello at the home of Reverend C.A. Striplin, a minister who had befriended me when I was pastor of Freeman Chapel Christian Methodist Episcopal (CME) Church in Hopkinsville. Reverend Striplin's impressions of the previous day's celebration were only mildly critical.

> Up there [Allensville] is no leadership. Up there, I mean, just an assembly. And I was just observing you know, nobody called together. It's just a practice they've been meeting. They play ball and they serve something—I didn't see this, I heard this—that they used to have a band come in. But up here it was just nobody called the other preacher or anything. Everybody is free and doing, you know. I was driving along—driving out you have to be careful—and I said, "Well, here we are sheep without any •
> shepherd." And everybody happy. They licking on ice cream, eating this one, pulling at one another just enjoying themselves away from the white folks.[15]

But he was severely critical of the celebration I was about to attend. "Now down there [Crofton] . . . the people have been full of rowdy, you know, likker drinking. I know they've had a few killings down there. You know, every two or three years they knock off one at Crofton."

Reverend Striplin's final remarks filled me with some apprehension as I approached Crofton's Bradley Park. The littered condition of the park only served to heighten my fears. Trash was everywhere. In finding a place to park, I had to steer my way through a maze of empty wine, whiskey, gin, and soft-drink bottles and beer cans which cluttered the landscape and roadway along with discarded candy wrappers, ice-cream cups, gnawed barbecue bones, half-eaten fish sandwiches, crumpled cigarette packages, empty matchboxes, cigar and cigarette butts, and solid paper napkins.

Automobile traffic in and out of the park followed a two-acre, Y-shaped, dusty, brown dirt road. The park road's two Greenville Road entrances joined midway in the park to form a single lane that ended at the baseball field clearing. Massive oak trees edged the two forks of this road providing daytime shade for the homemade stands of wire and wood where ice cream, barbecue, hot dogs, and white buffalo fish sandwiches were sold to the celebrants. The celebration merchants had also strung electric lines of red, blue, green, and orange 100-watt bulbs from the trees' branches to provide light for their night customers.

The gambling booth was located on the right fork of the road, well away from the other booths. Its crap table, a plywood rectangle covered with green felt and resting atop an empty oil drum, was discreetly hidden during the daytime in a clump of trees and underbrush ringing the park. The dozen or so young males who had gathered there sported uncombed naturals, impaled with Afro-picks, and had free-tail-flopping, barbecue-and-lipstick-stained shirts, rumpled pants, dusty shoes, and blood-shot eyes. They whiled away the bright daylight hours either playing tonk, signifying, laughing, leaning on the bright-colored jukebox popping their fingers to the blaring soul music, or poised in front of it rehearsing a new dance step, sipping wine from brown-bag-encased bottles, or taking tokes from joints cupped discreetly in their hands.

The thick aromatic billows of smoke filtering from the screened-in barbecue stand were a pleasant relief from the pungent wreath of marijuana smoke hanging over the gambling booth. An American Club sign, printed in red letters on a white background, hung over the cashier's window. It reminded me of an earlier discussion with Mr. Claude Snorton, Sr., concerning the Club's origin, "It wasn't no lodge. The first thing they called it was the . . . Afro-American Club. In the beginning when I started in it. Finally, we cut the 'Afro-' off and just had an American Club." And, peering through the booth's screen wall at the man barbecuing chicken parts and pork ribs over a "great long pit," I also recalled what Mr. Snorton had said about barbecuing at earlier 8th of August celebrations. "We had barbecue and we'd sell ham about two dollars a pound. . . . Another guy that worked with me called him Jimbo. He was a hell of a guy. Me and him we work all day and all night and then come home and rest a while and go back . . . we'd take it in shifts."[16]

The baseball diamond was deserted. No players were fielding grounders on the red clay infield or snagging flies in the outfield meadow; neither were there any fans seated in the rickety wooden grandstand watching a game or arguing with the umpire. This tranquil scene was apparently far different from earlier Crofton celebrations. Mr. Snorton attributed this waning of baseball's popularity to "young Negroes" dissipating their athletic talent in "wine" and "dope." He recalled playing on "a hell of a [Crofton] ball club" that once beat the Nashville Elite-Giants, a touring professional team in the old Negro leagues, and regularly played visiting teams which "would come out of Nashville . . . [and] Illinois . . . and play" on past holiday afternoons.

When I returned to my car, a novelty kiosk had been set up in the parking lot. The vendor was doing a brisk business selling his assortment of balloons, inflatable clowns and animals, stuffed gorillas, flying birds, straw hats, Hawaiian leis, beaded necklaces, toy watches, punch balls, whips, swagger canes, and American flags to young and old celebrants. The road leading out of town was deserted, in sharp contrast to Mr. Snorton's description of this same road during past celebrations: " . . . at one time they had five thousand. . . . And they'd be so many people out there they'd [be] parked from there [the church] clean back to Bradley Park . . . they used to run special excursions during that time from Evansville and Hopkinsville. They'd come in the morning. They'd get here at eight o'clock and leave at four. And we used to have special buses out of Nashville and Evansville. There'd be four or five Greyhound buses."[17] But there were no long lines of parked cars and buses to impede my exodus from Crofton during this 8th of August.

For the remainder of the summer and fall I transcribed tapes, wrote letters, read microfilm, built an Emancipation celebration bibliography, and planned my upcoming January 1st celebration field trip to Columbus, Georgia. Because of the holiday break I was able to take the family along. I selected the Columbus celebration for research and personal reasons. In terms of my research, this trip would allow me to conduct interviews and collect January 1st data in Nashville and Atlanta. Furthermore, the close proximity of Columbus to the Alabama border would afford me the opportunity of attending several other observances in the two-state area. Personally, it would give me the chance to treat my family to two nights of fun in Atlanta. The trip would also allow Janice and me the chance to introduce our daughter, Mary Ellyn, to such Afro-American cultural and historical landmarks as Nashville's Fisk University and Atlanta's Spelman College.

Mount Eagle's solitary pine trees, gnarled and dwarfed by the elements into serpentine configurations that would shame any award-winning bonsai, foreshadowed the brooding, southern Georgia pine forests that had been the scenes of countless lynchings, castrations, beatings, Klan rallies, and other rituals of southern racism.

Red and russet hues dominated the wintry southern landscape from Chattanooga to Atlanta. The run-off from spring and summer rains had sculpted the region's amber soil into an endless array of configurations. These same scarlet hills on which Dr. Martin Luther King, Jr., dreamed of brotherhood coming to "little black boys and little white girls" passed quickly before me. In other places, the groping tentacles and shriveled leaves of the brown, dormant kudzu vines covered clay ravines, abandoned houses, dilapidated barns, junked machinery, trees, telephone poles, guy wires, and any other stationary objects that lay in their paths in an efficiently relentless manner that reminded me of the way a dying, repressive social system of segregation had once strangled the region, fostering a proliferation of "white" and "colored" signs over lunch counters, bathrooms, drinking fountains, and other social accommodations.

I was charged with anticipation, on January 1, 1973, as I parked our car in the red clay parking lot of the New Providence Baptist Church, the site of Columbus's Emancipation celebration. Racing through my mind was the realization that in a few moments Janice, Mary Ellyn, and I would be experiencing a cultural ritual that members of my father's family had participated in. My paternal grandmother, Mrs. Anna Sanders Wiggins, while serving as a school principal, had actually sponsored January 1st celebrations at her school near Jackson, Georgia. And, more importantly, my father had participated in similar January 1st celebrations during his Georgia boyhood.

January Field Trip

I was about to turn a new page in my father's past. As a boy I had often thumbed through his worn, leather-bound, purple-backed college scrapbook, staring at his old baseball, basketball, and football photographs—he was a three-letter man—with their faint, white ink doggerel captions, in an effort to imagine what his Paine College days were really like. On other occasions I would take down from the living-room closet an old shoebox, loaded with a raft of baseball clippings, faded and brittle with age, and read all about his baseball exploits in such far-off places as Sioux Falls, South Dakota. But this ritual celebration, unlike the scrapbook's photographs and the shoebox's clippings, transcended time and would allow me to experience first hand the same freedom service that my father knew as a boy growing up in southern Georgia. It would give us much more to share.

The celebration site was a new, yellow-brick church with twin white columns and a pointed white wooden steeple. The neutral hues of the sanctuary's beige walls, yellow frosted windowpanes, hardwood floors, natural yellow-finished pews, pulpit, and three modern highback minister's chairs contrasted with the deep maroon carpeting that covered the pulpit area, as well as the center and two side aisles. Two choir stands, complete with microphones, flanked the pulpit area, where several gray folding chairs had been placed to accommodate the many participants. Two folding chairs and a portable lectern had been set up in the half-moon-shaped area between the altar rail and the pulpit.

Representatives from almost every social stratum of Columbus's Afro-American community could be found among the three hundred celebrants, most of whom were dressed in their Sunday-best black, blue, and gray suits, or yellow, red, green, and orange dresses. They were crammed into the sanctuary's two sections of pews. A few babies and several grade-school children also were present. Although the women celebrants outnumbered the men, Reverend Cloud's opening announcement implied that men held the prominent positions at this gathering. "Will the following people come to the platform: Brother E. Adams, Jr., Reverend H.L. Gladney. Mrs. Rosie Walker will come to the second platform. Mrs. Ethyln Kirby will come to the second platform."[18] The pulpit area was off limits to the women participants.

We stood and sang "Lift Every Voice and Sing," were led in prayer by Reverend Adams, heard the choir sing "More Love to Thee Oh Christ," listened to the reading of the Twenty-third Psalm, and sang "The Battle Hymn of the Republic," before Mrs. Rosie Walker walked to the "second platform" lectern and welcomed us: "Ministers of the gospel, Christians young and old, we the members of the New Providence Baptist Church welcome you with great anticipation. We have prepared ourselves to receive you, our guests, with open hearts and greetings of joyful love. We welcome you here today to share these services with us as we celebrate one-hundred-and-ten years of freedom. . . . From all of us to all of you we extend our heart-felt welcome." As Mrs. Walker returned to her seat, there was a smattering of polite applause and mumured affirmations of "amen" and "yes."

Next we stood and sang the civil-rights anthem, "We Shall Overcome," in the traditional call-response style heard in countless 1960s civil-rights news telecasts. Then Mrs. Ethyln Kirby also walked to the "second platform" lectern and read the Emancipation Proclamation. After slowly establishing eye contact with her attentive audience, Mrs. Kirby began to speak in the dramatic tones and cadences that we would hear again in the sermon.

> *Kirby:* America, I saw you grow. I saw your rocks and rills, thy woods and temple hills. America, I saw your military forces on land and sea . . . Alabama, Arkansas, Florida, Georgia, Mississippi, North Carolina, South Carolina, Louisiana, and Virginia . . . I saw you. I saw you ignore the warning of God and Lincoln's Preliminary Proclamation . . .
>
> *People:* Yes!
>
> *Kirby:* I can hear you, America. I can hear you at the Emancipation Proclamation, January 1, one thousand eight hundred and sixty three, issued by the President of the United States containing among other things the following: "To wit, I, Abraham Lincoln, President of the United States, by virtue of the power in me vested as commander in chief of the army and navy of the United States, order and declare that all persons held as slaves within said designated states and parts of states are henceforth forward shall be free . . ."
>
> *People:* Amen!

As I joined in the loud applause and heard the earnest cries of appreciation that immediately followed Mrs. Kirby's presentation, I was suddenly reminded of something that Dr. William Holmes Borders had said about the ritual during our stopover in Atlanta. "Whenever they found a person . . . who would really do it [read the Emancipation Proclamation] with understanding, it was a great and a glorious thing. But it's difficult to so find, for a person to get into it, vicariously, this reading of the Emancipation Proclamation so that it is a burning fire for the audience . . . every now and then we pick a person who was zealous; who knew it; who could share it. And when we did it was a woman most of the time."[19]

A violin solo of "Deep River" preceded Reverend George B. Thomas's celebration sermon that began with the twin themes of slavery:

> *Thomas:* There were 75 million or more of those whom we call slaves who were taken from Africa and brought to this land.
> *People:* Uh huh.
> *Thomas:* Notice now I said 75 million. How many million were wasted and lost in the process? Oh what a chapter of history if we were to look at it. It might shock us to understand it.

and Emancipation:

> *Thomas:* So He [God] said, "Black folk, I called you now up out of Egypt."
> *People:* Amen.
> *Thomas:* "The Egypt of slavery."
> *People:* Yeah.

Reverend Thomas concluded with a statement of the traditional belief that God has chosen these lowly, former slaves and their heirs to be His instruments of salvation for America.

> *Thomas:* "I called you out of the evils of segregation and degradation."
> *People:* Yeah.
> *Thomas:* We gonna get rid of the ghetto mentality.
> *People:* Yes, sir!
> *Thomas:* We're gonna get rid of the colored folks' mentality.
> *People:* Amen!
> *Thomas:* We're gonna get rid of the niggerized and the Negro mentality.
> *People:* Yeah!
> *Thomas:* We're gonna understand what the souls of black folks mean.
> *People:* Amen!
> *Thomas:* Because God has put into us the power of being a strange people.
> *People:* Amen!
> *Thomas:* And so the eyes of the world are saying, 'Well, if the Black folks in AMERICA don't serve the task or accomplish the task of humanizing the soul of this man, this nation and the people of this land, there is little hope for the salvation that would come for the fulfillment of God's purpose to the world."

After the sermon, I was introduced and allowed to circulate copies of my questionnaire among the congregation, during the rambling, humorous remarks of Reverend Howell.

> *Howell:* Do we have any new pastors among us? If so . . . will all pastors
>   stand. Give them a hand. Some of them gray and some of them old and
>   some of them young. . . .
> *People:* [*Laughter.*]
> *Howell:* Some of them good-looking and some of them bad-looking.
> *People:* [*Laughter.*]
> *Howell:* But they're pastoring. And I'm proud of their work and proud of
>   working with them. Yes. Brother Adams, the newly appointed pastor of
>   St. Mark's AME Church. Nice-looking young man. Watch out there!
>   Who was that said, "Yes, he is"?
> *People:* [*Laughter.*]

My quick scanning of the completed questionnaires that the ushers were
bringing to me turned up two references to a May 28th celebration date
that I knew nothing about.

After the benediction, two elementary schoolteachers, Mrs. Agnes
Hubert and Mrs. Lula Bass, sat with me on one of the front pews and
talked about the May 28th Emancipation date, as celebrated in the neighboring Alabama towns of Hachatubee, Eufaula, Clayton, Hatsboro,
Melville, and Pittsfield.

> *Bass:* We didn't spend too much time with the 4th of July.
> *Hubert:* Right.
> *Bass:* 'Cause we didn't care nothing 'bout those white folks day.
> *Hubert:* We didn't start to celebrate it until we got in the city.
> *Bass:* Until we got in the city. But you know what has actually happened;
>   the reason they don't celebrate the 28th like they used to? We have
>   become culturized like the man just finished speaking of; we've been
>   picking up these other folks' culture. We had our own day, but
>   now . . . everything is their day.[20]

Thanks to my successful field trip, my family and I were in a gay, light-
hearted mood as we drove away from the celebration site on Highway 80
toward Tuskegee Institute. There was not a cloud in the sky and the tem-
perature was in the mid fifties. As we drove down this sunny, southern road,
the car radio blared a play-by-play description of the Cotton Bowl football
game; Mary Ellyn peered silently out of the car's back window at the tall,
stately pine trees, while eating an ice cream cone; and Janice and I talked
about the celebration we had just participated in.

This was another cultural side trip for Mary Ellyn. In Nashville Janice
and I had shown her Fisk University and told her the story of how a choir of
ex-slaves raised enough money from singing spirituals to European royalty
to build historic Jubilee Hall. In Atlanta we had shown her the famous

"seat of Negro learning" with its proud institutions of Morehouse, Clark, Morris Brown, and Spelman Colleges, the Interdenominational Theological Center, and Atlanta University, where such cultural heroes as W.E.B. Du Bois, Benjamin E. Mays, Whitney Young, and Martin Luther King, Jr., had either studied or taught. Now we were capping her cultural enrichment with a visit to Tuskegee Institute, perhaps the most famous of all Afro-American institutions of higher learning.

Within an hour we were driving slowly through the immaculate campus, looking for a place to park. After parking we strolled over the neatly kept grounds, pausing to photograph our young daughter in front of such historical sites as the famous statue of Washington lifting the veil of ignorance from the unshackled slave, the new chapel, old Douglass Hall, the laboratory of George Washington Carver, and the home of the Institute's founder, Booker T. Washington. As we walked from site to site, Janice and I tried consciously, with all the solemnity of Williamsburg, Virginia, tour guides, to make the pretty pigtailed girl skipping between us aware of her history and heritage.

It was dark when we started back to Columbus, and our mood had quickly shifted from relaxed gaiety to quiet dread. Mary Ellyn, exhausted from all the walking, had fallen asleep on the car's back seat, but Janice sat next to me wide awake, anxiously staring ahead at the lonely highway, the infamous Highway 80 on which several civil-rights workers had been killed. As the road signs of Marvyn, Crawford, and other hostile little towns flashed before our car's headlights, I thought about a nasty experience that Reverend Parks had had in a similar southern town: "There was one town that had a sign, 'Nigger, run! If you can't read, run anyhow!' We stopped for gas and asked to use the restrooms. The man said, 'We ain't got no restrooms for niggers!' That's what he said, 'no restrooms for niggers!' I told him to stop putting gas in my car, and we drove on down the road."[21]

After what seemed like an eternity, we both breathed a sigh of relief as we spotted the flashing light of our motel sign; and we drove quickly toward the comfort of its light. As I carried the sleeping Mary Ellyn into our motel room I recalled something that Dr. Thomas had said earlier that day. "Let freedom ring. And yet its ring is hollow now. And yet its promises are still not ours. But we still say let freedom ring. But then deeper than words, let it ring into practice so that it might evidence that people of this land enjoy the right to be free."[22] The relieved look on my wife's face and the easing of the knot of anxiety within my stomach were reminders that indeed "freedom's promises are still not ours."

One month later, I experienced no such anxiety during my drive to Philadelphia to observe National Freedom Day. As with the May 28th and August 8th celebrations, chance had played a major role in my discovery of this celebration. While browsing through back issues of the *Pittsburgh Courier* in an effort to ease the eye-strain caused by several hours of squinting at microfilm accounts of Atlanta's January 1st celebration, I noticed this intriguing headline, "Emancipation was it January 1 or February 1 [?]." Included in the article was a historical summary of the celebration's origin: "Mayor [*sic*] R.R. Wright, Sr. . . . believed that not January 1, 1863 is the date the Black man's freedom began, but February 1, 1865, the day Lincoln signed the 13th Amendment which really made the Black free. Mayor [*sic*] Wright was so convinced that February 1, 1865 was the day Negroes were freed that he succeeded in getting President Truman to declare February 1 National Freedom Day."[23] This discovery sparked correspondence between myself, Dr. Mays—the author of the article—and Major Wright's youngest son, Emanuel. Mr. Wright sent me several old celebration programs and invited me to attend that year's celebration.

Overcast gray skies, freezing temperatures, and blowing snow were my companions on the Philadelphia trip. A blanket of snow covered the fertile Indiana, Ohio, and Pennsylvania farmlands. In eastern Indiana and western Ohio an occasional "I house" (so named because of its ubiquity on rural Indiana, Illinois, and Iowa landscapes) with its white walls, smoking twin red brick chimneys, and frosted windowpanes, appeared on the horizon.

The drive from Wheeling, West Virginia, to Philadelphia was the most nerve-wracking leg of my trip because of the slick, snow-covered inclines. Nor were driving conditions on the flat land much better. A recent snow,

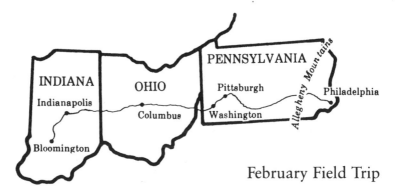

February Field Trip

high winds, and freezing temperatures had turned Interstate 76 into an obstacle course of snow drifts and icy bridges, conditions the truckers made all the more treacherous by splashing blinding sludge on my windshield as they sped by and buffeting the light front end of my rear-engine car, making it hard to handle.

But all that was finally behind me as I stood, along with about one hundred and fifty black bourgeoisie, in the rotunda of Independence Hall, gazing at the Liberty Bell. The celebrants were either teenage members of the John Rhodes Junior High School glee club or elderly, retired black professionals. The choir was uniformly dressed in white shirts and black pants or white blouses and black skirts. Their elders were fashionably attired in suits and dresses of black, blue, brown, and other subdued hues. During the next ninety minutes we sang "Lift Every Voice and Sing," were led in a flowery invocation, sang "My Country 'Tis of Thee," listened attentively to Mr. Emanuel C. Wright read Pennsylvania's National Freedom Day Proclamation, and watched solemnly as a small group of "distinguished citizens" placed a wreath at the foot of the Liberty Bell.

Our next service took place in nearby Congress Hall, a restored national shrine whose sterile, artificial atmosphere reminded me of Disney World and Six Flags Over Texas. We sang "The Star Spangled Banner" and "We Shall Overcome"; heard introductions ("Our guest speaker comes from a long tradition begun by the illustrious founder of African Methodism nearly two centuries ago") and an eloquent sermon that verbalized the patriotism enacted in the earlier wreath-laying ceremony at the Liberty Bell:

> Let the record show that we're not satisfied with anything less than that which all Americans enjoy: good housing, education, jobs, and above all that liberty and that justice that's given in our Constitution. Our fathers and our mothers sang "Freedom after while when we get home." But we are singing with the youth of our nation "Freedom now!" because we are at home. We're at home here in America. We're at home here in Philadelphia, Pennsylvania. We're at home here even in Georgia and Mississippi and Alabama. *This is our country!*[24]

We also heard witty post-sermon remarks, "Mr. Chairman and my friends, I'm too smart a man to speak after a bishop speaks. I learned that a looooong time ago. I'm a Baptist with Methodist inclinations."[25]

But the highlight of this service was the John Rhodes Junior High School choir's dramatic recitation, which wove selected passages from spirituals, the Constitution, a Martin Luther King, Jr., sermon, and Langston Hughes's poetry into a powerful paean to freedom. First, a girl stepped forward and said:

> *Girl:* Dr. Martin Luther King, Jr., 1965, "Today I want to say to the people of America and the nations of the world that we're about not to turn around. We're on the move now and no wave of racism can stop us."
> *Choir: I too sing, America! I am the darker brother!*

Next a boy stepped out of the choir's front row and continued this narrative pattern with a reference to the Constitution:

> *Boy:* The beginning of the Black man's freedom here in America as it was in the United States' Constitution. I will recite the law which gave our forefathers their freedom, the Thirteenth Amendment. "Neither slavery nor involuntary servitude except as punishment for a crime whereas the party has been duly convicted shall exist in the United States or any place subject to their jurisdiction. Congress has the power to enforce the article by appropriate legislation."
> *Choir: I too sing, America! I am the darker brother!*

I smiled and thought: Mrs. Kirby would be proud of them.

It was almost noon when we stepped outside into the cold winter's air for a brisk five-minute walk to the Ben Franklin Hotel for the Freedom Day luncheon. An integrated audience of over four hundred Philadelphians had paid ten dollars each for the privilege of sitting at formally set circular tables in a stately dining room with a cathedral ceiling and several gleaming, low-hanging chandeliers, and eating a gourmand's luncheon of "half grapefruit, braised top sirloin of choice beef covered in mushroom sauce, candied sweet potatoes, string beans noisette, assorted rolls and butter, coffee, tea, milk and sherbet."[26]

The celebrants were well groomed and expensively dressed in tailored suits and designer dresses. Several women had casually thrown their mink stoles over the backs of their chairs with the same nonchalance that the Allensville, Kentucky, baseball players had shed their cotton warm-up jackets on the sideline benches before the 8th of August game. Choirs, classical pianists, and aspiring divas entertained us while we dined. Mrs. Parks was right, some of us had truly come "From the pigpen to the palace."

The after-dinner speech by Mr. Mal Goode, the United Nations correspondent for ABC News, was hard-hitting. First he disarmed us with humor:

Goode: I said it to Dr. Davis and I've said it on other occasions, that we have become so sophisticated that we have forgotten the church and especially when we get two cars and we are able to buy whiskey by the case now. We used to buy it by the half-pint.

People: [*Laughter.*]

Goode: We have lots of clothes and three or four pairs of shoes and we get to church on Easter and New Year's Eve.

Shifting subjects suddenly, Goode boldly denounced American racism:

About a month ago, the man now gone from us, President Lyndon Johnson, told an audience at the University of Texas, "Despite the progress made in race relations," he said, "Black and white Americans are still on unequal ground." Is there a single one of us, black or white, Jew or Gentile, Catholic or Protestant, Republican or Democrat who would deny this to be a fact of life and [also] here in Philadelphia? And I come to your city at this celebration to ask any one of these more than three million in the metropolitan area, TELL ME WHY . . . TELL ME WHY THIS IS TRUE IN 1973!

He advocated busing:

Talk about busing. They were busing children for GENERATIONS! Busing white children to and fro across towns and through the counties when Black children were WALKING ROADWAYS IN THE SNOW AND SLEET AND MUD. AND THE MUD SPLASHING ON THEM FROM THE BUS WHEELS!

We talk about busing . . . even some Black children, some Black adults are opposed to busing. There's no great deal to busing. If it requires that it takes busing to give a child a quality education . . . THEN DAMMIT! LET'S BUS![27]

And praised the Black man's contributions to America's development:

Every time you pull up to a traffic light you owe a debt of gratitude to a Black man, Garret Morgan. Everytime you have a blood transfusion you owe a debt of gratitude to a Black man, Charles Drew. Every time you use a mask in a coal mine or any kind of period of destruction you owe a debt of gratitude to that same Black man, Garret Morgan. WHAT MOOOOOORE I ASK, DO WE HAVE TO DO?

We showered him with applause in a standing ovation as he returned to his dais seat.

The concluding segment of the luncheon was given over to awards. The Richard R. Wright Scholarship Award went to a young Afro-American male student who was admonished to "Take that scholarship, burn the midnight oil, and make good." Mr. Wright was given a surprise award "In appreciation for twenty-five years of continuous, meritorius service" to National Freedom Day. Members of the Women's Committee were recognized. A committee of young Afro-American businessmen was deputized by the group to study the plight of the city's Afro-American community and make a report at the next year's celebration. Finally, Dr. Davis dismissed us by saying, "If our work has been completed, thank you for coming, and tell 'em about it for next year so we can have twice as many people and ask for a larger hall. Thank you for coming and goodbye."

On the way out of the hotel, I bought a copy of Major Wright's biography, *Black Boy of Atlanta,* the final trophy of my four-trip search for freedom, and began reading it that night in my hotel room prior to beginning the long trip back to Bloomington and the continuation of my research.

CHAPTER 2

We too, have days of equal importance to us as
St. Patrick's Day is to the Irish. With sufficient
pride and leadership we can make ours of equal
note.

Irish Boys on Parade, Savannah Tribune *(1935)*

The Roots and Fruits
of Emancipation Celebrations

Contemporary Emancipation celebrations, whose structural and cultural origins can be traced to earlier slave holidays, have exerted continuing influence on Afro-American culture during the twentieth century. Numerous nascent cultural celebrations, often highlighting one or another of the many rituals and festivities that compose an Emancipation celebration, have spun off of these older, multi-celebratory freedom events. Furthermore, New Negro and some Black Cultural Nationalist ideologues have based their social theories of racial aesthetics, unity, and progress upon the traditional songs, dances, cuisine, and other expressions of Afro-American culture which these freedom celebrations have perpetuated and preserved since their inception.

The simple, leisure-time celebrations of the slaves were the cultural forerunners of these freedom celebrations. Slaves were allowed time off from their labor during certain periods of the calendar year. Saturdays and Sundays were normally set aside for rest and relaxation on the plantations,[1] and occasional celebrations were staged when there was a plantation visitor, or when a member of the master's family had a birthday or got married.[2] The most extensive of these slave holidays, however, were those seasonal celebrations observed annually when the two most critical plantation chores, planting and harvesting, had been completed. After the crops had been planted, chopped free of weeds, and grown to a mature size, slaves were normally given time off to frolic. This summer season in the slave calendar was called the "laid-by" period. (Interestingly enough, a significant number of August 8th and Juneteenth celebrants that I interviewed still referred to their celebrations as events that occurred after the crops had been "laid by.") July 4th (which one slave owner dubbed as "laying-by crop jubilee"), Election Day, and camp meeting were observed during this period.

Although some plantations celebrated Thanksgiving,[3] Easter and Christmas were the biggest slave holidays between the slack period of fall harvest and spring planting. Pinkster, a slave Easter celebration of parading, drum-dancing, games, drinking, and eating, was observed by up-state New York slaves as early as the eighteenth century.[4] Slaves also celebrated Easter in Alabama[5] and Louisiana.[6] Some slave masters extended the holiday to Easter Monday "if the work schedule permitted."[7] Christmas, however, was the longest and most universally observed slave holiday during this or any other period in the slaves' calendar year. In his autobiography, Frederick Douglass reported that the holiday lasted six days: "The days between Christmas and New Year's Day are allowed as holidays; and, accordingly, we were not required to perform any labor, more than to feed and take care of the stock."[8] Douglass also noted the various ways that the slaves "used" and "abused" this respite:

> Those of us who had families at a distance, were generally allowed to spend the whole six days in their society. This time, however, was spent in various ways. The staid, sober, thinking and industrious ones of our number would employ themselves in making corn-brooms, mats, horse-collars, and baskets; and another class of us would spend the time hunting opossums, hares and coons. But by far the larger part engaged in such sports and merriments as playing ball, wrestling, running footraces, fiddling, dancing, and drinking whiskey. . . .[9]

A small galaxy of related celebrations was also observed by the slaves during the Christmas holiday season. The most dazzling was John Canoe, a celebration observed by the slaves in eastern North Carolina, whose "basic structure" was depicted by one observer as being "a leader, an accompanying group of singers and marchers, gaudy costumes, strange head-pieces, instruments of bones and horns and percussive pieces."[10] The most depressing was New Year's day, which was sometimes celebrated on December 27 or 28 to allow the slaves ample time to return to their own plantations for another year of toil and separation from family and friends. The trauma of these New Year partings caused the slaves to dub this "heartbreak day."[11] To steel themselves against the impending despair of separation and slavery, some of the slaves attended fervent Watch Night Services on the last night of the year. The first minutes of the New Year found them on their knees in prayer. But for the remaining hours of darkness they were on their feet dancing the Ring Shout and frolicking until daybreak.[12]

Many of the slaves turned to alcohol as a means of alleviating the depression of slavery. Frederick Douglass wrote that the custom of tippling was so engrained in the slaves' holiday behavior, "it was deemed a disgrace not to get drunk at Christmas. . . ."[13] Douglass observed many slaves who worked all year to have enough money to buy, or produce to barter, for an ample supply of whiskey to keep them drunk throughout the Christmas season, so that "when the holidays ended, [they] staggered up from the filth of [their] wallowing, took a deep breath, and marched to the field. . . ."[14] According to Douglass, the slaves masters often encouraged this excessive drinking: ". . . the slaveholders not only like to see the slave drink of his own accord, but will adopt various plans to make him drunk. One plan is to make bets on their slaves, as to who can drink the most whiskey without getting drunk; and in this way they succeed in getting whole multitudes to drink to excess."[15]

This tradition is still much in evidence at most of the Emancipation celebrations that are convened outside of the church. Juneteenth observances in Brenham, Texas, had Afro-American deputies to control the drinking and general crowd behavior. Parade marshals at past September 22nd celebrations in Terre Haute, Indiana, performed the same duties. Unfortunately, sometimes they were not successful in their efforts at maintaining law and order among the celebrants. Reverend J.C. Cook told me that a fatal shooting "broke up" the May 28th celebration in Glenville, Alabama;[16] and Mrs. Elva S. Riggins described in a letter the excessive drinking and resulting violence:

> The beverages ranged from red soda-pop—a brand known as Knee-High [Nehi] was very popular!—"bootleg" whiskey in fruit jars, and "home-brew." I seem to recall an intoxicant that was not aged as long as "home-brew"; it was called "Sister-get-you-ready!"
> Unfortunately June 20th found our community buzzing with gossip "Who got stabbed with an ice-pick," or news of someone having cut someone else up with a straight-edge razor or a knife known as a "Dallas Special."[17]

Mr. Haywood Hygh's letter to me described the celebrations' excessive drinking and violence in a more cryptic style: "It was seldom that one of these events [Juneteenth] took place when there was not shooting and killing. Shortly after the brothers got full of white lightning, they were ready for action. The undertakers always made it their business to be around or have some of their friends on the look-out for prospects."[18]

Whiskey, however, was not the only refreshment served during the slave holidays. Barbecue was also consumed in great quantities at some Saturday night parties; and it was the main dish at all Pinkster, Election Day, Camp Meeting, and Christmas holiday feasts. Thomas Wentworth Higginson observed the traditional way in which this dish had been prepared at past slave holidays during his company's preparations to celebrate Emancipation Day in 1863. A December 30th entry in his diary notes the continuing disagreement regarding the proper cooking time: "Touching the length of time required to 'do' an ox, no two housekeepers appear to agree. Accounts vary from two hours to twenty-four."[19] While this New Year's Eve entry records the slow traditional way of cooking, which is still practiced at today's Emancipation celebrations: "Fatted, quotha! Not one of the beasts at present appears to possess an ounce of superfluous flesh. Never were seen such lean kine. As they swing on vast spits, composed of young trees, the firelight glimmers through their ribs, as if they were great lanterns."[20] This centuries-old cooking method has made the cry "baseball and barbecue" the proper description of the Juneteenth, August 8th, and May 28th celebrations observed in Texas, Arkansas, Louisiana, Kentucky, Tennessee, Georgia, Alabama, and Florida.

Dancing to lively music was another popular slave holiday activity that was adopted into Emancipation celebration observances. Election Day celebrations always featured a glamorous ball over which the Governor and his lady reigned.[21] Pinkster celebrants in Albany, New York, danced the "Toto" and other traditional dances to the accompaniment of drums on the village green.[22] John Canoe revelers danced a "type of dance which is danced backward with the hands behind the back."[23] "Cuttin' the Pigeon Wings"—whose folk choreography required the slave dancers to mimic a pigeon by holding their necks stiff while flapping their arms—and "Going to the East and Going to the West"—a courting dance that allowed the dancers to kiss without embracing—were two slave party dances.[24]

Judging from recorded slave narratives, however, "settin' de flo' with Jenny" and "Jigging" were easily the most entertaining and physically demanding of all the party dances. Crowds would quickly form around dance contestants who tried to perform intricate dance steps without spilling a glass of water that was balanced on their heads. One ex-slave woman recalled dancing the former dance:

Every gal with her beau and such music! Had two fiddles, two tangerines, two banjos, and two sets of bones. Was a boy named Joe who used to whistle, too. Them devilish boys would get out in the middle of the flo' and me, Jenny and the devil right with 'em. Set a glass of water on my head and the boys would bet on it. I had a great wreath roun' my head an' a big ribbon bow on each side, and didn't waste a drop of water on none of 'em.[25]

While a former male slave recounted a Saturday night jigging contest that took place on his plantation:

I must tell you 'bout the best contest we ever had. One nigger on our place was the jigginest fellow ever was. Everyone round tries to get somebody to best him. He could put the glass of water on his head and make his feet go like triphammers and sound like the snaredrum. He could whirl round and such, all the movement from his hips down. Now it gits noised round a fellow been found to beat Tom and a contest am 'ranged for Saturday evening. There was a big crowd and money am bet, but Master bets on Tom, of course.

So they starts jiggins. Tom starts easy and a little faster and faster. The other fellow doing the same. They gits faster and faster, and that crowd am a-yelling. Gosh! There am 'citement. They just keep a-gwine. It look like Tom done found his match, but there am one thing yet he ain't done—he ain't made a whirl. Now he does it. Everybody holds he breath, and the other fellow starts to make the whirl and he makes it, but just a spoonful of water sloughs out his cup, so Tom am the winner.[26]

Thomas Wentworth Higginson recorded hearing his troops "praying and 'shouting' and clattering with hands and heels"[27] throughout the Christmas night leading up to the first celebration of President Lincoln's issuance of the Emancipation Proclamation. The Ring Shout dance that Higginson heard was aptly described by Henry George Spauling, a white minister who saw one of these twenty- to thirty-minute-long communal dances performed at Port Royal, South Carolina:

Three or four, standing, clapping their hands and beating time with their feet, commence singing in unison one of the peculiar shout melodies, while the others walk around in a ring, in single file, joining also in the song. Soon those in the ring leave off their singing, the others keeping it up the while with increased vigor, and strike into the shout step, observing most accurate time with the music.[28]

Emancipation celebrations have perpetuated the slaves' holiday custom of dancing. Remnants of African drum dancing have been observed at some celebrations. At July 4th festivities in Como, Mississippi, participants celebrated this most American of all holidays with the African custom of dancing to fife-and-drum music.[29] In personal correspondence, Mrs. Carrye Bennett, a retired West Point, Mississippi, schoolteacher, informed me that during past May 8th Emancipation celebrations in the Magnolia State celebrants "would beat the drum, singing and dancing all night."[30] Drum-dancing was also observed at May 28th Emancipation celebrations in the Alabama towns of Eufaula and Rutherford. Afro-Americans in the neighboring state of Georgia also celebrated May 28 with drum-dancing. Reverend Thomas J. Flanagan told me that on May 28 in Thomaston, Georgia, celebrants "would beat that drum and barbecue goats and have a big time."[31] He also recited, rather haltingly, the poem, "When Uncle Lit Beat that Drum," which he was inspired to write after watching Thomaston's May 28th drum dancers:

> It was the 28th of May
> And merrymakers gay
> Hurrahed for the Emancipation.
> When Lincoln by decree
> Made black man free. . . .
> When Lincoln by decree
> Made all black men free
> And gave a new step to the nation.
> The day was fair,
> And the crowd was there,
> But somehow the spirit didn't come.
> Till Old Uncle Lit
> Stepped out. . . .
> Till Old Uncle Lit
> Hit the grit
> And began to beat that drum.
> The old drums rowded. . . .
> Went bow, bow, bow
> and Roddy, dow, dow and bip.
> And the mud. . . .
> And the dust flew
> As Uncle Lit's crew
> Danced. . . .
> Danced about beating that drum.[32]

Evening dances remain a popular festivity for Emancipation celebrants. Formal balls have been held at Jacksonville's (Florida) May 29th celebration,[33] and "Suppers"—evening dances—remain a fixture on the schedule of Juneteenth activities. Mr. Judson Henry recalled east Texas whites attending some Juneteenth dances:

> Seemed like white folks would enjoy that day just as well as we would. . . . They'd even come to our dances. Now it wasn't a social affair for them with us, but they would be crowded around there. . . . First experience I ever had on a ballroom floor was Pittsburgh. Man who had a orchestra there I don't recall. They had a good orchestra and . . . white folks would be congregated around there. They were enjoying it as far as looking, but not participating. But they would be out there until everything was over.[34]

Jitterbug dance contests have also been held at past Juneteenth celebrations.[35]

The pageantry of a parade is another slave holiday ritual that has been adopted by Emancipation celebrants. Master and slave alike enjoyed the spectacle of a mass of costumed slaves following their king through the streets, singing and dancing to the music played by the royal musicians. Eastern North Carolina's John Canoe, New York's Pinkster, and New England's Election Day parades were among the most colorful of these slave marches. Pinkster's King Charley led his parade, dressed as a British brigadier, a costume complete with "scarlet coat with gold lace and ribbons, buckskin smallclothes, blue stockings, black shoes with silver buckles, and tricorn hat with pompom."[36] An Election Day celebration eyewitness wrote that the highlight of the day was "a pompous and ceremonious parade" in which the slaves "decked themselves out in striking or fantastic costumes, and horseback or on foot accompanied their 'governor' through the streets."[37] Another observer noted that the governor's "parade days were marked by much that was showy, and by some things that were ludicrous. A troop of blacks, sometimes two and two on foot, sometimes mounted in true military style and dress on horseback, escorted him through the streets."[38]

Parades have been popular events at a wide range of Emancipation celebrations. Annual parades have been recorded at January 1st, April 16th, May 28th, Juneteenth, August 8th and September 22nd freedom celebrations. Professor Wesley Lyda recalled the pageantry of the lodge members who marched in past September 22nd parades in Terre Haute, Indiana: " . . . they had all this plumed stuff with the swords and blue jackets and all of that. Oh, they thought they were really something going down [Wabash Avenue]. Boy, you should have seen them!"[39] Mrs. Katherine Burton, a former Miss Goddess of Liberty in one of Brenham's

(Texas) Juneteenth parades, described her costume and the float she and her king rode on:

> The float would be a truck or something pulled by a car. And this float would have flowers. People would make roses or flowers out of crepe paper. And they would decorate these floats. I remember one I rode on was yellow and black. And we had yellow dresses and maybe black sashes and bows and ribbons on. And some would be pink. And some would be pink and white or blue. Just different. . . . And the queen would ride in front and she would have a king. And I don't know if she would ride in front or if that would be the last float. I don't remember. . . . And [the king] would probably be dressed in black pants and a white coat or something, and a bow tie. And she would have a pretty dress.[40]

Spirited athletic contests are another slave holiday custom that has been borrowed by Emancipation celebrants. At Christmastime the slaves would "run races,"[41] and an Election Day observer noted that on that holiday "the afternoon was spent in dancing, games of quoits, [and] athletic exercises."[42] Quoits, which is closely related to horseshoes, has been defined as "a game in which the quoits [flattened rings of iron or circles of rope] are thrown at an upright pin in an attempt to ring the pin or come as near to it as possible."[43] Fredrick Douglass cited "playing ball" as one of the more popular "sports and merriments" of a slave's Christmas holiday.[44] In all probability Douglass was referring to some variation of "rounders" and/or "townball," two forerunners of American baseball that were extremely popular with white southerners during this period.[45] The former sport is "a game of English origin that is played with ball and bat and that somewhat resembles baseball."[46] Boxing was the major attraction during the last days of Pinkster. One researcher of this Easter celebration has noted that "on Friday evenings there were usually fights to decide who was champion bully of the city."[47]

Afro-Americans still tell slave folktales of athletic competition. One popular "John" folktale revolves around that notorious slave trickster wriggling out of fighting the champion slave from the neighboring plantation. The bout occurred during a holiday period when all the slaves and master families from both plantations were present. The ring was a rough dirt clearing between the two rival groups of cheering slaves and masters. Three different conclusions to this folktale have been collected and published. In one climax John feigns possessing a superhuman strength that will allow him to hurl a heavy maul so high in the sky it will endanger heaven's angels: Grabbing the object, he looks heavenward, shouting, "St. Peter, move over, and tell Sister Mary to move out the way, and move baby Jesus."[48] The plantation bully believes John's claim and forfeits the fight. A second conclusion has John intimidating his stronger opponent by arriving late for the match so that all the spectators and his opponent can see him slap Miss Ann, the master's wife, after she has rebuked him for being late. His opponent is so traumatized by John's bold act that he runs away and loses the match. When John's master asks why John slapped his mistress, John replies: "Well, Jim knowed if I slapped a white woman I'd killed him, so he run."[49] And a third conclusion has the slave trickster intimidating his bigger opponent by arriving late for his bout and then kissing the master's wife, ramming his fist through a hole he had already secretly carved out of a tree, and kicking his master in the seat of his pants. The frightened slave gladiator forfeits the bout saying: "When I saw Little John kiss that white woman I got a little shaky. When he hit that tree my heart stopped beatin', but when he kicked that white man I had to go, for I knowed if that fellow kiss a white woman in front of a white man, then kick a white man and he say nothin', Lawd have mercy, what would he do to me?"[50]

Emancipation celebrations have carried on the slave tradition of featuring exciting sporting events. A handbill advertising the 117th Annual Observance of the September 22 Emancipation Celebration cited a list of "Kids and Adults Games" that included: "Catch the Greasy Pig, Climb the Greasy Pole, Watermelon Eating Contest, Hog Calling Contest, Softball Game, Horseshoe Pitching Contest and many other games."[51] The 1947 Juneteenth program in Karnack, Texas, listed these "5:00 pm Amusements": "1. Soft Ball Game, 2. Croquet, 3. Mule Race (bareback) [and] 4. Bicycle Race."[52] And a handbill advertising the 105th Juneteenth in Rockdale, Texas, informed its readers that its "Feature Attractions Will Be: Shetland Pony Races—Bicycle Races—Two Sack Race—Shoe Scramble Race—Barefoot Race—Softball Games (Boys and Girls)."[53]

Rodeos were popular Juneteenth athletic events. Mr. Overton Smith recalled one that took place in Patterson Flats, Texas: "I can remember they had calf-roping down there at the 19th of June tournament . . . they would run them horses down a steep [incline] and pick them rings off. See? I mean pick them off. . . . They was up on a pole."[54]

But baseball remains the most popular Emancipation celebration event. "Ball Game" is the simple listing that Daingerfield's (Texas) 58th Anniversary Juneteenth handbill gives to their featured athletic event of the day. Mr.

J.L. Donaldson, a former Juneteenth baseball player, recalled how the drama of these celebration contests electrified the white and black communities of such towns as Paris, Texas, his hometown:

> Usually when Commerce [Oklahoma] came to town on the 19th of June, or what have you, it was two days, a Sunday and Monday. Under normal conditions the town would close up when Commerce came to town to play, because during this time we had some what we thought at one time were the equivalency of a major-league ballplayer. And the city of Paris just closed up on Monday when Commerce was playing. Of course you couldn't hardly get a seat for the whites on Sunday. And it was a mess on Monday.[55]

Thus, the newly emancipated slaves inherited a wide variety of slave holiday rituals, which they drew from in molding their freedom celebrations. These celebrations fall generally into three categories. Slave communities' reactions to Emancipation ran the emotional gamut from sombre, religious thanksgiving to exuberant, carnal good times. From this widest of all possible ranges of human emotion the freed slaves and their descendants have fashioned celebrations that focus on thanksgiving, others that are devoted to good times, and still others that represent a combination of these two divergent emotional responses to Emancipation.

Some slaves chose to celebrate the news of their freedom with religious thanksgiving. In Allensville, Kentucky, the first August 8th celebrants gathered in Jim Phillips's barn to thank God with songs and prayers for giving them their freedom.[56] In New England, racially mixed congregations of free Afro-Americans and white abolitionists spent the last night of 1862 singing and praying for freedom in special Emancipation Watch Night Services.[57] In east Texas, the slave ancestors of Mr. Booker T. Washington Hogan celebrated their initial Juneteenth in 1865 with religious songs and prayers of thanksgiving: "It started in the church. The 19th of June celebrations really started as a camp meeting. Church meetings. They just prayed and sang and stuff like that. . . . It was a thanksgiving. It was just . . . really for the Negro. It was a method of thanksgiving, as it started out."[58]

The major components of this religious thanksgiving celebratory model, which were carried over from the slave Watch Night Services, are the singing of spirituals, praying, and preaching. The singing of a freedom anthem and the reading of a freedom document were two other rituals borrowed from the August 1st celebrations of West Indian Emancipation, which began in 1834, and which the free Afro-American community observed prior to Lincoln's issuance of his September 22, 1862, and January 1, 1863, proclamations of freedom. Abolitionist anthems such as "John Brown" and patriotic songs such as "America" were also sung. Thomas Wentworth Higginson recorded this account of the singing of the latter song at an Emancipation celebration that he attended on January 1, 1863:

> The very moment the speaker had ceased, and just as I took and waved the flag, which now for the first time meant anything to these poor people, there suddenly arose, close beside the platform, a strong male voice (but rather cracked and elderly), into which two women's voices instantly blended, singing, as if by impulse that could no more be repressed than the morning note of the song-sparrow.

> 'My County, 'tis of thee,
> Sweet land of liberty
> Of thee I sing!'[59]

And the Emancipation Proclamation was read instead of the West Indian Proclamation. This patriotic and religious thanksgiving mode of celebration provides the model for most contemporary January 1st observances.

But reverent thankfulness wasn't the only slave response to Emancipation; there were also early celebrations of sheer joy and good times. Paul Laurence Dunbar, the poet, recalled that his parents raced about screaming and beating pots upon receiving the news of freedom.[60] Mr. Charles Morgan told me that the initial Juneteenth celebration in his native Anderson County, Texas, was a joyous good time, devoid of any religious overtones:

> Well, the way it was explained to me, the 19th of June wasn't the exact day the Negro was freed. But that's the day they told them that they was free. . . .
> And my daddy told me that they whooped and hollered and bored holes in trees with augers and stopped it up with [gun] powder and light that, and that would be their blast for the celebration.
> [*Chuckles*] . . . Yeah, they'd tear a whole tree up. Be a hundreds of people looking at it.[61]

The central components of this exuberant, carnal, good-times model are borrowed from a wide variety of slave holiday celebrations. The culinary rituals of eating barbecue and drinking whiskey to excess, as well as the traditions of singing, dancing, and playing games all stem from the slaves' Christmas holiday season. Parading and gambling were good-time rituals derived from the slaves' Pinkster and Election Day celebrations. In April 1811, because of the former celebrants' "boisterous rioting and drunkenness," the Common Council of Albany passed an ordinance forbidding, among other things, the construction of a Pinkster booth "to collect in numbers for the purpose of gambling. . . ."⁶² This good-times celebratory model currently structures numerous Juneteenth, August 8th, May 28th, and various other warm-weather celebrations of Emancipation.

There was also a third variety of early Emancipation celebration that combined these two traditions. Just as the slaves' Christmas, Pinkster, and Election Day celebrations were designed to accommodate both the lost and saved segments of the slave community, so Emancipation celebrations have continued to provide, since their inception, some freedom rituals that will attract Afro-Americans of all persuasions and from all the socio-economic classes. This "Hallelujah/Good-Time" combination type of Emancipation celebration seems to be modeled after the old camp-meeting revivals, such as those that Mr. Clarence Morton attended as a boy in northern Tennessee:

> I tell you what, when I was a youngster, when I was a boy. You know, that's the way revivals was run. When a revival started, that's when they had their big crap game. They'd be in the woods, yes sireee. They'd come so close to the church and that's where they had it, yes sireee. . . . And the first thing when you go in, you go into the church. And the next place you get to is [serving] barbecue meat and stuff; the next place where they selling these birds and things like that; and back a little farther they selling the white lightning.⁶³

Some May 28th, September 22nd, August 1st, and Juneteenth celebrations have been based on this model that combines the sacred and the secular. Reverend J.C. Cook shared with me a May 28th anecdote that underscores how difficult it is to get both "saved" and "unsaved" Afro-Americans to unite in celebrating their Emancipation:

> I remember once on one Saturday . . . they opened up that Saturday night and the man who was going to preach. (The people in the church wasn't disciplined in being assembled; they was fellowshipping.) As so the man got to preaching and he yelled out. (It was raining just a little.) He yelled out: "THESE FOLKS GOING TO HELL!" One man stepped out who'd been drinking said: "LET 'EM GOOOOO, REVEREND!" [Laughter]⁶⁴

An examination of certain Emancipation celebrations' handbills and programs illustrates how celebration sponsors consciously scheduled events that would appeal to both of these groups. Sponsors of Gallipolis's (Ohio) 117th September 22nd celebration scheduled religious activities that included a Saturday afternoon concert featuring five area "Gospel Groups," a Sunday morning worship service, and an afternoon song ser-

ORDER OF SERVICE

12:00 Noon

Negro National Hymn ———————— "Lift Every Voice"

Prayer ———————————————— Rev. E. Adams, Jr.

Selection ————————— New Providence Church Choir

Scripture ———————————— Rev. H. L. Gladney

Selection ——————— Mount Pilgrim Church Choir

Welcome ———————————— Mrs. Rosie Walker

Selection ——————— New Providence Church Choir

Emancipation Proclamation —————— Mrs. Ethyln Kirby

Instrumental Solo ——————————— Dr. D. C. Grant

Introduction of Speaker ————— Dr. W. B. Howell, President

Speaker ———————————— Dr. George B. Thomas
Instructor, Interdenominational Theological Center
Atlanta, Georgia

Selection ———————— Mount Pilgrim Church Choir

Emphasis "Urban League" ———————— Rev. J. H. Flakes

Offering and Church donations ——— Finance Committee in charge

Selection ——————— New Providence Church Choir

Remarks ——————— Rev. J. H. Johnson, Vice-President

Benediction — Speaker

This program from a January 1st celebration in Columbus, Georgia (1973) is
an example of the religious-thanksgiving model of freedom celebration.

The Roots and Fruits of Emancipation Celebrations 37

139th
ANNUAL EMANCIPATION CELEBRATION
JACKSON PARK, WINDSOR, ONTARIO
BEING HELD
AUGUST 4, 5, 6, 7, 1972
PRESENTS
Black International "MISS SEPIA"
Beauty Contest

CONTESTANTS WANTED — QUALIFICATIONS:
Single, Black, Age 17-22; Closing Date July 15, 1972
FOUR DAYS OF CELEBRATING

★ **PETER MARCH'S CARNIVAL**

★ **AMATEUR TALENT SHOW**

★ **SUNRISE SERVICE**

★ **GUEST SPEAKER TO BE ANNOUNCED**

★ **FASHION SHOW**

★ **BEAUTY CONTEST - AUGUST 7, 1972**

DON'T FORGET OUR FAMOUS OPEN-AIR BAR-B-QUE PIT

Call for information: Windsor, Ontario, Edmund (Ted) Powell & Assoc., 1-519-258-3165

Call for information: Detroit, Mich., Jack Williams, 1-313-931-0979

☛ COME ONE ☛ COME ALL

The above flier (from Windsor, Canada) is an example of the evolution of the West Indian celebration of August 1, 1834, into the "good-time" variety of freedom celebration. The 1972 flier highlights such good-time elements as barbecue, a carnival, a fashion show, and a beauty contest.

The Gallipolis, Ohio, flier from 1980 (opposite) demonstrates how the celebration of President Lincoln's issuance of his preliminary proclamation in September 22, 1862, has evolved into a sacred-secular model of freedom celebration. Note the clear distinctions drawn between Saturday's secular events and Sunday's sacred activities.

EVERYONE WELCOME

TWO BIG HOMECOMING DAYS

117th ANNUAL OBSERVANCE

EMANCIPATION CELEBRATION

Saturday, Sept. 20, 1980   Sunday, Sept. 21, 1980

GALLIA COUNTY FAIR GROUNDS

STATE RT. 35   **3 MILES N. W. OF GALLIPOLIS**

GATES OPEN 8:30 A. M. EACH MORNING

SATURDAY PROGRAM — ACTIVITIES START AT 10:30 A. M.

Kids and Adults Games — Sponsored by FOCUS, Inc.
Catch the Greasy Pig, Climb the Greasy Pole, Watermelon Eating Contest, Hog Calling Contest,
Soft Ball Game, Horseshoe Pitching Contest and many other games. Prizes and Ribbons for Winners.

Cook and Bake Fair: Cake, Cookies, Pies, Rolls, and Favorite Dishes will be judged and Prizes and
Ribbons for the Winners. Then the food will be Auctioned off. Everyone Welcomed to Enter.

AFTERNOON

Bean Dinner, Crowning of Emancipation Queen for 1980, Talent Show,
Craft Demonstration—Della Brown Taylor, Charleston, W. Va.
Special Music By: "Sound Grove"—Clarence McCabe-Band Leader-Singer
Gospel Groups: Ethel Caffie—Charleston, W. Va., Dr. Francine Childs—Ohio University, Athens, O.,
Miracle Three Gospel Trio—Dayton, O., Corinth Trio—Corinth, O., Voices United—Gallipolis, O.
Arts and Crafts Display—Demonstrations

SUNDAY MORNING — 10:30 A. M.

Church Services—Invocation
Morning Messages—Rev. Vance Watson, Mt. Carmel Church, Bidwell, Ohio
Music: Combined Church Choirs
Special Selections

AFTERNOON

Greetings:
Special Music: Mt. Carmel Youth Choir, Bidwell, Ohio
Family Circle—Bidwell, Ohio, Voices United—Gallia County, Ohio
Speaker—Della Brown Taylor, Associate Professor, West Virginia State College, Institute, W. Va.

Concession Stands on the Grounds by FOCUS, Inc. and Others

Camping Facilities for Campers on the Grounds

Motel and 24 Hour Restaurant Close By

Admission Free   James Hogan, President

EVERYONE WELCOME

The Roots and Fruits of Emancipation Celebrations   39

vice featuring three gospel groups. Secular events planned included Saturday morning games, "Cook and Bake Fair," Saturday afternoon bean dinner, the crowning of the Emancipation Queen, a talent show, a craft demonstration, and special music by a local soul band. The 139th August 1st program for Windsor, Ontario, carried a similar schedule of activities. Religious events included a Sunday morning sunrise service and an evening song service with several local choirs. In addition to Peter March's carnival, other secular events staged at this celebration included "Kiddies Contests" on Friday, Saturday, and Sunday, an "Amateur Night" on Friday, a "Talent Show" on Saturday, a mammoth parade on Sunday, and a "Fashion Show" and "The Miss Sepia [Beauty] Contest" on Monday. In 1968 organizers of the Juneteenth celebration in Big Bluff Spring, Texas, shifted the observance date to July 4th and printed a program comprised of these sacred and secular activities. Religious thanksgiving activities included a 1:30 P.M. program consisting of a selection, prayer, reading of the Emancipation Proclamation, address, solo, and musical selections from a "visiting quartet." Secular good-time events enjoyed on that day included a 3:30 P.M. "free barbecue and basket dinner" and a 4:30 "baseball game."

These three types of Emancipation celebration have done much more than survive; they have also served as fertile cultural ground in which an impressive array of twentieth century celebrations and ideological movements have taken root and flourished. Some of these new cultural celebrations, like the older Emancipation celebrations, are geared toward the glorification of black womanhood Afro-American beauty contests, which were conceived in this century, stem directly from the Goddesses of Liberty and other Emancipation queens elected and crowned during past Emancipation celebrations. In the 1920s the fall national editions of the *Chicago Defender* were crammed full of stories and photographs of college homecoming queens at such Afro-American schools as Howard, Hampton, and Fisk. Miss Bronze America, Miss Sepia, and numerous other Afro-American beauty queens were crowned in the 1930s, 1940s, and 1950s.[65] In the 1960s and 1970s Afro-American coeds were also elected homecoming queens at some predominately white universities.[66] These last two decades also witnessed the selection of Afro-American women from Indiana, Kentucky, Ohio, and Wyoming as winners of their states' beauty pageants. And it was in the 1970s that Afro-Americans, motivated by the Black Power Movement, began to sponsor Miss Black America and Miss Black Teenage American beauty contests.[67] And in 1984 an Afro-American woman was finally crowned Miss America.[68] The series of events that ultimately led to this cultural first was initiated by the annual Emancipation celebration queen contests.

The tribute paid to the beauty and good grooming of Emancipation queens is the cultural forebear of other traditions in the Afro-American community. Since the 1950s *Ebony*, the Afro-American-owned, Chicago-based monthly magazine, has sponsored *Ebony* Fashion Fair, a national fashion tour.[69] Local civic, social, and religious Afro-American organizations sponsor these highly successful fashion extravaganzas in which the modern equivalents of the Goddesses of Liberty model the latest American and international fashions. Some Emancipation celebrations, such as the August 1st observance in Windsor, Ontario, have added fashion shows to their calendar of events.

As early as the late 1930s Afro-American Greek-letter and professional organizations have sponsored cotillions "to improve the social and cultural life" of Afro-American women.[70] These annual celebrations of Afro-American womanhood's social graces and moral values have expanded greatly since their inception. Washington, D.C.'s cotillion, which began as a small "dinner and banquet" that attracted a few hundred celebrants, has evolved into "a gigantic ball" with as many as fifteen hundred in attendance.[71] And the Philadelphia cotillion, whose seventeen hundred or more celebrants make it the largest of all of these coming-out affairs, annually gives a distinguished Afro-American, such as Roy Wilkins, their Jewelled Cross of Malta award to honor the awardee's contributions to racial advancement.[72]

The athletic traditions of Emancipation celebrations have also spawned a galaxy of new celebrations and new heroes in the twentieth century. During this century the Afro-American community's keen interests in boxing and running, events which had featured so prominently in Emancipation celebration and slave holiday sporting contests, widened to follow the fortunes of Afro-American sporting figures in national and international arenas. During the first three decades of this century, Afro-Americans took great pleasure and pride in watching Jack Johnson[73] and Joe Louis[74] become the first two men of their race to win the coveted world-heavyweight boxing championship. In 1936 they joined their fellow Americans in praising the four-gold-medal-winning Olympic exploits of Jesse Owens in the Berlin Games. The heroics of these three athletes are indelibly marked on the Afro-American consciousness. Johnson's disdainful threshing of Jim Jefferies, the former undefeated champion and first "white hope,"[75] and Louis's savage knockout of Max Schmeling, his first conqueror and symbol of Adolf Hitler's racial theory of Aryan supremacy,[76] are boxing triumphs that Afro-Americans still recount with pride.

But it was baseball, more than any other Emancipation celebration athletic contest, that has had the greatest impact upon Afro-American culture in the twentieth century. Out of those fiercely contested local games at countless August 8th and Juneteenth celebrations came such outstanding baseball players as "Rube" Foster, the east Texas minister's son who founded and managed the Chicago American Giants, the first premier Afro-American baseball team.[77] Former Juneteenth baseball player, Mr. Judson Henry, still recalled the thrill of being offered a tryout by Foster, almost fifty years later: "[The] guy who use to run the Chicago Black Giants, Rube Foster, he sent some papers for us to fill out and come and have a tryout with his club, which I figure we could have made. But, you know, that same spring we was supposed to go in and report to him, we all fell victims of smallpox."[78]

But founding the Chicago American Giants was not Rube Foster's greatest organizational achievement. In the second decade of this century he also founded and served as the first commissioner of the Negro National League, a sports institution that would leave its mark on Afro-American culture and radically alter American society before its demise in the 1950s. The financial success of Foster's league, which was comprised of teams in such midwestern cities as Cleveland, St. Louis, Indianapolis, Chicago, and Kansas City, ultimately led to the formation of a rival Eastern League that included teams in New York, Philadelphia, Washington, D.C., and other North Atlantic coast cities. A natural rivalry between these two leagues spawned two major sporting events. During the 1920s the two league champions played a fall World Series of Negro Baseball that was fervently followed by Midwestern and East Coast Afro-Americans and closely covered by such national Afro-American newspapers as the *Chicago Defender*.[79]

In the 1930s the same decade that the major leagues began their All-Star Game tradition, organized Negro baseball began their annual East-West All-Star Game tradition. This summer baseball classic, which pitted the best Negro players from both leagues, was an annual fixture on the Afro-American cultural calendar from its inception in 1933 until its demise in the early 1950s. Avid Afro-American baseball fans made annual pilgrimages from the South, Southwest, Midwest, and East to Chicago's Comiskey Park to see such outstanding players as Buck Leonard, Leroy "Satchel" Paige, "Cool Poppa" Bell, Josh Gibson, Roy Campanella, Monte

Irvin, Don Newcombe, Henry Aaron, and Jackie Robinson perform their diamond magic.

Robinson stands as the mightiest cultural hero of these Afro-American baseball stars. By successfully integrating organized baseball, an almost superhuman feat that taxed the limits of his athletic skills and personal resources, Robinson paved the way for integrating all of America's professional sports.[80] His athletic prowess also inspired other Afro-Americans to strive for excellence and social acceptance in other areas of American life. As the song says, "Did you see Jackie Robinson hit that ball? He stole home and that ain't all."[81]

In addition to beauty and sports contests—one event dominated by females, the other by males—Emancipation celebrations have perpetuated several other rituals which have also evolved into major influences on twentieth century Afro-American culture. Foremost are the celebrations' vibrant musical traditions which have spawned a series of cultural events focusing on music.

Beginning in the 1940s, the *Pittsburgh Courier* conducted an annual Negro musical poll. The format was simple and highly successful. The newspaper published a two-page listing of all the major Afro-American singers and musicians by categories. The readers would then vote for their favorite artists in the respective categories and mail their ballots back to the newspaper. The results of this musical plebiscite, along with pictures of the winners, were published in a later edition of the newspaper.[82] Since the 1960s, *Ebony* magazine has sponsored an annual Afro-American musical awards program. Their winners are selected by a panel of experts instead of by popular vote. The 1980s awards shows have been televised.[83] Two gospel music conventions have evolved in this century. In 1933 Reverend Thomas A. Dorsey, the father of gospel music, and Miss Sallie Martin founded the Gospel Singers Convention, an annual conference of Afro-American church choirs that is still in existence.[84] In 1969 the Reverend James Cleveland founded the Gospel Singers Workshop, another highly successful musical celebration that appeals more to younger gospel singers and musicians.[85] In the 1980s "soul" radio stations and Afro-American weekly newspapers have promoted Black Music Month celebrations. Every day in June soul radio stations air biographical sketches of a wide range of Afro-American musical artists followed by recordings of each artist. Weekly newspapers publish photographs or sketches of various artists along with an accompanying biographical statement which summarizes their lives and musical achievements.[86]

Emancipation celebration parades have proven to be the cultural fore-runners of several significant twentieth century annual Afro-American marches. When the Empire Lodge of Rochester, New York, invited Buffalo's Star of the West Lodge to join them in staging an August 1st parade, the host lodge printed posters which read, "A grand demonstration of the G.U.O. of Odd Fellows," whereas the Buffalo lodge's posters carried the message, "A grand Emancipation celebration."[87] One can interpret this disagreement in one of two ways: either the members of the Rochester Lodge were ignorant of the August 1st celebration or they were aware of it but did not choose to observe it. In either case this organizational mix up shows that by the 1890s some Afro-Americans wanted to parade for reasons other than for celebrating their Emancipation.

Beginning in 1899 thousands of Afro-American Elks, bedecked in "Gayly colored uniforms, with purple and gold and purple and white, tailored in many styles . . . ," paraded each summer through the streets of the city that was hosting their national convention.[88] In the 1920s Marcus Garvey's Universal Negro Improvement Association conducted annual spectacular parades, featuring Afro-Americans dressed in all types of military garb, through the streets of Harlem.[89] Since the 1920s the *Chicago Defender* has sponsored the Bud Billiken Day Parade. This annual August march through the South Side of Chicago was the brain-child of David Kellum, who also created the character for whom the parade was named. Parade marshals for this patriotic march include such national figures as Joe Louis, Duke Ellington, and Amos and Andy. During the 1930s crowds of fifty thousand were reported to have viewed the march.[90] In the 1940s West Indian immigrants to New York City began to celebrate an elaborate Labor Day Weekend Parade that featured costumed participants reminiscent of earlier August 1st parades.[91] The 1940s also witnessed the birth of the Orange Blossom Classic Football Game parade. Jacksonville, Orlando, and Miami Afro-Americans turned out to witness a dazzling display of floats, beauty queens, and the high stepping of the world-famous Florida A&M University marching band.[92]

Traditional musical genres, especially the spirituals and the blues, and folk ideas preserved in Emancipation celebrations have also served as the ideological springboards for Negro History Week celebrations, as well as for several new twentieth century Afro-American cultural movements. Carter G. Woodson, the Afro-American historian, founded the former celebration in February of 1926. Woodson selected the first two weeks of February because this period contained the birthdays of Frederick Douglass and Abraham Lincoln. Woodson's celebrations expressed in a more formal way the racial history that had been passed on orally by former slaves at earlier Emancipation celebrations. Woodson expressed his feelings on this matter a few months after celebrating the first Negro History Week, linking the very survival of the Afro-American race to the successful perpetuation of this history: "The Negro knows practically nothing of his history and his 'friends' are not permitting him to learn it. . . . [And] if a race has no history, if it has no worth-while tradition, it becomes a negligible factor in the thought of the world, and it stands in danger of extermination."[93]

The continued celebration of Negro History Week and its recent expansion to Black History Month are eloquent testimonies that Woodson's celebration "instill[s] [in] Afro-Americans a sense of pride and accomplishment . . ." similar to that fostered by Emancipation celebrations. W.E.B. Du Bois has also noted that Woodson "literally made this country, which has only the slightest respect for people of color, recognize and celebrate each year, a week in which it studied the effect which the American Negro has upon life, thought and action in the United States."[94]

The raison d'être of the New Negro Movement of the 1930s was traditional Afro-American culture, the very stuff from which Emancipation celebrations have been fashioned and maintained. Alain Locke and W.E.B. Du Bois, two of the major architects of this social movement, were both motivated by a desire to gain recognition for the significant contributions that Afro-American slaves had made to American culture. Locke wrote: ". . . for the present, more immediate hope rests in the realization by white and black alike of the Negro in terms of his artistic endowments and cultural contributions, past and prospective. It must be increasingly recognized that the Negro has already made very substantial contributions, not only in folk-art, music especially, which has always found appreciation, but in large, though humbler and less acknowledged ways."[95] Du Bois continued this theme of the rich endowment that Afro-Americans have bequeathed American culture: "We the darker ones come even now not altogether emptyhanded: there are today no truer exponents of the pure human spirit of the Declaration of Independence than the American Negroes; there is no true American music but the wild sweet melodies of the Negro slave; the American fairy tales and folk-lore are Indian and African. . . ."[96] Inspired by this kind of thinking, some Harlem Renaissance writers rejected European poetic forms. Langston Hughes, for example, wrote some of his earlier poems in the traditional AAB structure of the

Slavery (1619–1862)   1862–1865

Saturday/Sunday ——————————
- Dancing
- Drinking
- Barbecue
- Music
- Preaching

Pinkster ——————————
- Parading
- Dancing
- Drinking
- Sports
- Music
- Prayer

Election Day ——————————
- Parading
- Dancing
- Drinking
- Barbecue
- Music

August 1st ——————————
- Document Reading
- Anthem Singing
- Prayer
- Preaching

Christmas ——————————
- Dancing
- Drinking
- Barbecue
- Sports
- Music

John Canoe ——————————
- Parading
- Dancing
- Music

New Year's Day ——————————
- Dancing
- Music
- Prayer

EMANCIPATION CELEBRATIONS

Freedom (1865–Present)

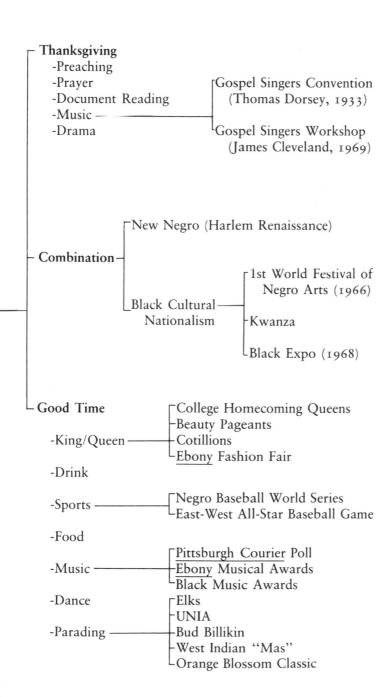

- **Thanksgiving**
  - -Preaching
  - -Prayer
  - -Document Reading
  - -Music ——— Gospel Singers Convention (Thomas Dorsey, 1933)
  - -Drama
  - Gospel Singers Workshop (James Cleveland, 1969)

- **Combination**
  - New Negro (Harlem Renaissance)
  - Black Cultural Nationalism
    - 1st World Festival of Negro Arts (1966)
    - Kwanza
    - Black Expo (1968)

- **Good Time**
  - -King/Queen
    - College Homecoming Queens
    - Beauty Pageants
    - Cotillions
    - Ebony Fashion Fair
  - -Drink
  - -Sports
    - Negro Baseball World Series
    - East-West All-Star Baseball Game
  - -Food
  - -Music
    - Pittsburgh Courier Poll
    - Ebony Musical Awards
    - Black Music Awards
  - -Dance
  - -Parading
    - Elks
    - UNIA
    - Bud Billikin
    - West Indian "Mas"
    - Orange Blossom Classic

blues;[97] and James Weldon Johnson used the structure and themes of traditional Afro-American sermons to compose some of his poetry.[98]

In the 1960s advocates of black cultural nationalism also turned to the well-spring of traditional Afro-American culture to validate their separatist ideology. On one occasion Larry Neal, one of the leading theorists of this ideology, wrote regarding the tension of double consciousness: "In some cases, the tension resolves in recognizing the beauty and love within Black America itself. No, not a new 'Negritude,' but a profound sense of a unique and beautiful culture; and a sense that there are many spiritual areas to explore within this culture."[99] Stephen Henderson labeled this Black Arts Movement "the cultural dimension" of the Black Power Movement.[100] Like their poetic counterparts in the earlier Harlem Renaissance, many of the poets in this era used the traditional narrative and musical forms of their people. Le Roi Jones used the intricate tonal and rhythmical patterns of jazz to compose his poems;[101] while other angry activists, such as H. Rap Brown, used the structure of the toast, a narrative poem which extols the sexual and pugalistic exploits of black men, to formulate their poetry.[102] And Nikki Giovanni recorded some of her poems while using the lush background music of a gospel choir directed by James Cleveland.

This movement in the arts also brought about some new cultural celebrations. During the month of April in 1966, the First World Festival of Negro Arts was held in Dakar, Senegal.[103] This celebration brought together black artists of the New World with their African counterparts. A second Festival was held in Lagos, Nigeria.[104] Kwanza, an Afro-American alternative celebration for Christmas, was introduced during the 1960s.[105] And in 1968 Reverend Jesse Jackson's Operation PUSH held the first Black Expo in Chicago. Since that time this cultural bonanza has been staged annually in Chicago and other midwestern cities such as Indianapolis. Like the original celebration, subsequent Black Expos have depended heavily on the participation of popular Afro-American singers and musicians to draw the masses of Afro-Americans to the maze of educational, political, and cultural booths. The list of artists who have performed at Chicago's Black Expo includes Roberta Flack, the Jacksons, Isaac Hayes, "Cannonball" Adderly, and Stevie Wonder.[106]

In essence, as the above diagram illustrates, these contemporary Afro-American celebrations are the latest cultural crop of fruit borne by the sturdy Emancipation celebration trees that were planted across the American historical landscape from 1862–65. And the taproots of those trees are firmly and deeply rooted in the survived, but not forgotten, era of slavery.

CHAPTER 3

*[During] early celebrations . . . slavery was
rehearsed, kept fresh in the mind and
emphasis laid indelibly in the minds of
youth that the Negro was once a slave.*

Atlanta Daily World *(1941)*

The Afro-American Saga

A primary function of freedom celebrations is to keep the Afro-American saga alive in the minds of celebrants. One newspaper editorial accurately described these events as "celebrations which rehearsed incidents of torture and privations, [and] narratives of hard and bitter experiences of the slave. . . ."[1]

The Afro-American saga is a commonly accepted story of the African's history in America. It has evolved over generations and been preserved and passed down both orally and in freedom celebration pageants. The saga has four epochs, with one overriding theme of a quest for freedom.

The Afro-American's glorious African past constitutes the first epoch. Scenes enacted from this period depict the glories of Egypt, Ethiopia, and other ancient African civilizations. Slavery is the second epoch, and depictions of this bitter period commonly include such episodes as the various forms of physical and psychological torture experienced by the slaves, the slave revolts, the underground railroad, and the evolution of the spiritual, the slaves' musical gift to American culture. Emancipation is the third epoch. Its chronicle includes such scenes as Abraham Lincoln's issuing of the Emancipation Proclamation, the Civil War, the courageous role of Afro-American soldiers, Lee's surrender to Grant, the superior morality of the slaves left behind to run the plantations while their masters were away at war, and the slaves' joy of experiencing freedom.

The fourth epoch encompasses the ongoing struggle for freedom that began for Afro-Americans, ironically with Emancipation. As one January 1st speaker expressed it, "Abraham Lincoln only partially emancipated our forefathers. We are not yet out of slavery. Negroes and whites alike are still in emotional slavery."[2] Major events in this era include the hopes and disappointments of Reconstruction, mass migrations from the South to the western frontiers and the northern industrial cities, Afro-Americans' participation in all the American wars, the civil-rights movement, the Supreme Court decision of 1954, the 1955 Montgomery bus boycott, the two marches on Washington, the assassinations of Martin Luther King, Jr., and Malcolm X, the election of Afro-Americans to Congress and various local offices, the rise of Black Nationalism, the urban riots, and the Afro-American's contributions of jazz, blues, ragtime, gospel, rhythm and blues, soul, and funk to American music.

Although random bits of this four-epoch saga appear throughout the freedom celebrations, the entire saga was best expressed as a unit in a series of historical pageants that were written especially for these observances. One of these pageants, *Born to Be Free,* was a Juneteenth drama that "enacted this history of the American black man through songs, dances, and dramatic presentations."[3] *O Black and Unknown Bards,* a "Jubilee-Pageant," was written for the 1938 September 22nd celebration held in St. Louis.[4] *Color Me Brown* was performed several times during the 1950s before Philadelphia celebrants of National Freedom Day. January 1st pageants include a 1937 production in Brunswick, Georgia, of *Out of the Darkness into the Light,*[5] a New Bern, North Carolina, staging in 1936 of *Up from Slavery,*[6] and two Atlanta, Georgia, productions: *Phrases for a Free People*[7] and *Freedom is a Hard Bought Thing,*[8] the latter a dramatic production that replaced the traditional Emancipation Day address. In addition, *Portraits: Brown Americans, Firm Foundations,* and *Bridging a Gap* have been produced during Negro History Week.

Folklorist Debbie Bowman Richards has defined these folk dramas as being: "episodic performances which: (a) employ a variety of techniques to focus attention; (b) exist as public action of a small, community level group, sharing a system of understood motives and symbols; (c) have a foreknown resolution; and (d) are related to game, play, and ritual."[9] Roger D. Abrahams has noted that these pageants are also characterized by "clowning, dancing, singing, instrumental music, bombastic speeches, and other highly stylized types of performance. . . ."[10]

The music and lyrics of the spirituals play a major role in these dramas. In some pageants "appropriate spirituals are sung [and] adapted to each scene of the pageant."[11] One Juneteenth celebrant recalled that these historical pageants "even dramatized the songs like 'Haven't Got Long to Stay Here.' "[12] "Steal Away" is dramatized in *O Black and Unknown Bards* and *Portraits: Brown Americans.* "Nobody Knows the Trouble I've Seen" is sung in *O Black and Unknown Bards.* "Go Down Moses" is woven into the scripts of *Portraits: Brown Americans* and *O Black and Unknown Bards.* "Motherless Child" and "Free at Last": are enacted in *Portraits: Brown Americans.* While "I'm Troubled 'Bout My Soul," "Roll Jordan Roll," "Swing Low Sweet Chariot," "We Are Climbing Jacob's Ladder," "It's Me, It's Me, Oh Lord," "My Lord, What a Mourning," "Certainly Lord," and "There's a Meeting Here Tonight" were all sung by the cast of *O Black and Unknown Bards.*

A clear illustration of the close relationship between these pageants and the Afro-American saga is the following description of *The Epic of a Race,* a historical pageant produced in Chicago's Soldiers Field during the 1933 World's Fair, which reads like another detailed statement of the Afro-American saga's various epochs and scenes.

> The pageant will be a fascinating presentation of the Negro's slavery with the slave revolts, the sorrow songs and the beautiful spirituals, the abolition agitation, the Lincoln-Douglas debates, John Brown's raid on Harper's Ferry, the underground railroad, the Civil War, the emancipation of the slaves, the reconstruction, Lincoln's assassination, the rise of the Ku Klux Klan, the educational crusade of the northern philanthropists, the ascendancy of Booker T. Washington and the advent of the jazz age.[13]

In this same vein, *Up from Slavery* has been characterized as a drama in which the "Struggles of [the Black] Race [are] Depicted. . . ."[14] And *Color Me Brown's* secondary title is appropriately enough, "A Story of Negro Progress and Achievements."[15]

Of all these dramas, *The Star of Ethiopia* and *Ethiopia at the Bar of Justice* do the best job of dramatizing the saga's themes of Africa, slavery, Emancipation, and continued struggle. The former pageant has been described as being "The Historical Pageant showing the progress of the Negro from Early Egyptian times to the present."[16] While the latter drama has been characterized as a pageant which gives "much attention to the strivings and achievements of the Negro. . . ."[17] W. E. B. Du Bois wrote *The Star of Ethiopia* for New York City's 1913 Emancipation Exposition, which celebrated fifty years of racial freedom and progress.[18] By Du Bois's account, the pageant was produced only two more times in the next three years: an October, 1915, production in Washington, D.C., and a May, 1916, production given in Philadelphia during the centennial celebration of the AME Church.[19] James McCoo's pageant, *Ethiopia at the Bar of Justice,* was first produced at the 1924 General Conference of the AME Church, held in Louisville. Since this initial production, McCoo's pageant has been annually produced at Negro History Week celebrations.

There were great disparities between the production of these two celebration pageants. *The Star of Ethiopia* was a religious extravaganza that cost almost $3,000 to stage. One ad boasted of a cast of "1,000 actors," a "200 voice chorus," "2 brass bands," and countless "Ethiopians, Nubians, Mohammedans, Egyptians, Freedmen, etc."[20] The pageant's plot was summarized by the herald in the drama's prelude:

> Here ye, hear ye! Men of all the Americas, and listen to the story of the eldest and strongest of the races of mankind, whose faces be black. Hear ye, hear ye of the gifts of black men to this world, the Iron Gift and Gift of Faith, the Pain of Humility and the Sorrow Song of Pain, the Gift of Freedom and laughter, and the undying Gift of Hope. Men of the world keep silence and hear ye this![21]

Each of the pageant's six episodes was introduced by the herald and four banner-bearers who held up signs announcing the setting, such as the African scene of "Forty Maidens Danc[ing] Before The Enthroned Pharaoh Ra, The Negro."[22]

Ethiopia at the Bar of Justice is a much more modest production. Its smaller cast includes: The Page, Justice, Leniency, Oppression, Mercy, Opposition, Ethiopia, History, First Slave from Africa, Haiti, Liberia, Crispus Attucks, Slave of '61, Civil War Veteran, Spanish War Veteran, Labor, Business, Professions, Womanhood, Negro Church, Declaration of Independence, Thirteenth Amendment, Fourteenth Amendment, Anti-Lynch Law, Public Opinion, Prophecy, and Love.[23] The pageant is set in the throne room of Justice, where Opposition has brought Ethiopia for judgment. Opposition and Justice introduce the play's theme in this early exchange, initiated by Opposition. "I appear before your bar to-day demanding that judgment be passed upon Ethiopia. She is doing too much; she is becoming too ambitious; she is flying too high; you must clip her wings."[24] And Justice responds: "Opposition, you forget that this is the Bar of Justice and not the court of Public Opinion! Let Ethiopia be called; let evidence be presented! Let her be placed in my balance and weighed against her deeds."[25] The play then unfolds with a series of characters appearing before the Bar of Justice either defending or denouncing Ethiopia.

These two celebration pageants reveal the Afro-American saga's ambivalent view of Africa. Civilized and uncivilized images of Africa are juxtaposed in these plays. In *Ethiopia at the Bar of Justice,* Opposition dismisses Africa as a "jungle and brier-patch. . . ."[26] And Liberia makes this self-disparaging remark: "In my land Ethiopia is building schools and industries and is sending civilization to the neglected sections of Darkest

Africa."[27] *The Star of Ethiopia*'s initial banner announces that the discovery of iron was made "in the deep and beast-bred forests of Africa. . . ."[28] This image of Africa as an uncivilized, jungle continent was also affirmed by a celebration editorialist who referred to Africa as "a country [*sic*] backward in civilization."[29]

But, on the other hand, both pageants also refer to Africa as a highly civilized continent. *The Star of Ethiopia* and *Ethiopia at the Bar of Justice* celebrate in song, dance, dialogue, costumes, and banners, such ancient African civilizations as Ethiopia and Egypt. *The Star of Ethiopia* extols Songhay; and *Ethiopia at the Bar of Justice* mentions Abyssinia and Sheba. The two Ethiopia pageants also confirm the belief held by many Afro-Americans that Africa is the cradle of civilization. Du Bois's second banner reads, "This picture tells how the meeting of Negro and Semite in ancient days made the civilization of Egypt the first in the world."[30] McCoo's character, History, tells his audience that not only has Ethiopia made significant contributions to ancient Greek and Jewish civilizations, but also "to Ethiopia is Egypt indebted for much of her early civilization. . . ."[31] (At the ceremonies I attended, Dr. Thomas and Reverend Williams echoed this folk idea in their respective Emancipation Day speeches. The former told his January 1st congregation that Africa was both an idyllic place which "had everything . . . all kinds of natural resources, mineral resources, vegetation and all the rest. There was never really any want." Africa was a "great continent where civilization was cradled and God first breathed and man became alive. In the dawn of history God was at work through a people, an African people."[32] While the latter minister proclaimed to his Juneteenth audience, "I'm proud that I'm a Black man! Because civilization started with God, with the Black man in Africa."[33])

The Star of Ethiopia and *Ethiopia at the Bar of Justice* present correspondingly ambivalent images of the Afro-American's African ancestors. In some instances Africans are presented as highly civilized; while in other cases they are portrayed as uncivilized savages. On the positive side, both pageants cite an impressive array of ancient black African royalty. Du Bois lists Mansa Musa, the enlightened ruler of Songhay; Candace of Ethiopia, the Queen of Sheba, a legendary beauty of antiquity; and Ra, "the Negro Pharaoh of ancient Egypt." In addition to the Queen of Sheba, McCoo's script makes references to Zerah, a king of Ethiopia who waged a losing battle with the King of Judah in 941 B.C.; and "Tirhakah, one of the most famous conquerors of ancient times. . . ."[34] On the negative side of Africa's image, both pageants present the masses of Africans as uncivilized. As the curtain rises on Du Bois's drama, a "dark figure of an African savage hurries across the foreground, frightened and cowering and dancing" in a futile attempt to quell the violent thunderstorm that has engulfed him.[35] Ironically, Dr. Du Bois, whose scholarship attests to his deep appreciation for African civilization, uses the pejorative term "savage" ten more times to describe the masses of Africans who follow in the wake of Mansa Musa, Ra, and other African nobility. McCoo's First Slave recalls "my primitive home" in Africa.[36] A January 1st editorial in 1933 echoed this degrading image of Africans, describing the African slave as being "unversed in the ways of an advanced people. He had no education. He was a savage."[37]

From Alex Haley's *Roots* back to slave-era stories of slaves who flew back to Africa in protest of their master's harsh treatment, Afro-Americans have long been fascinated with Africa. In the performing arts, beginning in the 1950s, there has been a steady series of films that treat the subject of Africa. *Soul to Soul,* a documentary of Afro-American musicians touring and playing concerts in West Africa,[38] and *Shaft in Africa,* a detective thriller that finds Harlem's best known detective in "the Motherland,"[39] are representative. On the stage, Eartha Kitt starred in *Timbuktu,* and Afro-Americans flocked to see this musical that glorified the ancient Songhay city of culture and learning.[40]

The theme of Africa is also central to the creeds and ideologies of several Afro-American politico-religious groups. Marcus Garvey's Universal Negro Improvement Association advocated a back-to-Africa movement.[41] Today the citizens of Yoruba Village of South Carolina are attempting to recreate Yoruba culture and religion in the New World,[42] and New York Rastafari cults believe that an African messiah will arise out of Ethiopia and lead all New World Africans back to Africa.[43] And all members of the radical group MOVE "use the surname Africa."[44] Stokely Carmichael, Robert Moses, and other disillusioned civil-rights activists moved to Africa as ex-patriots after the civil-rights era ended. Today Afro-American entertainers, athletes, writers, clergymen, and other affluent blacks make vacation pilgrimages to the home continent of their African ancestors.

The next episode in the saga dramatized by these two freedom pageants is that of slavery. Slave characters appear in both *The Star of Ethiopia* and *Ethiopia at the Bar of Justice.* The latter drama has two slave characters, the First Slave and the Slave of 1861, into whose mouth McCoo places this condemnation of slave masters: "For 250 years we toiled, but Opposition paid us no wages for our hire. We felled his forest, we tilled his fields, we protected his home, we nursed his children."[45] In 1943, Reverend William Holmes Borders made similar references to the slave in his Emancipation Day poem, "I Am Somebody": "I am a trustee in slavery. I protected my master's wives and daughters while he fought to keep the chains of slavery about my body."[46] Reverend Borders attributed the slave's moral superiority to his Christian religion which he practiced "at points better than my master from whom I learned it."[47]

How did this nightmare of human oppression begin? The First Slave said "Oppression lured me" into bondage.[48] The Afro-American saga has spawned a "red cloth" etiological tale to explain in greater detail how Africans were tricked into servitude by whites. According to one ex-slave's account:

> Granny Judith said dat in Africa dey had very pretty things, and dey had no red colors in cloth. In fact, dey had no cloth at all. Some strangers with pale faces come one day and dropped a small piece of red flannel down on the ground. All de black folks grabbed for it. Den a larger piece was dropped a little further on, and on until . . . de ship was reached, dey dropped larger pieces on de plank and up into de ship till dey got as many blacks on board as dey wanted. Den de gate was chained up and dey could not get back. Dat is de way Granny Judith say dey got her to America.[49]

Cudjoe Lewis, one of the central characters in *Portraits: Brown Americans,* is symbolic of the thousands of real-life Africans who told similar stories of being forced into slavery.[50] Charlie Smith, for example, claimed that when he was twelve years old white slave traders "recruited me— pulled me on the boat. . . ."[51] Silvia King said she "was married [and] had three children before [she] was stoled from my husband."[52] Susan Snow recalled her mother's capture this way: "Seem like de chief made 'rangements with some men and had a big goober grabbin' for de young folks. Dey stole my ma and some more and brung 'em to dis country."[53] This tableau was recently reenacted graphically in the television production *Roots,* in the scene where the young Kunta Kinte, who had left his village in search of wood to make a drum, was overpowered by slavers and sold into slavery.

Ethiopia at the Bar of Justice refutes the argument that uses the biblical account of Ham as a justification for slavery, which some slave masters and clergymen had made the linchpin of their apology for that institution. According to the story, Ham, who was perceived as being the mythological forefather of the African race, and his descendants were cursed with a life of servitude because he looked upon his drunken father Noah's nakedness. In McCoo's pageant Opposition tells History, "Turn to the first Book of Moses, read where Noah cursed the son of Ham." But Mercy forcefully dismisses this old argument: "This is one of the greatest fallacies used by Opposition to crush and throttle Ethiopia! Yes, Noah cursed the son of Ham, but God did not. And what was the condition of Noah at the time? Awakening out of a drunken stupor."[54] (In 1972, Dr. Thomas gave evidence of the continuing unpopularity of this negative image of African people when he reminded his January 1st congregation that, "In the dawn of history, God was at work through a people, an African people. . . .[55])

That slavery was an act of divine providence and that its consequences were ultimately beneficial is another notion examined. In *Ethiopia at the Bar of Justice* Opposition defends his enslavement of the First Slave as the only means of leading him to civilization. This idea has been often restated by Afro-Americans from all walks of life, such as Mr. Jerry Wilson, a local grocery store owner in Brenham, Texas, who confided to me that: "We shouldn't feel bad about the fact that our forefathers were slaves, because that was the way that I believe the Lord had it figured out that they could get over here and accomplish what they accomplished . . . In other words, I think it was a blessing."[56] Booker T. Washington made similar comments in his autobiography:

> . . . we must acknowledge that, notwithstanding the cruelty and moral wrong of slavery, the ten million Negroes inhabiting this country, who themselves or whose ancestors went through the school of American slavery, are in a stronger and more hopeful condition, materially, intellectually, morally, and religiously, than is true of an equal number of black people in any other portion of the globe. This . . . show[s] how Providence so often uses men and institutions to accomplish a purpose.[57]

And an Emancipation Day editorialist boasted: "God is in the Negro's corner and as was said in the days of the Queen of Sheba, 'THE HALF HAS NEVER YET BEEN TOLD.' "[58]

The half that has not been told is the belief that God has chosen the Afro-American community for the divine mission of saving America. The appropriately titled freedom celebration pageant, *Can Negroes Free America?*,[59] perpetuates the folk belief shared by many Afro-Americans that, "If we had not been a chosen race of the Almighty God, we would have been gone long ago."[60] Poet James Weldon Johnson urges his Afro-American readers to maintain "Faith in your God-known destiny! We are a part of some great plan."[61] Dr. Thomas echoed similar sentiments in his January 1st sermon:

"We are a religious people that has been blessed by God in a moment of strategy to be available to Him in some great work that He has not yet partaken of . . . Maybe God has chosen [us] as the redeeming soul of America."[62] And the celebration pageant *Color Me Brown* includes in its cast Dr. Martin Luther King, Jr., a leader who espoused similar views on several occasions.

But the majesty of this divine mission cannot make amends for the horrible suffering that the slaves endured for almost three centuries. The fourth episode of Du Bois's pageant dramatizes how the "race did suffer in Pain, of Death and Slavery and yet of this Humiliation did not die."[63] This misery is symbolized on stage by a silent Christlike figure "staggering beneath a cross and crowned with bloody thorns." The episode concludes with the huddled, cowering slaves singing, "Nobody Knows the Trouble I've Seen," as they shuffle off the stage bound in chains. In 1972, Reverend Williams made a personal reference to this pain in his Juneteenth sermon: "Oooh God! I used to listen to my great, great grandmother say she stood one day and watch them sell her mother. And from that day she never seen her before."[64]

Both Ethiopia pageants emphasize the history of active slave resistance to slavery. *The Star of Ethiopia* includes the militant spiritual, "O Freedom," which declares: "And before I'd be a slave/I'd be buried in my grave./And go home to my Lord and be free."[65] Similar sentiments are expressed by *Firm Foundations'* character Henry Highland Garnett, who in an 1843 speech urged America's slaves to: "Rather Die Freemen, Than Live To Be Slaves."[66] Gabriel Prosser,[67] who led over one thousand slaves in a revolt at Richmond, Virginia, on August 30, 1900, and Denmark Vesey,[68] who masterminded an insurrection plot against Charleston, South Carolina, in June, 1822, that involved as many as nine thousand slaves, are two slave revolt leaders whose exploits have been added to the Afro-American saga.[69]

But perhaps the most famous slave insurrectionist was Nat Turner, who led a bloody slave revolt on August 31, 1831, in Southhampton, Virginia that left sixty whites and more than one hundred slaves dead. Turner, along with thirteen other slaves and three free Negroes, were hung later.[70] The legend still circulates among Afro-Americans that the condemned Turner demanded coldly that his followers, "Die like men." *The Star of Ethiopia's* Fifth Episode banner introduces Turner and others in this manner: "The Fifth Gift of the Negro to the world, being a Gift of Struggle Toward Freedom. This picture tells of Alonzo, the Negro pilot of Columbus, of

Stephen Dorantes who discovered New Mexico, of the brave Maroons and valiant Haytians, of Crispus Attucks, George Lisle and Nat Turner."[71] *Firm Foundations* also repudiates the stereotype of the happy slave by recalling "two hundred recorded slave uprisings" as irrefutable evidence that many slaves were willing to fight and die, if need be, in order to secure their freedom.[72]

These slave revolts were the prelude to the Civil War and the era of Emancipation. Like all other wars, the War between the States had persuasive arguments to justify its human carnage. The celebration pageants dramatize the theological arguments for the war which circulated among the free and enslaved Afro-American communities of this era. *The Star of Ethiopia*'s Sixth Episode features Sojourner Truth, the fiery abolitionist, asking Frederick Douglass, after the execution of John Brown, "Frederick, is God dead?" And finally, the despondent Douglass replies, "No, and therefore slavery must end in blood."[73] *Ethiopia at the Bar of Justice* has this same question posed by The Church: "When the way seems dark, when the path is rough, I bid Ethiopia look above and ask, 'Is God dead?' "[74] George Lisle (*The Star of Ethiopia*), Henry Highland Garnett (*Firm Foundations*) and Richard Allen (*Portraits: Brown Americans* and *Color Me Brown*) are Afro-American clergymen from the slave epoch who adhered to the abolitionist's creed: "Am I not a man and a brother?,"[75] which was based on the biblical argument that God made all men from one blood.

This "one blood" theme has remained popular with freedom-day speakers for more than a century. At an 1827 celebration of New York Emancipation, the Reverend Nathaniel Paul confidently predicted the abolition of slavery in America and every other "part of the habitable world" in this manner: "It [Emancipation] is certain because that God has made of one blood all nations of men, and who is said to be no respecter of persons has so decreed. . . ."[76] Frederick Douglass excoriated self-righteous white Americans who supported slavery in his July 4, 1852, Independence Day address: "You profess to believe 'that of one blood, God made all nations of men to dwell on the face of the earth,' yet you notoriously hate, and glory in your hatred, all men whose skins are not colored like your own."[77] I heard the same Scripture quoted more than a century later in a similar appeal for universal brotherhood, when Mr. Mal Goode told his integrated, middle-class National Freedom Day audience: "We must come to a realization, simple as it may sound, that 'God has made of one blood all nations of men.' And we are his children, brothers and sisters all."[78] And at the

Juneteenth I attended, Reverend Williams expanded this biblical theme for his Afro-American working-class congregation. After quoting Acts 17:26, "And He has made of one blood all nations of men to dwell on the face of the earth,"[79] Reverend Williams wove the thread of this theme into the Creation Myth by arguing that the original blood of Adam is found in all branches of mankind.

Both Ethiopian pageants cite several black New World freedom fighters who fought for this belief. In McCoo's play the character Hayti boasted: "I gave to the world Louverture [sic] and a Dessalines,"[80] two champions of Haitian Independence. In Du Bois's drama Crispus Attucks says, "I am Crispus Attucks, an Ethiopian. My blood was the first to flow for American freedom. When, on Boston Commons, the first blow was struck to break the chain of English tyranny, I fell as a martyr to the cause of civilization in the western world."[81] Du Bois's cast also includes the Civil War Veteran who recalls proudly the major role played by Afro-American soldiers in the success of the Union Army:

> I represented Ethiopia in the Civil War. I am a Union Soldier. I fought for Old Glory. Who says that Ethiopia has done nothing for civilization? When civilization was about to fail in America, Ethiopia saved it. When State after State was seceding; when the stars were falling in quick succession from our flag, I and my black comrades stepped beneath them, caught them upon the points of our bayonets and pinned them back to Old Glory! Yes, the spirit of John Brown moved in Ethiopia, and Ethiopia saved the day.[82]

Abraham Lincoln, the commander in chief of the Union army, also appears in both Ethiopian pageants. A bust of Lincoln is displayed during *The Star of Ethiopia's* Sixth Episode, the "Gift of Freedom." And in *Ethiopia at the Bar of Justice* the Slave of 1861 gives this divine messianic description of President Lincoln: "He [God] called His Moses Abraham Lincoln. I heard Him say, 'Go down, Lincoln, go down, away down in Dixie Land, and tell Opposition to let my people go.'"[83]

There are numerous Abraham Lincoln stories in the Afro-American saga. The "slaves talk[ed] a heap about Lincoln,"[84] especially about Lincoln's efforts "to set 'em free."[85] There was a cycle of stories centering around the Union president's conflict with Jefferson Davis, the president of the Confederacy. According to one legend, the Civil War began after these two leaders met in South Carolina, where "Lincoln said, 'Jeff Davis, let dem niggers go free.' Jeff Davis told him, 'You can't make us give up our property.' Den de War started."[86] And southern white children taunted

This sheet music cover from 1881 illustrates the central role that barbecue has long played in Afro-American social gatherings. Courtesy of the Lilly Library, Indiana University.

This sheet music cover (1863) depicts the black Union soldiers fighting for their freedom. Note the Confederate soldier retreating from the fire. Courtesy the Lilly Library, Indiana University.

This sheet music cover (1884) captures the intimate association supposed to exist between ex-slaves and the mule, the animal, according to legend, ridden by a black Union soldier from Washington, D.C., to Texas to spread the news of Emancipation. Courtesy of the Lilly Library, Indiana University.

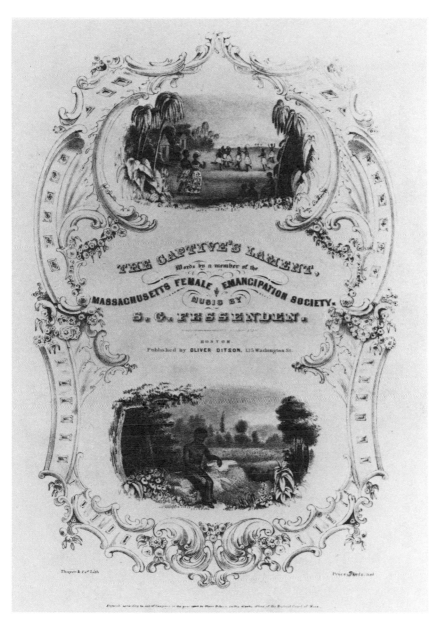

The slave's obsession with freedom is the topic of this sheet music cover, ca. 1860. The enslaved African in the lower drawing seems to be reflecting on his past freedom in his native Africa. Courtesy of the Lilly Library, Indiana University.

This Currier & Ives illustration, 1860, depicts President Lincoln, the great Emancipator, playing baseball, the most popular game at warm weather Emancipation celebrations. Courtesy of the Lilly Library, Indiana University.

FREEDOM TO THE SLAVES
Proclaimed January 1st 1863, by ABRAHAM LINCOLN, President of the United States.
"Proclaim liberty throughout All the land unto All the inhabitants thereof." ___ LEV. XXV. 10

President Lincoln is portrayed as the Great Emancipator in this Currier & Ives illustration, ca. 1865. Note President Lincoln stepping on the slave's shackles with his right foot as he lifts the newly emancipated slave with his left hand. Courtesy of the Lilly Library, Indiana University.

PRESIDENT LINCOLN AND SECRETARY SEWARD SIGNING

THE PROCLAMATION OF FREEDOM

JANUARY 1ST 1863.

"Upon this act, I invoke the considerate judgment of mankind, and the gracious favor of Almighty God."

This Currier & Ives illustration, 1865, captures one of the most significant events in black American history: President Lincoln signing the January 1, 1863, Emancipation Proclamation, a document which is still read annually at contemporary Emancipation celebrations. Courtesy of the Lilly Library, Indiana University.

Thomas Nast has juxtaposed images representing the inhumanity of slavery and the new dignity of Emancipation in this *Harper's Weekly* illustration, 1865. The drawing's left side depicts such slave scenes as the

O Freedom! Afro-American Emancipation Celebrations

auction block; the right side portrays scenes such as that of the
emancipated slave being paid for his labor. Courtesy of the Lilly Library,
Indiana University.

The moment of Emancipation is the subject of this *Harper's Weekly* illustration, 1865. Stories of such slave encounters with the Union army still circulate in the lore of some black American families. Courtesy of the Lilly Library, Indiana University.

their slave playmates with the rhyme: "Jeff Davis long and slim,/Whipped old Abe with a hickory limb./Jeff Davis is a wise man, Lincoln is a fool,/Jeff Davis rides a gray, and Lincoln rides a mule."[87]

The slaves also created and circulated a cycle of legends which were based on the motif of President Lincoln slipping into Jeff Davis's Confederate states incognito in order to spy on the inhumanity of slavery. According to one of these legends, Lincoln was able to "see how the niggers come in on Saturday and drawed four pounds of meat and a peck of meal for a week's rations. He also saw 'em whipped and sold."[88] Lincoln's role as a recorder of slavery's injustices is another manifestation of the slaves' God whom they sang about in their spiritual, "My Lord is writing all the time. He see all you do and He hears all you say. My Lord is writing all the time."[89] Singular accounts have been published of Lincoln traveling south as a worker who spied on slave masters' books,[90] a tramp who slept at a southern inn and carved his name between the table leaves,[91] and a peddler who defended Abraham Lincoln while conversing with a southern belle.[92] There are multiple accounts of President Lincoln touring the South as some nameless dignitary. As a mysterious visitor, Lincoln slept in "Old Mistress' bed" and carved his name on the bedstead;[93] he visited Texas slaves who didn't "know who he was";[94] he had breakfast at a North Carolina plantation and told the master that "our sons are conceiving children by slaves and buying and selling our own blood, and it will have to be stopped."[95] He held secret meetings with slaves and told them that they were "his black brothers."[96]

There are also numerous legends which depict President Lincoln as the Great Emancipator. During my field trip I heard Reverend Williams tell his Juneteenth audience, "God saw fit a hundred and seven years ago that Abraham Lincoln sign into law that it was wrooooong for any man, anywhere, whether he was black or white, he was brown or white, to be in slavery."[97] According to one story in this vein, Lincoln "made a solemn vow before God that if General Lee was driven back from Maryland he would give the slaves their freedom."[98] Two stories have been collected which have Lincoln leading the Union army onto plantations and freeing the slaves. In one account, black Union soldiers tell the slave cook, "You ain't got no more master and no more missus. You don't have to work no more." In the other story President Lincoln opens the smokehouse and tells the newly emancipated slaves, "Help yourselves; take what you need; cook yourselves a good meal!"[99]

Some of the stories are not as complimentary about Lincoln's motives for emancipating the slaves. One such account has an alcoholic Lincoln being jolted out of his drunken stupor by one of his aids telling him that he had freed the slaves during his latest binge.[100] Another legend explains the crack in the Liberty Bell: "Do you know they got the crack in the Liberty Bell? Well, it happened this way. The whites were mad at Abraham Lincoln for all he'd done to free the Negro. They told him about it and Lincoln told them, 'I'd wade up to my neck in blood before I'd forget my race.' When the whites heard that good news they rang the Liberty Bell 'till it cracked."[101] This legend's blood-wading motif appears in other Lincoln narratives. In one slave narrative, a former slave recalls, "The white folks said they'd wade blood saddle deep before they'd let us loose."[102] And two others are attributed to Lincoln himself. Speaking to defeated southerners in Atlanta, Lincoln is supposed to have said, "Many of you agreed to turn the Negroes loose, but Jeff Davis said that he would wade in blood up to his neck before he would do it."[103] And, according to the Afro-American saga, Lincoln also made this declaration to a southern slave master, "Before I'd allow my wife and children to be sold as slaves, I'd wade in blood and water up to my neck."[104]

The actual moment of Emancipation is an implicit theme in both Ethiopian pageants. If called upon, any of the Freedmen in *The Star of Ethiopia* could have provided dialogue that reflected the etiological freedom legends of the Emancipation celebrants. Some 8th of August celebrants observe this summer date because they were freed in the winter when it was too cold to celebrate.[105] Two cycles have also sprung up around the delayed message theme. A popular legend among Juneteenth celebrants is that the white slave masters withheld the news of freedom from their slaves from January 1 to June 19 in order to make another crop.[106] One celebrant told me that "The Negroes was freed on January 2nd [*sic*]—what year I done forgot—but the white decided that he would not free him in the state of Texas until the crop was gathered."[107] Some other Juneteenth legends argue that the slave masters killed the freedom messenger when he came in order to make another crop.[108]

Like the witnesses of any other important historical event, the emancipated ex-slaves entered anecdotes into family lore that captured their personal moments of freedom. At earlier celebrations ex-slaves would "recollect it all . . . when the 'kernal' stood on the porch of the big house an' told 'em they wuz free. . . ."[109] In another Emancipation memory, a slave receives the news aboard a wagon.

I had a friend—I wish she were here to tell you—her uncle or granddaddy or something was on his way . . . seemingly his boss or master had sent him someplace to get a load of flour or something, and he was on his way back when he met a white man. And he told him, "Well, you're free now." He said, "Sure enough. Do you mean that?" He said, "Yes, you're free." Said he said, "Thank you." Said he got out and left the wagon right there [*laughter*]. Said he didn't even complete his journey to carry it back. He said, "I'm free. I'm not going any farther." She tells that. I don't know if that's true or not, but she was telling that the other day.[110]

By the same token, the black Civil War Veteran in *Ethiopia at the Bar of Justice* could have affirmed hearing military legends of Emancipation similar to those still circulated among Juneteenth celebrants. Some of these stories center around General Gordon Granger, the Union officer who landed at Galveston on the 19th of June and spread the good news of Emancipation throughout east Texas.[111] Another group of Juneteenth legends revolves around a nameless Afro-American Union soldier who spread the word of freedom throughout the southwest by mule. One version of this legend was told me by a celebrant who had first heard it from his eighty-six-year-old father: "an ex-Union soldier (Negro) rode a mule given him by Abraham Lincoln. Yessuh, all the way to that section of the country. And when he got to Oklahoma, he informed the slaves that they were free. From there he went to Arkansas and Texas. It was the 19th of June when he arrived in Oklahoma."[112]

The fourth epoch of the Afro-American saga as enacted in the celebration pageants is that of a continuing struggle for full freedom on the part of emancipated ex-slaves. This struggle is fully dramatized in *Ethiopia at the Bar of Justice*. James Weldon Johnson's "Lift Every Voice and Sing," the "Hymn of the Race," whose lyrics celebration speakers have based their sermons on,[113] is sung when Ethiopia initially appears before the bar of justice. During his 1973 January 1st speech, Dr. Thomas cited the song to illustrate the constant struggle that Afro-Americans have waged since their Emancipation: ". . . as the song sang earlier [says] 'God of our weary years. God of our silent tears.' And we have come over ways that with tears have been watered. We've come that way. I'm talking about our fathers and mothers who have come through pain and want, and suffering, and fire and torture, and castration, and lynching and DEATH AND HELL AND ALL!"[114]

The celebration pageants' casts are chock full of cultural heroes and heroines who have led or represented the race in some courageous way during this era of struggle. Booker T. Washington, labeled "an interpreter and savior of the New South"[115] in a January 1st editorial, is a character in *Portraits: Brown Americans* and *The Epic of the Race*. There is a large cycle of Booker T. Washington stories and anecdotes in the Afro-American saga. Afro-Americans in all sections of the country talked about him eating dinner at the White House. And during the era of segregated schools, Afro-American students in the southern public schools were told the story of how the newly freed young Washington desired an education so badly he walked over a hundred miles to Hampton Institute, slept out of doors, and earned admission to the school by cleaning a room so thoroughly that when the schoolmistress inspected the room with a white handkerchief she couldn't find any dust.[116] The moral to be learned from this Washington exemplum was crystal clear: Afro-American children, you must struggle to improve your condition in America.

Major R.R. Wright, Sr., the founder of National Freedom Day, has a legend associated with his childhood that reflects also this attitude of defiant struggle. The scene is Atlanta, where an abandoned railroad box-car has been converted into a schoolroom for young Wright and other recently freed ex-slaves. One day General O.O. Howard, the Commissioner of the Freeman's Bureau, visits the crowded schoolroom and asks the young scholars, "What shall I tell the children up north about you?" At which young Wright springs from his seat and answers, "Tell 'em we're rising."[117] Reverend Stevenson alluded to this story during the 1973 National Freedom Day celebration: "You will remember many years ago when little Richard R. Wright was in school and the great character came to Georgia to make a speech and wanted to know what message he must carry back. And he was told by this little lad, 'Tell them we're rising.'"[118] Once again the note of struggle is struck. Afro-Americans are not to be intimidated by the poverty of their surroundings; they must struggle against it and rise.

The Afro-American worker, typically the "last hired and the first fired," during this period, appears in the casts of both Ethiopian pageants as a symbol of the race's struggle for economic parity with white laborers. In McCoo's drama, Labor says, "The world stands upon my back."[119] Du Bois's herald proclaims: "Hear ye, hear ye, of the Sixth and Greatest Gift of black men to the world, the Gift of Freedom for the workers."[120] McCoo mentions the significant contributions that Afro-American workers have made to American civilization.

The American colonies were a failure till I came to their rescue. Even the soil of Dixie refused to yield its crop of fleecy cotton till it heard my voice, singing in plaintive melody, as I buried the seed within its bosom. I have followed the hoe and plow with laughter and with song; I have performed those tasks which all others shirk, yet without which America would not be great. Without me the wheels of industry would not be great. Without me the wheels of industry would not turn, commerce would cease, chaos would reign supreme.[121]

The Ethiopian pageants's labor characters are theatrical extensions of John Henry and Shine, the overworked and underpaid work heroes of the Afro-American saga. The latter hero was an exceptional worker ("he didn't need no crew"[122]) who had the unenviable task of working in the heat and grime of the Titanic's boiler room.

Well, on aboard that ship they had
a man named Shine.
He ran up to the Captain, said,
Captain, Captain, don't you know,
There's a leak in your boiler-room floor?[123]

Ironically, Shine, the lowly laborer, was the only person to survive the sinking of the Titanic.

Now when the news got to the port,
the great Titanic had sunk,
You won't believe this, but old Shine
was on the corner, damn near drunk.[124]

The lowly Afro-American laborer has struggled against great odds and survived.

John Henry, the railroad workman who died from exhaustion brought on by a steel-driving contest with an industrial steam drill, is a more tragic hero. Afro-American balladeers sing of this contest of labor:

John Henry kissed his hammah;
White man turned on steam
Lil'l Bill held John Henry's trusty steel,
'Twas the biggest race the' worl' had ever seen,
Lawd, Lawd,
The' biggest race th' worl' had ever seen.[125]

And John Henry's heroic death.

John Henry, O, John Henry!
Blood am runnin' red!

Falls right down with his hammah to th' groun'
Says, "I've beat him to th' bottom, but I'm dead,
Lawd, Lawd,
I've beat him to th' bottom but I'm dead."[126]

Reverend Williams mentioned the economic exploitation of Afro-American workers in his Juneteenth sermon:

Williams: We're being underpaid on many jobs.
People: Amen!
Williams: And some of us are still living on plantations.
People: Amen!
Williams: Mississippi, Alabama, and Georgia.
People: Yes!
Williams: Some of us here in Texas are still working for 50 cents a day.[127]

The struggle for legal justice is also dramatized in *Ethiopia at the Bar of Justice,* when Anti-Lynch Law declares: "I am for Ethiopia! I am the Anti-Lynch Law. I had a hard fight to pass through the legislative bodies; they tried to discredit me in the courts. I come here to ask if Justice has lost sway?"[128]

This character is central to the Afro-American's epoch of struggle. In fact, our inability to pass an anti-lynch law has been one of the major disappointments of this era. In 1936 Senator Robert F. Wagner drew loud cheers from over fourteen thousand September 22nd celebrants when he announced that a federal anti-lynching bill sponsored by him had been introduced into Congress.[129] In 1956, Congressman Charles Diggs reported to January 1st celebrants in Atlanta what he had found in his investigation of the Emmett Till lynching.[130] Despite the valiant efforts of senators and congressmen such as Wagner and Diggs, the United States Congress has yet to pass an anti-lynch law.

Despite this legal setback, some progress has been made in the struggle for justice under the law, and the removal of Jim Crow Laws from southern law books has spawned a cycle of Afro-American jokes that alternately celebrate or poke fun at these achievements. There are a raft of civil-rights jokes, for example, about integrating a segregated restaurant—with a variety of punchlines. In some versions a lonely demonstrator stands in line for several months and finally forces the owner to wait on him, only to find out that the restaurant doesn't serve soul food.[131] A variant has the demonstrator seated in the restaurant and ordering a series of traditional dishes, such as collard greens, candied yams, okra, pork chops, chitterlings, etc., only to be informed by the waiter that the restaurant does not serve any of these dishes. Leaving in a huff, the Afro-American demonstrator declares to the white patrons and waiter, "Y'all ain't ready for integration!"[132] Other humorous narratives attack southern customs that place Afro-Americans in an inferior social position. One popular civil-rights joke attacked the demeaning southern custom of expecting Afro-Americans to go to the back door of white homes and to address all whites, regardless of their ages, as "Mr.," "Mrs.," or "Miss":

> Negroes getting mean now. They ain't taking no more stuff off the white man. Like this mad Negro who went up to these white folks that he's worked for all his life and said, "Ain't gon be no more Mister Charlie. It's just Charlie from now on." Then he looked at his wife and said, "Ain't no more Miss Ann. It's just plain Ann from now on." After saying this the Negro turned in a huff to leave. But when he got to the door he turned again and said, "An another thing! Ain't no more Mississippi! It's just plain 'Sippi from now on!"[133]

The oppressive southern judicial system has also been satirized by freedom-day speakers and celebrants. An Atlanta January 1st speaker drew gales of sarcastic laughter from his audience by citing the case of Max Ingram, a black farmer from Yanceyville, North Carolina, who was given a stiff prison sentence for "leering" across a field at a seventeen-year-old white girl.[134]

Some jokes dramatize the physical dangers often experienced by southern blacks who dared register to vote or the superhuman feats they were asked to perform to obtain the right to vote.[135]

Some of the freedom pilgrim's jokes satirize the South's Jim Crow laws and customs. One narrative asserts with tongue in check that Afro-American pipe smokers had to ask for "*Mr.* Prince Albert" when buying a can of that tobacco, because a white man's picture is on the can;[136] they also insist with a straight face that Afro-Americans had to stick their heads in a laughing barrel, if they felt the urge to laugh in the presence of whites.[137] Freedom pilgrims convulse in gut-wrenching laughter at the joke about the faithful down-home brother who, when southern whites put him on the radio and television so that he could tell the world just how fairly he was being treated, yelled "Help!"[138] Freedom celebrants also chuckle at the joke about the young northern Afro-American who asks God if He will go South with him and help him claim his inheritance only to hear God reply "Have no fear. I'll be with you . . . at least as far as Memphis."[139]

These jokes allow Afro-Americans to survive and cope with the many disappointments of this epoch of struggle for first-class citizenship. The sustaining role played by this humor is reflected in a remark of one former January 1st speaker:

> The Indian met the white man,
>   cursed him and died.
> The Negro met the white man,
>   laughed and multiplied.[140]

This traditional humor, together with histories, songs, and stories of the African's experience in the New World, is annually expressed in freedom celebration addresses and dramatized in celebration pageants. By these methods the celebrants are reminded of the essence of the Afro-American saga, whose message is this: Celebrants, always remember that your African ancestors were a free and highly civilized people, who were kidnapped and forced into almost three hundred years of slavery, partially emancipated, thereby making it necessary for you, current sons and daughters of Ethiopia, to continue your often frustrating and sometimes dangerous struggle for first-class citizenship in the land of the free.

CHAPTER 4

*I think that on the first day of January, we ought
to call our children in, we ought to eat some
bread and water symbolizing the diet of our slave
forefathers in the slave ships.*

Benjamin L. Hooks,
Executive Secretary of the NAACP (1979)

A Circus of Symbols

Afro-American freedom celebrations are symbolic circuses whose three big-top rings of fellowship, worship, and entertainment offer kaleidoscopes of cultural celebration and racial determination. Just as the "kids of all ages" in the larger society annually trek to the circus tent to see "death-defying acts," hear the blood-curdling roars of caged wild animals, and smell the mouth-watering aroma of freshly cooked circus cuisine, so a large number of Afro-Americans annually return to their childhood homes and attend freedom celebrations which reaffirm their cultural identity through an intricate system of symbolic sights, sounds, and smells.

Celebration fellowship is closely associated with the concept of home. The 117th annual September 22nd celebration in Gallipolis, Ohio, and the 106th annual August 8th Emancipation homecoming celebration in Allensville, Kentucky, were advertised on their respective fliers as festivals to which "Everyone [is] Welcome"[1] and "Where Old Friends Are Met and New Friends Are Made."[2] Home, the destination of these freedom pilgrimages, has numerous meanings. Physically, it is that domicile in which the celebrants grew up before moving away as adults. But, spiritually, terms like "down-home" refer to "a sense of place"[3] shared by a particular group of people. Socially, "home" implies a much broader kinship system than the nuclear family; it is a "sentiment of corporateness,"[4] or a cultural concept which "reflects the intermingling of nuclear family members, other kinsmen, and non-kinsmen."[5] This "sentiment of corporateness" is best illustrated in the community churches such as the AME Church that I visited in the all-black Griffin community. Denominational affiliation has traditionally been a means for Afro-Americans to establish a meaningful sense of community fellowship. Sociologist E. Franklin Frazier noted "that a Negro when asked to identify the people in the adjoining community replied: 'The nationality in there is Methodist.' "[6] In short, freedom celebrants make annual pilgrimages to several cultural homes.

Many celebrants return to their family homes for a few hours or days of intimate fellowship with members of their extended family. The modest dwellings in which some of them were born, and all of them were raised, not only hold precious memories of family births, deaths, weddings, birthday parties, first dates, wedding anniversaries, etc., they also stand as triumphant symbols of the older generation's determination and mother-wit. If they could talk, many of these cottages could tell stories similar to that of August 4th celebrant Mrs. Mary Morris who told me how her parents negotiated the purchase of her childhood home with a paltry five-dollar downpayment. Furthermore, these neat cottages are crammed full of important symbols of family and communal values. Family patriotism is symbolized in the official pictures of family members who served in the armed forces, the silver star window hangings, and the pictures of Presidents Abraham Lincoln, Franklin D. Roosevelt, and John F. Kennedy. Racial pride is expressed in the photographs of Booker T. Washington, Martin Luther King, Jr., and other group leaders that are hung on the walls, and the old recordings of Nat "King" Cole, Billy Eckstine, Count Basie, Duke Ellington, and other Afro-American artists, which are dusted off, played, and danced to during their stay. A respect for education is reflected in the high school and college graduation photographs of family members and in the diplomas that are displayed in the living rooms of these homes. And the family's traditional Baptist-Methodist faith is symbolized in the crosses, pictures of Jesus, sculptures of praying hands, the family Bibles, and such plaques as: "Prayer Changes Things," "Earth Has No Sorrow That Heaven Cannot Heal," and "God Bless This House" which adorn the walls.

Celebrants also make the Emancipation Day homecoming trip to experience the pleasure of eating authentic down-home cooking. During the rest of the year they nourish their appetite for down-home cooking by eating occasionally at neighborhood rib joints, chicken shacks, and cafes. Urban Afro-American communities are dotted with numerous examples of food being used as an effective symbol of a "sentiment of corporateness." Tucked away in the urban brick and mortar landscape are barbecue joints selling Tennessee, Georgia, or some other down-home-state style of barbecue; neighborhood markets that advertise their produce under such names as "Kys." (the regional brand name that Indianapolis grocers use to advertise chitterlings to their Kentucky migrant customers); and soul food restaurants that daily prepare and sell down-home breads (cornbread, cracklin' bread, and biscuits), vegetables (collard, turnip, and mustard greens, candied yams, black-eyed peas, red beans and rice, fried okra, fried green tomatoes, green beans, pigeon peas, and squash), meats (fried chicken, shrimp, oysters, white buffalo, and catfish, neckbones, chitterlings, ham, gumbo, burgoo, and barbecue), and desserts (apple, peach, and cherry cobblers, sweet potato, transparent, pecan and apple pies.) But for this one weekend, the celebrants will have the luxury of once again eating these and other down-home dishes in the places where they were introduced to them: their childhood homes.

Barbecue is the most popular down-home dish served at these celebrations. Mr. Paul Darby, a Juneteenth celebrant, noted the special cultural significance ascribed to barbecue: "They really set aside that day for special cooking—you didn't eat the same thing, you know, like everyday—that day you had special food, barbecue beef, mutton, pork, everything is 'specially set aside for that day."[7] And Mrs. Bennie Mae Smith recalled the fun and fellowship associated with visiting the celebration's barbecue site: "And the night before at several places they are barbecuing whole hogs. And they barbecue whole hogs and have them spread out on these pits. And that's fun too to run around to these barbecues. It is great fun to meet somebody you haven't seen for ages."[8]

The celebration's barbecue pit is another fitting symbol of slavery and Emancipation. The cultural importance of the pit is evident in the fact that many urban barbecue merchants prefer the adjective "pit" to "southern" when advertising their culinary wares. Some barbecuers have gone out of business rather than alter their traditional pit cooking method to conform with current sanitation standards.[9] From Texas to Kentucky, celebrants refer to the "sense of place" and time symbolized by "pit barbecue." Mr. Lovelady of Rockdale, Texas, apologized for not barbecuing "the old way [where] you need to dig a hole and have *a pit* [my italics]."[10] A 1972 handbill from Windsor, Ontario, reminds its reader: "Don't Forget Our Famous *Open-Air Bar-B-Que Pit* [my italics];" and Allensville's August 8th "bills" promised their readers that "THERE WILL BE PLENTY OF GOOD OLD FASHIONED PIT-COOKED BAR-B-Q" for them to eat. These crude earthern ovens are stark symbols of that "old" time when slavery was a reality in this current place of mirth and freedom.

From Windsor, Ontario, to Waco, Texas, celebration barbecuers cook their meat in the same traditional way: the meat is roasted slowly on a grill laid over white-hot ashes taken from a smoldering pile of hickery logs.

During the eight-to-ten-hour period of cooking, the animal carcass is turned over regularly and sopped with specially prepared hot, medium, and mild barbecue sauces. "They don't rush it" is the way one celebrant succinctly summarized this celebration cooking ritual that was practiced at the first January 1st observance held in 1863.[11]

The aroma of the pork drippings sizzling in the white-hot hickory ashes, which one celebration reporter has described as being "as exotic as Paris perfume,"[12] is a powerful olfactory symbol. It conjures up in the minds of the older celebrants memories of past good times spent around similar pits with family members and friends, now deceased or absent. The distinctive smell of these slow-rising spirals of smoke also link celebrants with their slave ancestors who smelled this same aroma during their slave social gatherings and their initial freedom celebrations. In other words, celebration barbecuing allows each new generation of freedom celebrants to recreate in rite and symbol their ancestors' original observances of Emancipation.

The pigs barbecued over these pits are themselves rich in symbols of slavery and freedom. Early arriving freedom pilgrims to Allensville's August 8th celebration are treated to the re-enactment of the centuries-old ritual of slaughtering, gutting, scalding, scraping, singeing, and cleaning hogs. Witnessing this farm ritual evokes memories of the celebrants' pastoral southern childhood and slave stories that their grandparents used to tell, such as the one of the recently emancipated ex-slave who exercised his freedom by rejecting his former master's slave wage of the hog's head, feet, entrails, and tail for slaughtering and dressing his hog. He tells his former master, "Well, Old Marster, I can't because I'm eating further up the hog than that now . . . I eat spareribs, backbone, pork chops, middling and everything else."[13] The folktale uses these better cuts of pork, which were reserved for the ruling class during slavery, as metaphors for the ex-slave's freedom. It also gave to Afro-American speech the phrase, "eating higher on the hog," a saying that many visitors to the celebration pits use to symbolize racial and/or personal progress. Given this close socio-historical association with the pig, freedom celebrants also understand that racial progress is being expressed in the Juneteenth motto: "From the pigpen to the palace,"[14] and that a January 1st speaker was chiding them for living beyond their means when he said, "You've got pork chop tastes and neckbone salaries."[15]

Some barbecue pit frequenters have relatives and friends who have developed a much more negative set of pork symbols. The Black Muslims refuse to eat soul food on the grounds that it will perpetuate a slave mentality among the Afro-Americans who eat it.[16] Muslims also disdain eating pork because they perceive the pig as being symbolic of the hated white man.[17] Soul food has also been used by some Afro-Americans as a symbol of social class. Eldridge Cleaver once argued that: "The eating of Soul Food is counter-revolutionary black bourgeois ideology."[18] Ironically, many of the middle class Afro-Americans that Cleaver excoriated shy away from traditional soul food for health reasons. They argue that the high concentration of pork in soul food (aside from being served as chitterlings, pork chops, barbecued ribs, ham, liver, neckbones, and pig feet entrees, pork fat or drippings are also used to season such soul food side dishes as white, red, black, pinto, butter, and green beans, black-eyed peas, cabbage, collard, mustard, and turnip greens; and bits of pork skin are even baked in cornbread mix to make "crackling bread") and an over reliance on frying often leads to obesity, high blood pressure, and heart trouble.[19] But most freedom celebrants, at least during the duration of their homecoming stays, perceive all of the middle class's eating of broiled meats and fresh salads as a culinary capitulation to "the ways of white folks."

Freedom celebrants also come home to worship in their down-home Baptist and Methodist churches. At the turn of the century a common saying among the faithful was, "If you meet a Negro and he isn't a Methodist or Baptist, then you know somebody's been messing with him."[20] These two denominations are deeply rooted in the urban Afro-American community. Chicago's Mount Olivet Baptist Church and Philadelphia's Mother Bethel AME Church are two examples of how denominations that were small community-based churches in the rural south grew to be huge institutional congregations of several thousand worshippers in the urban north. Afro-American urban churches promote fall and spring revivals, musical programs, productions of *Slabtown Convention* and other religious dramas, and many of the other religious activities and rituals formerly carried on by the family based down-home church. Most of these urban churches cater to the varied musical tastes of their congregation by having senior choirs that sing hymns and anthems, young adult choirs that sing spiritual arrangements, and a gospel choir that sings contemporary gospel music. Black urban ministers promote a sense of corporateness among smaller segments of their large congregations by organizing all of the natives of a particular southern state into home state clubs.

Afro-Americans who have emigrated to urban areas can also experience their religion outside of their neighborhood churches. Soul radio stations devote a significant period of their broadcast time to live broadcasts of local church services and to commercial recordings of gospel music and sermons. Some religious shows' hosts encourage their listeners to phone in prayers. A few soul stations sponsor touring gospel artists in public concerts in neighborhood auditoriums. Community record shops and newsstands supply urban Afro-Americans with the latest gospel and sermon recordings and tapes and with current copies of *Jet, Ebony,* the *Chicago Defender,* the *Pittsburgh Courier,* and the *Baltimore Afro-American,* which publish regular religious columns and occasional feature articles on major religious personalities.

But the freedom pilgrims who return home for annual Emancipation celebrations experience their traditional Baptist-Methodist religion first-hand, not filtered by tapes, records, radio, television, print, or any other urban customs. For one special Sunday, these cultural crusaders become down-home Baptists or Methodists again and renew once more their down-home religious allegiances. Methodist and Baptist pilgrims can experience again their traditional cultural rivalry, as in this fond August 8th remembrance of Mrs. Bennie Mae Smith: "And there was a time when the Methodists had their picnic at their church and the Baptists would have theirs at their church. I remember at one church the band was standing up playing, 'Will there be a star in my crown?' And the band at the other church started playing, 'No Not One [*laughter*].' Well, anyhow, there was always a lot of fun. I mean you could talk about it from one year to another."[21] And at the Sunday morning worship services they might sing the old spiritual that declares:

> My mother says it is the best
> to live and die a Methodist.
> I'm Baptist bred and Baptist born
> and when I'm dead it'll be a Baptist gone![22]

Howard Thurman, the noted theologian, mentioned "these denominational frictions" in his autobiography. One of his favorite aunts was a Methodist through marriage, a transgression that evoked in his staunch Baptist family "an unspoken awareness that she was a bit queer."[23]

These traditional denominational divisions were clearly evident at Allensville's August 8th celebration site, where the Baptists and Methodists operated separate barbecue booths on either side of the church lawn. This denominational division of space not only increased the coffers of the two local churches, it also enhanced the opportunities for socialization of the celebrants who had come home to see old church members and friends.

Baptism best epitomizes these "denominational differences" which separate homecoming celebrants. Since slavery Afro-American Baptists and Methodists have debated the proper mode of this rite of church membership. The former denomination advocates immersion, but the latter denomination allows its converts the choice of baptism by sprinkling, pouring, or immersion. Howard Thurman recalls representing the "Baptist kids" and arguing this central theological issue with the son of the Methodist minister, who "was the spokesman for the Methodist kids" during school recess. The Methodist boy justified his group's traditional sprinkling procedure by quoting John the Baptist's words to Jesus, "I baptize you with water." Young Howard Thurman rejected the argument with this apology for the Baptist mode of baptism by immersion, "Yes, but the Bible says, when Jesus was baptized, 'He came up out of the water,' and that could only mean that Jesus had been down under."[24]

Although the homecoming Baptist and Methodist celebrants disagree over the proper mode of baptism, they both agree that baptism, like all other adult cultural rites of passage, symbolizes all of the central values of down-home religion. First, it dramatizes the religious community's "saved"-or-"lost," Christian-or-sinner view of humanity. Second, baptism confirms the down-home church's belief in heaven and hell, which is illustrated in one AME bishop's childhood remembrances:

> There had been a current theological tenet that a child was not responsible for his sins until he was 12 years of age. Up to that time his parents, particularly his mother, were responsible for him. If he died before he was twelve, he was sure to go to heaven, whether converted or not; but if he died unconverted after twelve, hell would be his portion. For that reason, there was always a frantic effort for boys of twelve and over to be converted. I was not sure of this belief but I did not want to take any chances.[25]

Third, baptism requires each new convert to make a public confession of faith; these halting, often highly emotional statements, mark the convert's initiation into the traditional congregational role of providing oral support for the church services with loud "amens" and fervent testimonies.[26] And, four, baptism's emotional emphasis signifies that the convert is joining an adult community that perceives emotion as an integral part of its religion;

the baptism candidate, like his elders, has "felt" the spiritual presence of God in his soul in a way that some describe as "fire shut up in my bones."[27]

Nowhere does the ethos of the down-home church burn brighter than in the traditionally preached sermon. Freedom pilgrims come home with the hopes of hearing one of the area preachers deliver in his own distinctive style such traditional sermons as "dry bones and the eagle stirred his nest."[28] Down-home preachers, like down-home blues singers and musicians, have their own distinctive preaching styles. Dr. William Holmes Borders, a master preacher in his own right, recalled that the Reverend L.K. Williams, the east Texas native son who grew up to become the famous pastor of Chicago's Mount Olivet Baptist Church, "was essentially a biblical preacher with a large number of country illustrations and a magnificent sweet tenor voice . . . [who] along 'bout the close . . . would holler and turn that tenor voice over." However, he noted that the Reverend C.L. Franklin, a Mississippi Delta native whose recorded sermons are popular with many Afro-Americans, had a preaching style which was much rougher in vocal quality. "But Franklin is a whooper, a Mississippi whooper. And he can whoop like I like it. And I finished five or six schools and got eleven doctorate degrees and he can whoop like I like it. That Negro can put his hand back of his head. . . . He can whoop, too. I'm telling you."[29] James Weldon Johnson, who immortalized the down-home preacher and his traditional sermons in his collection of poems entitled, *God's Trombones: Seven Negro Sermons in Verse,* described the type of traditional preaching that the homecoming celebrants hope to experience during their down-home visit.

> The congregation sat apathetic and dozing. He [the preacher] sensed that he was losing his audience and his opportunity. Suddenly he closed the Bible, stepped out from behind the pulpit and began to preach. He started intoning the old folk-sermon that begins with the creation of the world and ends with Judgment Day. He was at once a changed man, free, at ease and masterful. The change in the congregation was instantaneous. An electric current ran through the crowd. It was in a moment alive and quivering; and all the while the preacher held it in the palm of his hand.[30]

Although homecoming pilgrims may not experience such a demonstration of preaching during their stay, they are certain to sing spirituals, those slave songs whose themes of freedom, justice, and hope still have a special relevance for the celebrants. These sorrowing songs portray the slaves' physical environment as a hostile one. One of the spirituals often sung at these freedom celebrations declares: "This world is a howlin' wilderness.

This world is not my home."[31] The spirituals' metaphorical portrait of this "howlin' wilderness"—presumably the slaves' vision of America—includes images of stormy, dark nights, deep and wide rivers, lonesome valleys, slippery, muddy clay paths, rocky roads and high mountains.

"Hell" is another popular Afro-American metaphor for America. Frederick Douglass described his condition as being "left in the hottest hell of unending slavery."[32] After slavery an Afro-American farmer said of his native Georgia: "This land was a little Hell, . . . I've seen niggers drop dead in the furrow, but they were just kicked aside, and the plough never stopped."[33] A Black Muslim tune declares: "The white man's heaven is the Black man's hell."[34] Emam Muhammad, son of Elijah Muhammad, theorized that, "America has survived the days that it existed as the pit of hell on this earth."[35]

The spirituals portray the struggle against racial oppression in a variety of metaphors—some having to do with difficult movement through space, some with the threat of adverse physical conditions, some with endurance and the passage of time. The songs are replete with spatial metaphors and with references to lateral, upward, or downward movement. For example, difficult lateral movement is expressed in the lyrics: "We'll inch and inch along,/Jesus will come by-and-by,/And inch by inch till we get home,/Jesus will come by-and-by."[36] Arduous upward movement is conveyed in lines like: "Lord, I'm climbin' high mountains, Tryin' to get home."[37] And downward movement is expressed in the dire warning: "O the downward road is crowded, crowded with unbelievin' souls."[38]

Darkness and violent storms are two metaphors of adverse conditions that recur frequently in the spirituals. "Dark midnight, was my cry, dark midnight was my cry, dark midnight was my cry, 'Give me Jesus' ";[39] and "O stand the storm, it won't be long, we'll anchor bye and bye,"[40] are representative samples of these metaphors that depict the slave as operating in an essentially hostile environment.

Frequently, the spirituals celebrate the slaves' sheer ability to endure, and metaphors depicting movement through time—from old to new or from night to day—are also common. "I looked at my hands and my hands looked new! I looked at my feet and they did, too!"[41] and "I prayed and I prayed, I prayed all night long. I prayed and I prayed until I found the Lord!"[42] are two examples of such temporal metaphors, and the bold refrain, "Hold on! Hold on! Keep your hand on the plough! Hold on!"[43] is a call to further endurance.

The spirituals' common tableau of a weary slave walking, running, stumbling, marching, inching, climbing or creeping his or her way out of this "barren land" is an effective symbol of both individual and racial progress. In some rare instances this lonely sojourner is aided on his or her way by several types of heavenly transportation such as the heavenly train: "When the train comes along, when the train comes along, I'll meet you at the station when the train comes along";[44] or by heavenly ships, "O, the old ark's a movering, a movering, a movering, the old ark's a movering, and I'm going home";[45] God's chariot, "Swing low, sweet chariot, Coming for to carry me home";[46] or angelic wings, "One of these morning bright and fair,/Way in the Kingdom;/Going to hitch on my wings and cleave the air,/Way in the Kingdom."[47]

This spiritual theme of the weary traveler struggling through a hostile landscape, while leaning and depending on God, with only an occasional lift from heavenly transportation, still surfaces in the lyrics of such contemporary Afro-American songs as Thomas Dorsey's gospel classic, "Precious Lord," a favorite freedom celebration selection that Dorsey wrote in 1932 to assuage his grief over the death of his wife and their still-born child.[48]

Dorsey's composition conforms to many of the criteria for a spiritual, as described above. First, the song is sung by a tired, weary traveler who confesses, "I am tired, I am weak, I am worn." Second, Dorsey's alter ego describes his difficult journey through adverse conditions, as "Through the storm," "through the night," and asks that he be led "on to the light." In the second verse Dorsey repeats the darkness motif, "When my way grows drear," before turning to "the river" (one of the obstacles most frequently mentioned in the spirituals' metaphorical wilderness). Like the slave pilgrim in "Deep River," Dorsey's singer stands at the bank of this wide river trusting in God's ability to provide a chariot, ship, or wings to lead him "home" to heaven on the other side.

Elements of the spiritual form also appear in many celebration anthems. As early as 1862 free Afro-Americans sang "John Brown" at their July 4th celebrations and referred to it as "our national air."[49] In 1863 they sang "America" at one of their initial January 1st celebrations.[50] "The Battle Hymn of the Republic" and "The Star-Spangled Banner" have also enjoyed a long tradition of being sung at these freedom celebrations. W. C. Handy's "The Afro-American Hymn" had only limited success with Emancipation Day celebrants. However, Charles A. Tindley's "I shall Overcome," Madame A.C. Bilbrew's "This Is Freedom Day," and James Weldon Johnson's "Lift Every Voice and Sing" are still sung during contemporary freedom celebrations. The continued popularity of these last three songs is due in no small measure to the large degree to which their composers borrowed from the spirituals' metaphorical trove.

The civil rights anthem, "We Shall Overcome," is based upon "I Shall Overcome," a gospel song composed by the Afro-American minister Charles A. Tindley during the first decade of this century. Although originally written to enhance Reverend Tindley's worship services, by the early 1940s "Negro Textile Union workers adapted the song for their use. . . ."[51] Soon afterward "union gatherings all across the south" were singing such adapted verses as "We shall organize." And during the 1950s white and Afro-American civil-rights demonstrators stood, clasped hands, swayed rhythmically, and sang: "We Shall Overcome."[52]

There are several elements of the spirituals' system of metaphors in the lyrics of this civil-rights anthem. First, there is the image of the weary pilgrim traveler: "We'll walk hand in hand." Second, the motif of an ability to endure over time is expressed in verses like: "We shall overcome," "The truth will make us free," "The Lord will see us through," and in the repeated "someday." The chorus conveys an abiding faith, reminiscent of the spirituals, in God's ability to guide the singers safely to their goal; "Oh, deep in my heart, I do believe./We shall overcome someday."

Madame A.C. Bilbrew, a California actress, composer, and playwright, composed National Freedom Day's anthem, "This Is Freedom Day," just before the civil-rights movement began in earnest. Although originally written to be sung by the assembled celebrants, it was sung as a solo during my field trip visit to Philadelphia. The audience did not even join in on the chorus.

Madame Bilbrew's lyrics do not draw on the spirituals' metaphors as extensively as "We Shall Overcome" did, probably because of the former song's more middle-class origins and intended audience. In verse one, however, we find the darkness motif ("From our chaotic darkness, amid a din of strife") and the movement from nighttime to daytime ("Dark night is past./Morn breaks at last"). Madame Bilbrew uses this same motif in the second verse; "The night is gone./Welcome the dawn." And her final verse contains a storm: "The storm is past./We are safe at last." References to a weary pilgrim traveler or to an essential belief in God are missing from Madame Bilbrew's lyrics. Unlike "We Shall Overcome," which affirms that "The Lord will see us through," Madame Bilbrew's song turns to the judical power of nations as the ultimate force for social change: "That might has failed, right prevails and justice has full play." Certainly the absence of these two important spiritual metaphorical motifs may help explain the diminishing popularity of this freedom anthem among the masses of Afro-Americans.

On the other hand, James Weldon Johnson's "Lift Every Voice and Sing" continues to increase in popularity. Johnson's song was originally written to be "sung by school children—a chorus of five hundred voices"[53] at a February 12 celebration of Abraham Lincoln's birthday held in Jacksonville, Florida, during the first quarter of the century. Although personally moved to "tears" and "feverish ecstasy" during the song's composition, Johnson didn't expect that in less than "twenty years the song [would be] sung in schools and churches and on special occasions throughout the South and in some other parts of the country."[54] Nor did he envision the NAACP adopting it as its official anthem. But perhaps the most gratifying recognition that Johnson's song received was that his fellow Afro-Americans began to paste "printed or typewritten copies of the words . . . in the backs of hymnals and . . . songbooks."[55]

The spirituals' metaphorical system is clearly present in Johnson's lyrics. In verse two we find the lyrical image of the tired pilgrim traveler: "Yet with a steady beat, have not our weary feet,/come to the place for which our fathers sighed?" There are numerous metaphorical references to America's hostile social landscape. In the first verse Johnson uses the darkness motif: "Sing a song full of the faith that the dark past has taught us"; and the penultimate line of this verse contains a reference to temporal movement: "Facing the rising sun of our new day begun." The second stanza has several references to the race's struggle through space: "Stony the road we trod" and "We have come, over a way that with tears has been watered./We have come, treading our path thro the blood of the slaughtered." Johnson concludes this stanza with another reference to darkness, now giving way to light: "Out of the gloomy past, 'til now we stand at last/Where the gleam of our bright star is cast." And his song concludes by powerfully affirming a belief in God: "Thou who has by Thy might,/Led us into the light."

In essence, Johnson's song is an anthem of Afro-American folk religion. Despite the frustrating stasis of their struggle for freedom, Afro-Americans continue to steadfastly believe that God is their primary agent of liberation. Johnson's pen captured this paradox of social immobility and immovable religious faith in the opening two lines of the second stanza: "bitter the chast'ning rod,/Felt in the days when hope unborn had died." The ironic metaphor of hope pictured as a lifeless fetus captures the depths of despair felt by Afro-Americans who, despite America's revered tradition of freedom, remain oppressed citizens in a free society.

This poetic expression of racial frustration and social inertia is not new to Afro-Americans. Two ornithic metaphors for oppressed hope have long been popular. First, the image of the pilgrim traveler as a wingless creature bound to his earthly sorrow appears in such spiritual lyrics as, "Sing a ho that I had the wings of a doze; I'd fly away and be at rest."[56] Henry Bibb's slave narrative includes a similar image: "Oh, that I had the wings of a dove, that I might soar away to where there is no slavery. . . ."[57] Contemporary Afro-American novelists Toni Morrison[58] and John McCluskey[59] have incorporated this theme of would-be human flight into their writing: Both Morrison's *Song of Solomon* and McCluskey's *Look What They Done to My Song* open with tragicomical scenes of characters attempting to fly—one plunging to his death, one left dangling ignominiously from the limb of a tree. Suppressed hope portrayed as a caged bird is another ornithic metaphor used widely by Afro-Americans. The traditional sermon, "The Eagle Stirreth Her Nest," is an oral elaboration of this tableau. According to one rendition of the sermon the caged eagle, like the pilgrim traveler and Henry Bibb, becomes "dissatisfied" with his earthly condition when, "A flock of eagles flew over and he heard their voices."[60] Post-slavery literary uses of this metaphor include Paul Laurence Dunbar's poem, "Sympathy,"[61] whose opening line, "Now I know why the caged bird sings," was the title of Maya Angelou's first autobiography.[62] W.E.B. Du-Bois cited the bird metaphor to illustrate the frustration of Afro-American youth trapped in the cage of American racism: "And their weak wings beat against their barriers,—barriers of caste, of youth, of life; at last, in dangerous moments, everything that opposed even a whim."[63] Kelly Miller used the same metaphor in counseling young Afro-Americans to forsake bravado in their battle against American racism: "The caged eagle [that] beats his wings into insensibility against the iron bars of his prison-house is accounted a foolish bird."[64]

Afro-American folk religion, like Johnson's song, has always counseled its members to believe that God is the ultimate force in this world and that by being faithful to Him you can help Him change this world and assure yourself a place in Heaven. Johnson's first line captures the "earth to glory" ethos of Afro-American folk religion, which is ritualized in the rite of baptism, vocalized in sermons and spirituals, and dramatized in such religious dramas as *Heaven Bound* and *In the Rapture*.[65] The entire last stanza makes direct reference to the Christian faith. And the fourth line, "Keep us forever in the path, we pray," is reminiscent of the Christian "path" often mentioned in spirituals: "Watch out my sister how you walk on the cross/Yo' foot might slip an' yo' soul get lost!"[66] The folk church's world-view of humanity as being either saved or lost is represented in the line: "Lest our hearts, drunk with the wine of the world, we forget Thee." The song's last line affirms an undying faith and patriotism: "True to our God, true to our native land." The song's close association with the Afro-American ethos explains why Mrs. Leila Blakey recalls her Monticello, Georgia, childhood community as a place where "you could hear it ["Lift Every Voice and Sing"] sung on the road, in the fields, just as we sing now the pop songs."[67]

In some instances the lyrics to "Lift Every Voice and Sing" are printed in celebration programs, whose pages are also rich repositories of other significant cultural symbols. Their pages are crammed full of pictures, photographs, and drawings of past and present Afro-American and American freedom fighters. Photographs of Abraham Lincoln, "The Emancipator"; President Harry S. Truman, signer and sponsor of the National Freedom Day Bill; Congressmen James P. McGranery, Francis J. Myers and Robert McGarvey, Co-sponsors of the National Freedom Day Bill; and Major R.R. Wright, Sr., the "Founder" of the celebration, are published in the National Freedom Day programs. Baseball pioneer Jackie Robinson's sketch, along with a biographical statement, appears in the 1972 August 1st program for Windsor, Ontario. American freedom icons such as the American flag, the Statue of Liberty, and the Liberty Bell are also published in several National Freedom Day programs. February 1st programs publish such freedom documents as the Emancipation Proclamation, the Declaration of Independence, the Thirteenth, Fourteenth, and Fifteenth Amendments, local, state, and federal proclamations, and letters from Presidents Franklin D. Roosevelt, Harry S. Truman, and John F. Kennedy.

The homecoming celebrants return annually down-home to have a super Saturday night of fun. Saturday is the traditional day for fun, just as Sunday is the day for worship. This traditional division of the Afro-American weekend is expressed in this blues lyric:

> The Eagle flies [payday] on Friday
> and Saturday I go out to play.
> Sunday I go to church
> I kneel down and pray.[68]

Celebrants often tell a joke about a good-timing Afro-American who gets drunk every Saturday night. Every Monday morning finds him standing before the judge to arrange bail. One morning the judge finally asks the man in exasperation why he persists in this pattern of behavior, to which the man replies: "Your Honor, if you ever was a nigger on Saturday night, you'd never want to be white again."[69] It is this sort of high "good times" that celebrants look forward to having with their parades, baseball games, and "suppers." As one Juneteenth participant said, the average celebrant "didn't care a thing about the thanksgiving prayer and that type of thing. All he wanted to do was get to the ball game and get some booze, corn likker, whatever I may use [*chuckles*]. That's what they were looking for— good times."[70]

Parades have been annual good time rituals at January 1st, September 22nd, August 8th, and May 20th celebrations for a long time. A September 22nd celebrant recalled that the parade marshall "kept order and seed that everybody, you know, didn't get out of line. That's all he did. See one gettin' out of line he'd go to him and tell him, 'Now we can't have that going on. You'll have to do that drinking somewheres else.'"[71] But prominently displayed amid all of this revelry are numerous important cultural symbols.

One of the parade's primary functions is to depict "the progress of the race from slavery. . . ."[72] Consequently, several interesting symbols of slavery appear in these marches. Brooklyn's annual Labor Day "Mas" parade, a celebration of Trinidad's Independence, includes the "jab molasses" or "molasses devil" in its line of march. These frightening figures, whose lineage goes back to Trinidad's initial 1834 Emancipation celebration, have been described as "men who chained themselves together and, nearly naked, smeared themselves from head to foot with oil and grease [and] paraded mutely, almost funereally, transfixing spectators with inhuman stares, scaring children and appearing in diametric contrast to the general gaiety of the celebration."[73] At one August 1st celebration march members of the "Son of Uriah," who were "dressed in black robes, white trousers and three-cornered cocked hats, decorated with black and red . . . [and] carried an axe [which] indicated the doom of the slaveholder."[74] As late as the 1930s, emancipated slaves served as parade marshalls at various January 1st[75] and September 22nd[76] parades.

Because clothing had been one ubiquitous symbol of servitude in America, the neat dress of these ex-slave paraders served as an important symbol of their emancipated status. After Denmark Vesey's slave revolt in 1821, some states passed legislation restricting the dress of slaves.[77] And one of the more popular, personal freedom rites was the scene of emancipated ex-slaves shedding, like metamorphosing butterflies, their drab, coarse flax garments and adorning themselves in colorful, smooth, hitherto-forbidden silk clothing. A newly freed Virginia coachman celebrated his liberation by dressing in his former master's clothing.[78] One Confederate diary included three examples of slaves changing dress to mark their emancipation. A slave named "Eben" was reported to have "dressed himself in his best" and "run to meet his Yankee deliverers";[79] and in two instances, ex-slave women engaged in this sartorial ritual of freedom. One entry bemoaned the sight of "Negro women, dressed in their gaudiest array, carryi[ng] bouquets to the Yankees."[80] Another entry expresses indignation over the knowledge that "ladies' maids were dressing themselves in the mistresses' gowns before their very faces and walking out."[81]

The neat dress code of today's freedom parades also symbolizes the homecoming parader's elevated social status. The linking of dress with social status was evident in America as early as 1651 when Massachusetts legislators passed a law prohibiting "men and women of meane condition" from wearing "the garb of gentlemen" and "persons of greater estates, or more liberal education. . . ."[82] A 1955 sociological study conducted in a small North Carolina town documented the fact that any Afro-American male who did not wear work clothes during the week was labeled "a smart nigger."[83] And a 1974 study contends that the dress code of some Afro-American men serves to "raise self-esteem, aid status symbolization, and cushion the traumatic effects of a subordinate position."[84] This is why celebrations like Juneteenth have always been viewed as special days when you "bought your new shoes, your new clothes and dressed up. . . ."[85]

African Liberation Day paraders are dressed and groomed in a way that reflects their raised African consciousness and Black Nationalist ideology. Instead of suits and dresses, they are dressed in colorful *dashikis*. Men often wear skullcaps knitted in the red, black, and green colors of Black Nationalism. In the past, some male marchers have worn a single black leather glove in honor of Tommy Smith and John Carlos's demonstration during the Mexico City Olympics.[86] Others wore a medallion with this image stamped on it.[87] In addition to African necklaces, women paraders also wear rings featuring Black Nationalism's tri-colors as well as silver, gold, or copper earrings shaped in the form of the African continent.

Male and female marchers in the African Liberation Day parades have symbolized their racial pride and nationalist ideology by wearing their hair in either an "Afro," cornrow, or dreadlock hairstyle. Many "Afro" wearers view their hairstyle as a symbol of cultural liberation from the second-class social status that they associate with the "process," an older hairstyle that uses chemicals to straighten or "process" the wearer's crinkly hair straight.

This idea was expressed during the mid-1960s in a "soul" recording that asked its listeners: "How you gonna get respect, you haven't cut your process yet?"[88] And a poet of this era mused: "Just because you wear a natural baby/don't mean you ain't got a processed mind."[89] Cornrow wearers adapt this African-derived hairstyle to their nationalist ideology by weaving Black Nationalism's tri-colors into their rows of intricately plaited hair. The dreadlock wearers' hairstyle indicates membership in the Rastafari Movement, a Jamaican-based religious sect that believes that a black messiah will rise up out of Ethiopia and lead all New World blacks back home to Africa.[90]

Black Nationalist or American flags are carried in the various freedom day parades. The American flag has long been a popular symbol of patriotism with Emancipation Day marchers. Celebration color guards carry it at the head of the parade; bands, drum-and-bugle corps, lodges, and military units carry it; dignitaries ride in "beautiful flag-draped cars"; children along the parade route wave miniature flags; and Old Glory's red, white, and blue colors crop up as buntings on buildings along the mainstreet parade routes. In another context, African Liberation Day paraders express their nationalistic ideology by waving the red, black, and green Black Nationalist flag. It can be seen in our era at the head of the various local and state delegations that have come to such regional celebration sites as Washington, D.C., and Chicago. During the 1930s it was unfurled in Terre Haute, Indiana, at a September 22nd parade by the local chapter of the Black Cross Nurses Unit. And from the time Marcus Garvey arrived in America until the time of his deportation (1916–1927), Black Nationalist flags were popular ideological symbols in the parades sponsored by Garvey's Universal Negro Improvement Association. In all of these contexts the three colors stand for the same values: red symbolizes the African blood shed during the slave trade, black represents the color of the African people, and green symbolizes the fertile continent of Africa to which adherents have vowed to return and start a mighty black civilization.[91].

Parade posters and flyers, which are either carried by the marchers or posted along the parade routes, are two other popular vehicles of expressions for Black Nationalism. African Liberation Day paraders carry picture posters of such nationalist ideologues as Malcolm X and Patrice Lumumba. A popular poster displayed during the 1970s' African Liberation Day marches featured an unshackled fist banging against an iron gate, with the caption: "Black/Struggle/Shall Prevail."[92] Another popular poster image features sketches of the United States interlocked with the continent of Africa. A 1982 Indianapolis Black Expo poster had the state of Indiana drawn inside the continent of Africa. And a 1983 Dayton-sponsored celebration of Afro-American culture produced a poster with the outline of the state of Ohio superimposed upon the northern edge of the African continent.

Cars and floats are popular at freedom parades, and lending your car to be decorated as a float or driving it yourself are two long-standing freedom parade traditions.[93] Owning a Cadillac or some other expensive car has long been a way for Afro-Americans to demonstrate an elevated social status. Dr. King alluded to this practice, saying he longed for the day when men would not judge success by "the size of the wheel-base on your automobile. . . ."[94] And Afro-Americans have created a great deal of folklore around this theme of the Cadillac being a symbol of upward mobility. They tell the joke of the Afro-American who drove his new Cadillac on one down-home trip, but "when he got to Memphis, he parked his Cadillac and caught a bus into Mississippi."[95] Another Cadillac joke involves a northern "bad nigger" who rebuffs a white gas station attendant's efforts to intimidate him because he is driving a Cadillac. The Cadillac owner flips an apple in the air, coring, peeling, and cutting it into applesauce with his razor before it hits the ground. After witnessing this frightening display of skill, the intimidated gas attendant asks politely if the man wants his oil and water checked too.[96] Afro-American speech is sprinkled with such proverbial sayings as "You've got Cadillac minds and wheelbarrow pocketbooks."[97] And: "The only thing black I want is a Cadillac."[98] These shiny parade vehicles were also mentioned by one Emancipation Day speaker who chided his audience with this automotive observation: "We get mad when we see a Negro riding in a Ford, but we say nothing when we see a white riding in a Cadillac."[99]

After the parade at typical Emancipation celebrations, paraders park their cars around the local baseball diamond and enjoy the entertainment of the annual Emancipation Day baseball game. Mr. Judson Henry recalled the high drama of one Juneteenth game between teams from Jefferson and Daingerfield, Texas, in which he made the winning hit for Daingerfield: "It was tied up 2 and 2 going into the last half of the ninth inning. . . . And I come up with two outs, two strikes, and I hit that ball right across the centerfield fence. . . . And when they [the Daingerfield fans] got through having a time down there [at home plate], they taken me up about sixteen dollars." Mr. Henry concluded with this observation of baseball's value to Afro-American communities during the first quarter of this century: "Well,

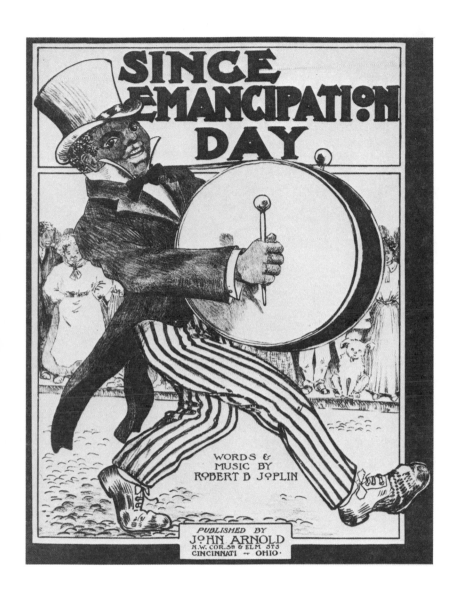

This sheet music cover, ca. 1900, portrays the parade tradition that has evolved with the celebration of Emancipation. Courtesy of the Lilly Library, Indiana University.

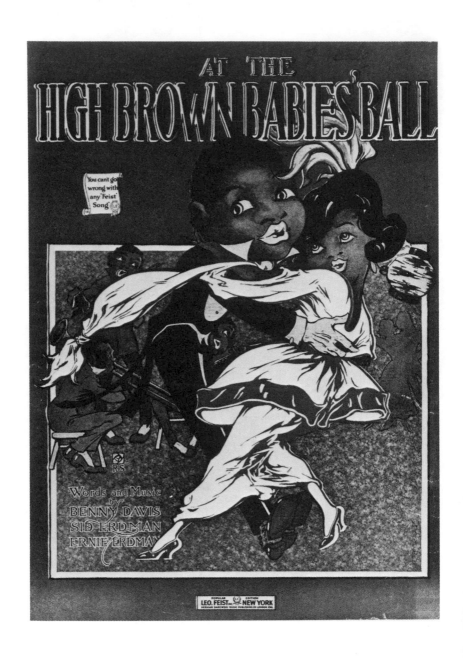

Emancipation celebrations have often included dances, such as the one illustrated on this sheet music cover, ca. 1890, among their events. Courtesy of the Lilly Library, Indiana University.

The pageantry of an Emancipation celebration parade is conveyed in this sheet music cover, 1896. Note the waving spectators and strutting band. Courtesy of the Lilly Library, Indiana University.

Photograph of the Elkton, Kentucky, Cornet Band, ca. 1930, which played at past August 8th celebrations in Allensville, Kentucky. Front row, from left to right: Sam Wisdom (Mrs. Slaughter's father), Milton Marshall, Emmerson France, Will Penick, Jessup Weathers. Back row, from left to right: Levon Underwood, Jimmy Roberts, _____, _____, Thomas Russell. Courtesy of Mrs. Mary Slaughter, Indianapolis, Indiana.

actually that [baseball] was the biggest sport we had back in them days, because every little hamlet and town would have a baseball team."[100]

As Mr. Henry's observation rightly suggests, baseball is inextricably wrapped up with American history and culture. Jacques Barzun argues that, "Whoever wants to know the heart and mind of America had better learn baseball."[101] And President Herbert Hoover once said, "Next to religion, baseball has furnished a greater impact on American life than any other institution."[102] Two presidential anecdotes illustrate Barzun's and Hoover's remarks. According to legend, Abraham Lincoln, who was playing in a game of baseball when the national nominating committee came to confer the Republican party's nomination on him in 1860, sent word that "they'll have to wait a few minutes till I make another hit."[103] And President William Taft initiated the ritual of American presidents throwing out the first baseball of the season,[104] an American spring rite that rivals in cultural importance the Japanese Emperor's planting of the first shoot of rice in May.

Baseball remains a popular symbol of American democracy at these down-home freedom celebrations. For more than eighty years, these celebrations' simple baseball games were the only community events which drew southern whites and Afro-Americans together in any semblance of brotherhood. Local white merchants would close up their stores and join many of their customers at the annual Juneteenth and August 8th baseball games.[105] In some rarer instances, these celebration playing fields were the first sites of integrated contests between local Afro-American and traveling white teams several years before Jackie Robinson integrated organized baseball in 1945. January 1st speaker, Dr. William Holmes Borders, used the game as a metaphor for American democracy in a 1965 celebration address that he delivered in Stamford, Connecticut. In Dr. Borders's narrative, Washington, D.C., was the baseball diamond on which the anti-American visiting team of prejudice, ignorance, ill-will, stupidity, "Jim Crow," and hatred battled the American home team of truth, the Bill of Rights, the Constitution, sanity, intelligence, the Declaration of Independence, and eternity. At the homeplate of justice stood Mississippi Governor Ross Barnett wielding the bat of Southern customs. But, like the mighty Casey, Southern slugger Barnett strikes out on a blazing fast ball thrown by the NAACP's ace pitcher, Attorney Thurgood Marshall.[106]

Freedom celebration baseball games are spectator events, but the post-game dance "supper" is a good-time communal activity in which all of the celebrants can engage. Afro-American musical and dance forms have been

LEST YOU FORGET!

Emancipation Day
Celebration,

Tuesday Eve., Sept. 22, 1908
AT TOMLINSON HALL.
Under the auspices of the following well
known clubs:
THE SUMNER LEAGUE,
THE IRON LEAGUE,
THE TOUSSANT L'OVERTURE CLUB,
THE EAST END TAFT CLUB.
Addresses will be delivered by Hon. J. Milton Turner,
St. Louis, Hon. James H. Williams of Rushville.

Chorous of 100 voices under the direction of Prof. Frank
Johnson,
Music by the Famous Iron League Band.
ADMISSION FREE. Doors open at 7 P. M.

The American flag is the dominant symbol in this September 22 celebration advertisement carried in the *Indianapolis Recorder*, 1908. Photograph by Indiana University Photograph Services.

1st Batallion U. R. K. of P.

Emancipation Day

Celebration, Uniform Rank Field and Gala Day

MONDAY, SEPT. 23, '12
State Fair Grounds.

$50 in Gold to the winning visiting companies; many other features, all day long such as motorcycle, automobile and horse races; 100 yd dash, pole vaulting, band concert and speaking. Street parade at 1 p.m sharp, with floats and Uniform Rank.

The committee has spared no pains to make this a gala success and this occasion will be an annual affair It is is requested that the public will decorate their homes & business places. Good car service day and night

Com:— Segt. Wm. Morton, chm; Corp. Rogers Cary, sec.; Col. J. M. Porter, teeas

Admision   -   -   25c.

A bust of President Lincoln, a spread eagle, and an American shield are the major symbols of this September 22 celebration advertisement published in the *Indianapolis Recorder*, 1912. Photograph by Indiana University Photograph Services.

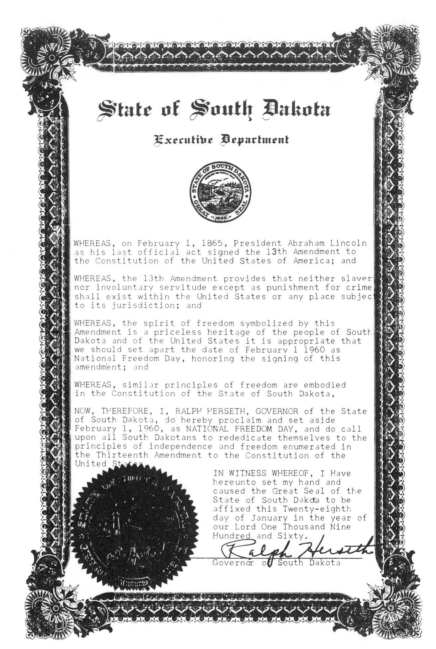

State of South Dakota

Executive Department

WHEREAS, on February 1, 1865, President Abraham Lincoln as his last official act signed the 13th Amendment to the Constitution of the United States of America; and

WHEREAS, the 13th Amendment provides that neither slavery nor involuntary servitude except as punishment for crime shall exist within the United States or any place subject to its jurisdiction; and

WHEREAS, the spirit of freedom symbolized by this Amendment is a priceless heritage of the people of South Dakota and of the United States it is appropriate that we should set apart the date of February 1 1960 as National Freedom Day, honoring the signing of this amendment; and

WHEREAS, similar principles of freedom are embodied in the Constitution of the State of South Dakota,

NOW, THEREFORE, I, RALPH HERSETH, GOVERNOR of the State of South Dakota, do hereby proclaim and set aside February 1, 1960, as NATIONAL FREEDOM DAY, and do call upon all South Dakotans to rededicate themselves to the principles of independence and freedom enumerated in the Thirteenth Amendment to the Constitution of the United States.

IN WITNESS WHEREOF, I Have hereunto set my hand and caused the Great Seal of the State of South Dakota to be affixed this Twenty-eighth day of January in the year of our Lord One Thousand Nine Hundred and Sixty.

Ralph Herseth
Governor of South Dakota

This National Freedom Day Proclamation, which was issued by the governor of South Dakota on February 1, 1960, is representative of the proclamations issued by most states and collected annually by the sponsors of National Freedom Day. Usually one of these documents is read aloud during the celebration. Courtesy of Mr. Emanuel C. Wright.

Souvenir Program

Twenty – Second

ANNIVERSARY CELEBRATION

OF

NATIONAL FREEDOM DAY

Friday, February 1, 1963

CEREMONIES

INDEPENDENCE HALL

6th and Chestnut Streets
Philadelphia, Pa.
at Four P. M.

MOTHER BETHEL A.M.E. CHURCH

6th Street below Pine Street
Philadelphia, Pa.
at Eight P. M.

A bust of President Lincoln and the Statue of Liberty's torch are the two symbols of freedom on this National Freedom Day program cover, 1963. Courtesy of Mr. Emanuel C. Wright.

an integral part of these observances since their inception. Mrs. Bennie Mae Johnson wrote on a celebration questionnaire, "My father said when the people were told about their freedom, some shouted, danced, yelled, some beat on washtubs and hit plates together. They were so glad." She continued with this personal observation of celebration drum-dancing.

> On the 28th of May some of the same things are relived. Dancing, singing, etc. In some of the more recent years large and small drums was purchased. Different ones would beat the drum to a beat that everyone is familiar with. You could see different ones dance their troubles away. There would be several large-size boys, age 11 to 13, carrying the drum through the crowd. Usually older men would do the drumming, while the boys would carry them. A group of people form and some one jump in the circle and dance. Sometimes alone and sometimes a group.[107]

However, the dancing to down-home blues played on a piano or "six-string guitar" is the most popular form of celebration dancing.

This latter form of dancing continues to be an important element in Afro-American culture. Albert Murray has noted that "dance . . . seems to have been the first means by which human consciousness objectified, symbolized, and stylized its perceptions, conceptions, and feelings."[108] And Jeff Titon contends that "there is good reason to suppose that a people's traditional music and the way they behave when performing it are symbolic expressions of broad cultural pattern and social organization."[109] W. C. Handy first observed the deep cultural significance of blues music and dance during the intermission of a dance he was playing in Cleveland, Mississippi, when a "local colored band," consisting of a guitar, mandolin, and string bass, played the blues, and a "rain of silver dollars began to fall around the [musicians] outlandish, stomping feet. . . ."[110] A quick learner, Handy used this same blues form while introducing "The St. Louis Blues." "I tricked the dancers by arranging a tango introduction, breaking abruptly into a low-down blues. My eyes swept the floor anxiously, then suddenly I saw the lightening strike. The dancers seemed electrified. Something within them came suddenly alive. An instinct that wanted so much to live, to fling its arms and to spread joy, took them by their heels."[111]

Freedom celebration dancers use blues dancing to celebrate their down-home roots. Particular regions are represented in such regional dances as the Texas Twist, the Georgia Crawl, and the Swamp Shimmy (Florida).[112] The miming dances of down-home animals, such as the Grizzly Bear, the Buzzard Lope, the Horse, the Turkey Trot, the Turtle Twist, the Bunny Hug, the Fishtail, and the Funky Chicken,[113] as well as the choreographing of past farm chores like Walking the Dog and Holding the Mule, trigger memories of down-home life. Special mention should be made of the role played by the mule, a beast that has been a particularly important symbol for Afro-Americans since slavery. He is often used as a symbol of labor. A cycle of slave narratives associates the mule with the drudgery of bondage. In one of these folktales the mule utters this note of social protest to his slave driver: " 'Ain't it awful, us poor mules and all the niggers have to work all the time, and the white man gets all the money. Don't never get any rest. All we get to eat is beans and hay.' "[114] Emancipation was summarized in the phrase, "40 acres and a mule." A popular contemporary joke draws upon this mule-Black man relationship for its humor. After many unsuccessful attempts at getting his favorite worker to return home, an irate white boss sends his northern vacationing black worker this criptic telegram: "Dear John, MMMMM!" As John hurriedly packs to leave, he explains to his city relatives that the telegram means: "Meet My Mule Monday Morning!"[115]

The mule has also been associated with the liminal social status of Afro-Americans. Slaves and mules were often lumped together as subhuman beasts of burden, as illustrated in this Booker T. Washington anecdote: " . . . I remember that I asked one coloured man, who was about sixty years old, to tell me something of his history. He said that he had been born in Virginia, and sold into Alabama in 1845. I asked him how many were sold at the same time. He said, 'There were five of us; myself and brother and three mules.' "[116] Today the lowly social status of the mule and Afro-Americans is summarized in the saying: "Kill a mule, buy another. Kill a nigger, hire another."[117]

The mule has been totally integrated into Afro-American speech and folk expressions. Some blacks have labeled their moonshine whiskey, "white mule."[118] A stubborn person is often called "mule-headed." A dependable individual is often referred to as a "bank mule."[119] And bluesmen have used the mule to fashion such lyrics as "I worked for you like a Goergia mule," to convey the notion of fidelity, and "another mule is kicking in my stall," to refer to a cuckolded lover.

The mule was a prominent freedom symbol during the civil-rights era. Mule-drawn wagons appeared in the Poor Peoples' March on Washington, symbolizing the abject poverty of many Afro-Americans. Later, one of these crude, mule-pulled wagons bore the body of Dr. Martin Luther King, Jr., to his grave, poignantly capturing the humility and scope of Dr. King's ministry.[120]

In addition, then, to these animal mime dances, satiric dances such as the White Boy and the Watergate symbolize the heroic quality required of each dancer living in this "howlin' wilderness." Albert Murray argues persuasively that blues dances are "rituals of self-expression" in which the dancers and musicians engage in an endless round of "confrontation . . . improvisation . . . affirmation . . . celebration."[121] Murray also sees these blues steps as yet another manifestation of the spirituals' metaphorical arduous journey through America's hostile landscape: "What the customary blues-idiom dance movement reflects is a disposition to encounter obstacle after obstacle as a matter of course."[122]

Every year the sensuous sounds of the blues, the smell of barbecue, and the stimulation of political oratory lure large numbers of Afro-Americans from big urban areas to down-home celebrations. And there they engage in the numerous symbolic rites of fellowship, worship, and entertainment that make up these annual freedom pilgrimages.

[Emancipation Celebrations] have been those schools of citizenship and the training of a new group in the army of struggle for the realization of first-class citizenship for all people.

Atlanta Daily World *(1955)*

The Politics of Protest

Since their inception, Emancipation celebrations have remained important, annual, grass-roots political forums for Afro-Americans. Furthermore, their persistent protest of the Afro-American's status as a second-class citizen—expressed through an unrelenting barrage of resolutions, proclamations, petitions, NAACP membership drives, militant speeches, civic committee reports, parades, voter-registration campaigns, boycotts and numerous other political stratagems—have helped create and maintain the political climate that has spawned much of this century's political activity among Afro-Americans. These simple freedom celebrations, especially in the South, made significant contributions to such Afro-American political gains as: the repeal of Jim Crow laws in public accommodations and education; the elimination of the poll tax, white primaries, and other means of voter restriction; the significant increase in Afro-American voters; the surge in the number of Afro-Americans elected to a wide range of local, state, and national offices; the proliferation of Afro-American caucuses and conventions; and the historic presidential campaign of Jesse Jackson.

Emancipation celebrations remain political forums for protest against the numerous forms of overt and covert racism perpetrated against Afro-Americans. Memories of these racist acts are vivid for many celebrants. One celebration speaker described his audience's second-class status during the 1920s in this manner: "They still had not experienced American freedom in its essence. They were receiving fringe benefits if any benefits at all. And they were closer, at that time, to the borderline of slavery than now. . . . . Their earnest desire to be free . . . just made your heart jump. . . . At that time they were not allowed to vote."[1] One celebrant I interviewed spoke of the Ku Klux Klan's role in keeping Afro-Americans second-class citizens. He recalled the terror that a simple act in defiance of the Klan brought to his home:

> When as a boy I can remember how the KKK used to parade up and down Wabash Avenue. And a red KKK sign . . . (If you go by the house, 16th and Oak Streets, you'll see a telephone pole and a KKK sign was put around that telephone pole) and my father tore it down. And he and Dr. Carrol got in the living room . . . at our house over there with shotguns, expecting the KKK to come through and take punitive action against them. However, the KKK never did that.[2]

Unfortunately, an all-too-frequent consequence of such blatant acts of racial hatred and implied violence was the creation of an intimidating social climate which deterred some Afro-Americans from attending their communities' Emancipation celebrations. One Georgia celebrant said that January 1st "was a day of jubilation and joy practically for most of the people. 'Course we had some Uncle Toms around there who hated to get out and some of them didn't get out."[3]

Celebration speeches frequently made reference to acts of racial oppression. A former celebration speaker recalled how he described a particular form of white-collar racism in his January 1st speech:

> And I mentioned the late attorney Bob Booker, who had . . .gone to the State Supreme Court and got them to overturn . . .to throw out . . . to repeal . . . (During that time the Arkansas legislature had enacted some . . . laws that would require certain organizations like the NAACP . . . to submit their membership rolls and things like that. And the purpose was to see who the members were, and people could be harassed if they had state jobs and what have you.) And it was through Mr. Booker, who took that thing to court, and the Supreme Court threw it out.[4]

Celebration speakers also sought solutions for these covert and overt tactics of racial oppression. A former January 1st celebrant clearly expresses the intensely political role that the celebrations could fulfill:

> I can remember in particular after we had had one celebration, oh it was about, say, a few weeks later. That some discussion had come up between one plantation's helper and another. And in the argument well, I think one had gotten the better of the argument. So one tells his [boss]. And that led to getting his boss riled at this Negro foreman of the other farm. And so much so that he came out to the other farm to kill him. Shot at him but missed. And so lost his life because he missed. Because this other fella got him. . . . And it worked out all right for our brother, because everybody was on the hush hush. Then . . . all incidents like that would be brought up at the next celebration, letting you know that you

still are not free and until you have gotten to the place where *you* yourselves can *stop these things,* you will not be free.[5]

The primary means by which organizers of these celebrations attempted to elevate Afro-Americans to first-class citizenship was by mobilizing celebrants into a united political bloc. One January 1st celebrant recalled how this racial organization was undertaken by a local political group:

> Its [January 1st celebration] sponsored by the Civic League, and they had oooh I suppose an appeal for membership in the Civic League and a kind of . . . an idea of talking about what the Civic League had done and how they had done it. Not just for that year, but primarily giving the people an idea of what the Civic League is all about, which is supposedly civic pride, community involvement . . . non-partisan, you know, political involvement.[6]

Another January 1st celebrant cites his celebration as being a favorite recruiting device for the local chapter of the NAACP:

> Atlanta through the years has had this Emancipation Proclamation celebration on January the 1st. And it is sponsored by the National Association for the Advancement of Colored People here. And it usually, the Association, brings in some outstanding speakers to speak about liberation, advancements that the Blacks have made, and the importance of Blacks continuing to work together for the advancement of Black people. . . . And usually we carry a very good crowd at our Emancipation Proclamation here. . . . The reason is we've had it so many years, and it's during that time when we try to get our membership built up in the NAACP. The five-hundred-dollar members and other persons who just want to make a contribution.[7]

And a September 22nd celebrant remembers the theme of political unity being sounded by a celebration speaker. "There is one thing that sticks with me about Oscar De Priest's [speech] emphasizing that Black people need to register and vote. And perhaps organize . . . to organize themselves into a power bloc so that they could make demands of politicians. And that would be one way to get your goals. I remember that."[8]

The sense of unity derived from the celebrations has manifested itself in numerous ways. Staging parades through the downtown areas of the cities and towns hosting these freedom celebrations has been one popular means of making the larger American society aware of the Afro-American community's desire for first-class citizenship. A former September 22nd celebrant described how the freedom parades attracted white and black citizens in his hometown. "If my memory serves me right, one of the mayors of Terre Haute might have participated in an automobile or something like that. But it was mostly black people who were in the parade itself. Now all up and down Wabash Avenue there were blacks and whites. And also the stores put up some bunting indicating the celebration of the Emancipation Proclamation."[9] Atlanta's January 1, 1944, celebration was highlighted by a massive parade of military units, fraternal organizations, civic clubs, Boy Scout troops, high school marching bands, floats, and decorated cars "down several of the main streets and avenues of the city."[10] The 1976 Juneteenth parade in Anderson, Texas, which was led by a flag-waving Uncle Sam, wound its line of mounted cowboys, colorful floats, and decorated cars around the town square, before heading out to the picnic site.[11]

The political significance of such parades was clear as early as 1886 and 1887 in Washington, D.C.'s April 16th parades. In the first year a group of distinguished leaders of the city's Afro-American community called upon President Grover Cleveland and formally requested that he review their Emancipation day parade as it filed past the White House. President Cleveland refused their request, causing a local reporter to write: "We believe this is the first time that he [President Cleveland] has refused to review any organization that asked for that courtesy. The thought very naturally arises, did he refuse in this case because the organizations were composed of colored men? Perhaps not, but it looks that way."[12] In 1887 President Cleveland changed his mind and reviewed the April 16th parade as it moved past the White House.[13]

The sense of political unity generated by Emanipation celebrations also manifests itself in the celebrants' turning inward to take care of their local communities. Many freedom celebrations sponsor community improvement projects. The January 1st celebrations of the 1930s frequently took up donations for the surviving ex-slaves.[14] An Atlanta January 1st celebration provided free bags of food and coal for needy Afro-American families.[15] An offering of food for the poor was also raised at the January 1st celebration I attended in Columbus, Georgia. In the interest of improving their environment, Atlanta's January 1st celebrants resolved to eradicate all "Immoral nuisances in Negro neighborhoods";[16] while their counterparts in Chattanooga conducted a plebiscite which denounced the "legalizing of cocktail bars in Chattanooga."[17]

Politically united freedom celebrants also draft resolutions which publically protest their second-class citizenship status. In 1945 Atlanta's January 1st celebrants resolved to recruit "10,000 additional registered voters," celebrate "Walter White Day," take an active role in the Seventh War Loan Drive, expand the program of the Atlanta NAACP chapter, express their dissatisfaction with the administration and policies of the Colored Boys Farm, and fight to resolve ". . . the issue of the White Primaries, the Poll Tax, Discriminatory School Facilities, Unequal salaries for teacher [sic], Immoral nuisances in Negro Neighborhoods, Recreation and the whole fabric of discriminatory segregation."[18] Five years later, in Indianapolis, January 1st celebrants resolved to vote out of office those members of Congress who failed to support President Harry S. Truman's fair employment practice and civil-rights laws.[19] In 1955 Atlanta's January 1st celebrants resolved to resist the delaying tactics of Southern segregationists to stall the implementation of the Supreme Court's school desegregation ruling of May 17, 1954, and to protect Negro teachers from losing their jobs because of this edict.[20] One year later, Birmingham's January 1st celebrants showed that they had caught the defiant spirit of the nearby Montgomery bus boycott, when they issued this resolution:

> Whereas the economic status of the Negro citizens has greatly enhanced the development and progress of the several states of the United States.
> Be it resolved that housewives and other persons concern themselves with a selective use of their purchasing power as both a self-defense economic weapon and as an aid to winning first-class citizenship.[21]

Politically organized freedom celebrants also give various forms of formal recognitions to individuals who have made significant contributions to their struggle for first-class citizenship. Indianapolis's January 1st celebrants drafted a resolution commending President Truman's efforts on behalf of civil rights.[22] And Birmingham's January 1st celebrants issued this glowing commendation for participants in the historic Montgomery bus boycott:

> The Emancipation Association of Birmingham and Vicinity make the following commendations:
> 1. That the citizens of Montgomery, Alabama be commended for their uncompromising and determined stand in resisting the undemocratic and unchristian practices of the Montgomery Bus Lines and the City of Montgomery, Alabama in discriminating and segregating its own local citizens solely on account of race.
> We further commend the citizens of Montgomery, Alabama for refusing to accept anything short of that which they are entitled to as full citizens of the State of Alabama and the United States of America.[23]

Emancipation celebrations also give awards to those individuals whose lives best typify this struggle for freedom and first-class citizenship. Appropriately, ex-slaves were the first honorees, serving as parade marshals, gracing the head tables of the celebration dinners, and rendering remarks or prayers at numerous programs.[24] In 1935 one of the highlights of Atlanta's January 1st celebration became the awarding of the "27 Award," which was given by the 27 Club "to the person having rendered the most outstanding service during the year."[25] (Past recipients include Dr. Benjamin E. Mays, the former president of Morehouse College.) And the sponsors of the National Freedom Day celebration began giving the National Freedom Award in 1963. The award, which was given posthumously to the educator, Dr. Horace Mann Bond, in 1973, was described this way by Mr. Emanuel C. Wright:

> . . . the National Freedom Award is given to men or women—although we haven't given [it to] women yet—persons who have consistently been in line with the concept of the National Freedom Day Association. Now we haven't [given it to] . . . radicals, people who come up overnight and some who come up overnight and then fade away. But over the long pull that they have . . . consistently believed in the rights of people and . . . believed in goodwill and harmonious understanding among all people. And worked consistently toward that goal.[26]

The annual selection of these courageous, freedom-loving men and women provide the celebrants with role models to identify with and to pattern their actions after in their own struggle to achieve first-class citizenship.

No right of citizenship is stressed more at these freedom celebrations than the right to vote. One former January 1st speaker reminded his audience of the heroic efforts of one local citizen to secure for them the right to vote in the primary elections:

> I mentioned the fact that Professor Robinson, James Robinson, who way back was president of what was called the Arkansas Negro Democratic Association. And how he worked in order to make it possible for Negroes to vote in the Democratic primaries here. Because there was a time right here in Arkansas when Negroes couldn't vote in the Democratic primary. They either had to wait until the general election or not vote at all. It was Dr. Robinson who took this thing to court.[27]

Other speakers urge the celebrants to register and vote in all elections. If Afro-Americans exercise the right to vote in an intelligent and unified manner, the speakers argue, they can eliminate the socially restrictive racial barriers that stand between them and first-class citizenship. This theme has been sounded by an ever lengthening line of keynote speakers. Dr. Mary McLeod Bethune told January 1st celebrants in Macon, Georgia, "those who don't have the use of the ballot should get it, and those who already have it should use it."[28] J. Wesley Dobbs told Chattanooga's January 1, 1952, celebrants: "We had less than five hundred registered Negro voters in Atlanta fifteen years ago, now we have twenty-five thousand registered. It was definitely the Negro vote that elected the present mayor of Atlanta and, as a result of his election, we have colored police riding in squad cars."[29] In 1956 Congressman Charles Diggs advised Atlanta's January 1st celebrants to use the ballot to remove Dixiecrat James C. Davis from Congress and keep former governor Herman Talmadge out of the Senate. Congressman Diggs also reminded his audience of the respect that is accorded a group of people who vote: ". . . you and I have seen attitudes change when registration goes up. . . ."[30] In 1984 Reverend Jesse Jackson urged Mississippi's August 8th celebrants to register and vote.[31]

Emancipation celebrations played a major role in the massive shift of Afro-American voters from the Republican to the Democratic party. One Juneteenth celebrant recalled how the older celebrants justified being Republicans:

> Well, I tell you what I know since I been celebrating [Juneteenth]. Back in my day, way back yonder, and you know the old folks used to tell us that they were enslaved. The white folks had 'em enslaved, and they had 'em working on farms, and they . . . drove them, worked 'em just like animals. Beat 'em and just all this, that, and the other. You know the older folks could just tell us different things how they done 'em, how they treated 'em. So it come around a time when Abraham Lincoln got elected president. He was a Republican wasn't he, Reverend Parks? 'Cause they say all Negroes ought to be Republicans. That's what they tell us now. But the Republicans act so bad, but that's what they say, the Negro ought to be because that's who freed him, what little freedom we did get.[32]

A September 22nd celebrant remembered the prominent Afro-American Republicans who used to speak at the celebrations he attended as a boy:

> And then they would attempt to bring some outstanding Negro leader, so many times an outstanding speaker. I remember they had Roscoe Conklin Simmons. He was one of the speakers, you know. . . . But the one that sticks with me the most, of course, is Oscar De Priest. And he was a Republican as I recall. And we had quite a Republican politician in Terre Haute named Grace Edwards who was quite a speaker herself, quite a dynamic speaker. And the one I'm referring to, she introduced Oscar De Priest with a lot of flourish and so forth. And, of course, being a

> Congressman, you know, it meant quite a bit and he gave quite a stem-winding address.[33]

Newspaper accounts confirm that the majority of celebrants were loyal Republicans from Emancipation through the first three decades of this century. A newspaper report of Terre Haute's September 22nd celebration in 1888 noted that, after Frederick Douglass's "non-political" keynote address, one of the celebrants "made a violent Republican harangue, greatly to the distress of many present and particularly if [sic] those members of the committee who had pledged their word in soliciting subscriptions from Democrats that there would be no politics at the celebration."[34]

However, this ardent Republican loyalty was shattered during the presidential election of 1936. A graphic illustration of this internal political bickering evolved out of New York City's celebration of September 22nd, which was broadcast over a national radio network to twenty-five other Emancipation celebrations. More than fourteen thousand Afro-Americans crammed into Madison Square Garden to celebrate the seventy-fourth anniversary of President Lincoln's issuance of his preliminary proclamation, hear a letter read from President Roosevelt, cheer political remarks by Representative Caroline O'Day and Senator Robert F. Wagner, and ratify a resolution that called upon the celebrants to switch their political party affiliation from the party of Lincoln, the Great Emancipator, to Roosevelt, the father of the New Deal. The resolution challenged the celebrants to "emancipate ourselves from the mere party shibboleths, even though this may shatter tradition and ancient loyalties." It further urged these prospective voters "not to be shackled by the slavery of dead issues of a day long past," encouraging them to unite with other "forward-looking citizens" and "carry forward the real spirit of Abraham Lincoln by supporting the social and economic program of our great President, Franklin D. Roosevelt."[35]

Opposition was not long in coming. A group of clergymen headed by AME Bishop David H. Simms, who supported the Republican candidate, Governor Alf Landon, held a meeting at the Republican party's New York State Committee headquarters at which they protested the Democrats "attempted perversion of the sacred principles of the Emancipation Proclamation" and issued this counter-resolution of party loyalty:

> We regard the Republican party as the one party capable of meeting the issues of this campaign. While we frankly recognize that like every political party there may have existed grounds for minor criticisms as to

the achievements of the party in the past, we nevertheless herein express our profound conviction that our party history, spirit, vitality, platform and candidates are the instruments through which this country can be restored to normalcy.[36]

But their plea failed to elicit a positive response from the mass of Afro-Americans, who bolted from their traditional Republican party affiliation and, for the first time in their history, voted in large numbers for the Democratic candidate, landslide winner Franklin D. Roosevelt. Their sentiments were aptly expressed by one of the speakers at the 1936 celebration of September 22nd in Gary, Indiana: "At last we Negroes have realized that voting Republican will not aid in the further emancipation of southern Negroes. . . . We are asked why we deserted the Republican party. We did not desert it, we were kicked out of it. The Democrats merely accepted us."[37] The shift in Afro-American voter registration begun in these 1936 Emancipation celebrations marks the beginning of today's political reality that the majority of Afro-American voters are primarily registered Democrats.

The spoken word plays a major role in the politicization of the freedom celebrants. A January 1st observer remembered the political tone of the celebrations' prayers: "And we would have an invocation. And I better call it a prayer, because it was a little long for an invocation. Where even in this prayer there was almost a sermon about all the things that may be happening. That was the way we had in those days I am sure of letting everybody know what had happened and how we should feel about it."[38]

Freedom celebrants are also annually politicized by the reading of some freedom document in the course of the celebration program. In 1860, before Emancipation, celebrants of July 4th in North Elba, New York, heard "Rev. C.G. Prindle . . . read the Declaration of Independence, in a full and clear voice."[39] And after the opening prayer in the 1859 August 1st celebration at Geneva, New York, celebrants heard "Augustus Jeffrey, Esq., read the Act of British Emancipation . . . in a clear, unfaltering voice, and with much spirit and emphasis."[40] Since Emancipation, freedom celebrants have made the reading of the Emancipation Proclamation a favorite ritual. A January 1st celebrant placed this reading almost on a par with the celebration's keynote address. "There would always be an appropriate program with a speaker, an outstanding speaker. And certainly the reading . . . the Proclamation. And some good reader was especially chosen to do this. Some person who read especially well. And it was an honor to be chosen to read the Emancipation Proclamation."[41] Another January 1st

Emancipation Day Drill Team, Owensboro, Kentucky. Copyright © 1982, *The Courier-Journal.* Reprinted with permission.

Attorney Yvonne Watkins reading the Emancipation Proclamation at an Emancipation program held in Indianapolis, Indiana, January 2, 1984. Courtesy of the *Indianapolis Star.*

African Liberation Day Concert, Louisville, Kentucky. Copyright © 1980, *The Courier-Journal.* Reprinted with permission.

Photograph of a drum and bugle corp marching down Ouellette Avenue in the August 1st West Indian Emancipation Day Parade in Windsor, Ontario (1971). Courtesy of the *Windsor Star*.

celebrant recalled how the annual reading of this document heightened his political awareness: "The Emancipation Proclamation served to me more as a go forward basis for blacks. We've come here now to celebrate, to reappraise, retrospect on where we've come from and set the directions and the routes in which we are going and traveling."[42] These ritualized readings of freedom documents have a politicizing effect upon the celebrants in that they remind and reassure the observers that they are legal, full-fledged citizens of the United States of America and deserving of all the rights and privileges that accompany that status.

Sponsors of some Emancipation celebrations have taken this proclamation-reading ritual one step further and annually solicited freedom proclamations from various levels of American government. During the first two decades of this century, the organizers of Terre Haute's September 22nd celebration prevailed upon the mayor to issue a proclamation praising the observance. And in 1918 Mayor Charles R. Hunter issued a statement calling upon Terre Haute's citizens to decorate their homes and businesses in honor of the occasion and in remembrance of President Lincoln, praising the colored citizens for their progress, and concluding with the words: "Let us celebrate this day in a fitting manner and give the colored people of the city a wonderful ovation on this, their day of all great days."[43]

National Freedom Day sponsors have had great success collecting proclamations from the United States' fifty governors. Mr. Emanuel C. Wright told me:

> Surprisingly, we have gotten proclamations from I believe all the states except . . . Mississippi [*chuckles*]. I don't [believe] we've received one

a.

b.

c.

d.

e.

Freedom Souvenirs: a) This January 1, 1863, medallion, cast in 1906, was given to me by Mr. Robert Lee Perry of Tyler, Texas. b) One of the buttons worn by supporters of legislation to make Dr. King's birthday a national holiday. c) Booker T. Washington centennial stamp, issued in 1956, depicts the noted educator's Virginia birthplace. d) This Jackie Robinson commemorative stamp shows Jackie stealing home against the Yankee's Yogi Berra in the 1956 World Series. It was issued in 1982. e) An Abraham Lincoln commemorative stamp, depicting Thomas Ball's Emancipation Monument in Lincoln Park, Washington, D.C., was issued in 1940 to commemorate the 75th anniversary of the passing of the 13th Amendment.

The abolitionist medallion (opposite), whose images and inscriptions are based on the Josiah Wedgwood medallion (1730–95), was also used as a one-cent coin during the depression year of 1838. This is perhaps the first American coin depicting the figure of an Afro-American. Courtesy of the Lilly Library, Indiana University.

The above illustration appears on a program for an exhibit of nineteen paintings by Burford E. Evans. The exhibit was "I Remember Juneteenth." 1972. Courtesy of Mr. Burford E. Evans.

The African Liberation Day poster (opposite) is representative of the many posters annually glued to trash cans in Washington, D.C., on or before each May 28 to commemorate African Liberation Day.

AFRICAN LIBERATION DAY '77

"The Core of the Black
Revolution is in Africa, and
Until Africa is united
under a socialist ·
government, the
Black man throughout
the world lacks a
national home!"

"The U.S., South Africa,
Rhodesia, and Israel,
Enemies of Africa and all Mankind!"

MALCOLM X PARK
16th & EUCLID, NW
10 AM SATURDAY
28 MAY 1977

 **All-African People's
Revolutionary Party**

BOX 3307, WASHINGTON, DC 20009 (202)

from Mississippi. . . . And of course a few of the states in the Northwest said, "We don't have any colored people in our state and we don't know anything about segregation." And, "We don't think the proclamation will have any meaning in our state." So you couldn't fight that.[44]

The 1964 National Freedom Day program featured copies of proclamations from the states of Pennsylvania, Illinois, Maryland, New York, Oregon, Texas, West Virginia, Iowa, Kansas, Kentucky, Michigan, Missouri, Nebraska, Ohio, and South Dakota. The 1973 celebration program carried a reproduction of the proclamation issued by Pennsylvania Governor Milton J. Shapp, which read in part: "Each year on February 1st, we commemorate the anniversary of the signing of the 13th Amendment to the Constitution of the United States of America by President Abraham Lincoln, which abolished slavery forever from our nation and guaranteed freedom for all Americans."[45]

The 1963 National Freedom Day program carried a reproduction of President John F. Kennedy's presidential proclamation commemorating the centennial anniversary of the issuance of the Emancipation Proclamation. President Kennedy's statement cited the Thirteenth, Fourteenth, and Fifteenth Amendments as constitutional documents that "guaranteed" equal rights for Afro-Americans, noted that "the goal of equal rights for all our citizens is still unreached," urged all Americans "to observe the centennial by appropriate ceremonies," and reminded the nation that ". . . the Emancipation Proclamation expresses our Nation's policy, founded on justice and morality, and that it is therefore fitting and proper to commemorate the centennial of the historic Emancipation Proclamation throughout the year 1963."[46]

The major political focus of these celebrations is on their keynote addresses. As one January 1st celebrant put it, "the feature is always the speaker. It's always, even in Michigan, some guy that brings up the history of the movement. You know what I mean, of the Emancipation of Negroes. . . ."[47] Another celebrant remembered that these speeches were the highlights of many Juneteenth celebrations: "I remember that young people in their teens would work to have money on that day. We'd go to the picnic and somebody was always selected from the community or adjoining community that they looked up to as a leader, some minister or teacher to talk about how far we had come. . . . And they had these rousing freedom speeches. . . . Big picnics and speeches . . . had a platform for the speakers to speak on."[48]

A wide variety of speakers have graced these freedom celebrations.

Local white politicians often spoke at these affairs, and many of them donated food for the celebration meal. One Juneteenth celebrant recalled that "if it [Juneteenth] was near time for an election, county election or city election, sometimes the officials would come out and talk to the people. Sometimes the candidates that spoke would give them half a beef or something of that sort."[49] Another Juneteenth celebrant said, "Yes, they would invite the candidates out to speak. . . . And the primary now comes off . . . in August, . . . But it used to be in June, and they'd have the candidates; all the candidates would come out and speak. And then generally . . . the candidates would give the beef. The man running for sheriff or judge or something, he'd give them the beef. And another one would give the bread."[50]

President Franklin D. Roosevelt prepared two political statements that were read to freedom celebrants during the presidential election year of 1936. January 1st celebrants who attended the services at New York City's St. Marks Methodist Episcopal church heard his letter giving presidential recognition to the date as well as lauding their progress as a race: "Few events in our history are of greater significance than the freeing of the slaves. As we go back to the date when the Emancipation Proclamation was issued by the great Lincoln and down through the years, decade by decade, we are profoundly impressed by the steady progress which the Negro has made since January 1, 1863."[51] Later in the year, those in attendance at the September 22nd celebration held in Madison Square Garden heard another letter from President Roosevelt that also sounded the positive note of racial progress: "The record which our Negro citizens have made in their own personal and racial development and their contribution to the material advancement of our country and to the promotion of its ideals are well known."[52]

Black speakers, however, are the most popular orators at these freedom celebrations. Whether a local or national freedom figure, the speaker "was always the man who could fire them up. The pride in the race and that, the day of our freedom, and how thankful we ought to be, and how much progress we've made."[53] A January 1st celebrant spoke of a former celebration speaker in hyperbolic terms that call to mind some of the protest humor of the civil rights era:

> See in Alabama I remember Clifton Madison . . . was the speaker one time. . . . Clifton Madison then lived in Hobson City, and he was the first Negro down in that way to vote, because there you had to be able to recite the Constitution in verbatim. By memory. And he was the first person,

white or black [*laughter*]. But that's what you had to do, you know, those were evasive schemes, and he was the only one could do it. And he was the first.[54]

Roscoe Conklin Simmons was one of the more popular freedom celebration speakers during the first quarter of this century. A January 1st celebrant remembers Mr. Simmons's oratorical style and physical appearance:

> Now as far as I can remember . . . he was silver-tongued. Of course there were no mikes in those days, but he had the voice that could command the attention of his audience. Now these are the things I heard, because I never knew him. And as near as I remember about his description, he was a man of good stature. And I don't remember if they said he was a very big man, but of good stature, because he was always spoken of as a "fine looking gentleman." And he had polished manners. I remember those things.[55]

She also spoke of his appeal as a celebration speaker:

> Well, if you remember I told you that he was the man of the day. Now bigger towns, course, would have him. We only got the excerpts of these people who had heard him. Now a small town like Monticello could not afford Mr. Simmons. He would more than likely go to Atlanta, Macon, or . . . Savannah would have him. But our little town would have to take who had heard him. . . . And in their speeches could say, I quote from Roscoe Conklin Simmons thus and so. And of course, that got everybody's attention who wanted to hear what Simmons had to say. And I think today, if we could have had what we have now and his voice preserved, you know, where it could have been—for instance like we do about Martin Luther King—children who have never seen him can hear his voice and see his precious picture in the paper. I am sure I never saw him personally. I mean actually saw the man. But we just heard so much about him and always at these celebrations.[56]

The celebration speeches delivered by speakers like Clifton Madison and Roscoe Conklin Simmons, like those of Dr. King, were often filled with an emotional, religious fervor. A January 1st celebrant recalled that "Sometimes some of those speeches, you know, would really get your [back up]. So that you would want to let loose some of that fire now. . . . I mean some of the speeches were so filled with . . . religious fervor that you just had to shout. And sometimes they were mixed. Sometimes the speaker would know that these are deeply religious people. They would use a background of possibly the Red Sea and all that kind of thing."[57] Another January 1st celebrant confirmed this observation: "I can remember [in] the keynote that they stressed . . . that last verse of that Negro National Anthem, 'God of our weary years, of our silent tears,' you know, 'keep us forever in Thy path we pray. Lest our hearts, drunk with the wine of the world, we forget Thee. Less our feet stray from the places our God where we met Thee.' You know."[58]

Celebration speakers reverberate myriad themes off of this traditional, emotional, religious sounding-board. The Madisons and the Simmonses continue to make a clarion call for racial unity. A January 1st speaker mused over the latent economic power possible in racial unity: "I have a dream myself. I so very often thought of the fact that if every Black church in the city of Columbus, Georgia, every member in every Black church, would give one dollar a month. Do you know how much money we would have? Have you ever thought about that? And how we could become incorporated and we could establish our housing projects and establish our shopping centers and, at the same time, create jobs for our people."[59] Reverend Tascherean Arnold challenged his 1953 January 1st audience to strive for economic unity, ridiculing those "Negroes [who] haven't been convinced that the white man's ice is not colder than the Negro's ice despite the fact that both of them got the ice at the same plant."[60] At Montgomery's January 1st celebration in 1946, Dr. William Holmes Borders reminded his audience that "intelligent Negroes must remain with the masses. They very much need each other. Apart, both will perish."[61] Congressman Charles C. Diggs also expressed this same idea during his 1956 January 1st address in Atlanta, when he told his affluent audience: "The Negro doctor, dentist, minister, teacher, etc., 'have got to stop trying to be a big fish in their own little pond, and come out and help. . . . There's not a Negro professional man in the United States who doesn't owe all he is today to the NAACP.' "[62] While on February 1, 1973, Mr. Mal Goode told his upper-middle-class audience that they were "just luckier" than the "wino" and "narcotics addict" that they passed on the street.[63]

Charismatic speakers of the Madison and the Simmons variety also constantly sound the strident theme of social protest. A January 1st celebrant said, "They mostly talked about how the colored man is being pushed back, kept back."[64] And a sponsor of many August 1st celebrations recalled two past speakers who had spoken against injustice: "Milton Henry, he, you know, he's really a militant. And I told him, I said, 'Look, old pal,' I said, 'Tell it like it is, but *tone* it.' [*chuckles*] 'Because I've got to live here.' [*laughter*] But he put on a beautiful one. And then Dr. Abernathy when he came over here, I told him, 'Tell it like it is.' And he told it like it is and it was beautiful, beautiful."[65] Many celebration speakers, like Mr. Mal Goode, protest the racial inequalities of America's judicial system:

> There is no need for a dual system of justice in our courts, where one man is white, steals $100,000 from a bank, and gets five years probation in the courts. But in that same court the next day they bring in a Black man who stole a television set, and he gets five years in the penitentiary. An unequal system of justice. Go to your penitentiaries across the length and breadth of this state . . . and you'll find that sixty percent of the inmates are BLACK! Does that mean that we are criminally inclined? Ooooh no! That means that there is a dual standard of justice.[66]

Better education is often proposed as a solution to American racism. A January 1st celebrant remembered hearing this solution discussed as a child:

> What freedom really meant to us—and that has been sometime ago, because the time I am speaking about is between fifth grade and eighth grade times there at Monticello Training School, uh, Jasper County Training School. Freedom to us as children maybe did not have too much impact. Because as we had been taught by our parents, you accept what we are able to give you and always reach for the top. And to get to the top you must have education. Every child was geared to learn, and on these celebrations in particular all of the speeches were geared to learning. The child must know all—to make a better living. The top is what we want. We want a day when all of us can be free, and you can't be free unless you *know!* Because until you know, the person that *does* know will always take advantage of you. That was one thing that was brought up in our minds.[67]

Another January 1st celebrant recalled a celebration speaker urging his audience to learn more about how their city government worked:

> . . . the interesting thing last year in connection with this Emancipation Proclamation celebration was the fact that the speaker emphasized the fact of blacks getting involved in city planning. Too often when cities, in the South in particular and I imagine in the North, too, begin to plan their cities they put the blacks out on the edges don't you see. And there are no . . . blacks are really not involved. What he was suggesting was there is money available for blacks to learn how to plan and how to get the skills and get the jobs and the jobs will be there for them.[68]

An uplifting, patriotic note is struck in many celebration speeches. One Juneteenth celebrant noted that "These speeches would play up the achievement of the black man, our culture and our society. They were geared toward the enriching of the self-concept. In other words, you played a role and you had a right to be proud."[69] While another Juneteenth celebrant said, "They were admonished, you know, to be good citizens. . . . They would mention that he [Afro-Americans] always obeyed all the laws, and he fought in all the battles and that nobody could point their finger at him for being a traitor. I've heard that and I guess I've heard it fairly often, because my father dinned it into us also [*chuckles*]. But I did hear that. I can recall that in this note there would be his attainments and how he hasn't reflected anything but credit on himself since being free."[70]

Emancipation speeches frequently climax with the joyous promise of total future freedom. A January 1st celebrant recalled the effect that these speeches had upon the people in her community after they were over:

> In our neighborhoods, even though we lived far apart, after a speaker had been there for this type of celebration, we would gather—mostly we would gather at our home because we lived in the parsonage, and everybody in the community looked up to the ministers of the community. And then we rediscussed all of these things. And they—parents—thought that it was very good for children to hear *all* of the things that were being said *after* the celebration. What things could be done in our own little community that we could someday—maybe far off—could actually someday get real freedom.[71]

Bishop Ernest Hickman told a February 1st audience: "So today we are to encourage our fellow man to help God to make a better world by permitting a better world to begin in us. So that out of the valley of suffering, agony, and pain shall come a vision of a new day and a new social order."[72] And February 1st keynote speaker Mr. Mal Goode shared this futuristic vision of America with his audience: "Grant us a vision of our nation, a nation of justice where none shall prey on others, a nation of plenty where vice and poverty shall cease to fester, a nation of brotherhood . . . a nation of peace where order shall not rest on force, but on love for all the nation."[73]

The continuous political activity of Emancipation celebrations has helped create the social climate necessary for the emergence of several of the twentieth century's Afro-American political organizations, which are dedicated to the realization of this new day of freedom and brotherhood. The Niagara Movement, which flamed across the American historical landscape from 1905 to 1909 before merging into the NAACP in 1910, issued resolutions of protest which are consistent in theme and tone with similar statements issued by Emancipation celebrants. From their Harper's Ferry conference, W.E.B. Du Bois and other angry young Afro-American men issued this statement of political protest whose tone is reminiscent of Emancipation Day resolutions: "Never before in the modern age has a great and civilized folk threatened to adopt so cowardly a creed in the treatment of its fellow-citizens, born and bred on its soil. Stripped of verbose subterfuge and in its naked nastiness, the new American creed says: fear to let black men even try to rise lest they become the equals of the white."[74]

The civil rights era is marked by the emergence of several Afro-American religious and political organizations whose founding principles and major objectives are clearly extensions of the Emancipation celebrations' tradition of political protest. Dr. King's Southern Christian Leadership Conference, which is also the parent organization of Jesse Jackson's Operation Breadbasket and the surrogate parent of Jackson's Operation PUSH, has continued to address such Emancipation celebration issues as voting, jobs, and housing. Its annual conventions, like those of the NAACP, the Urban League, and Operation PUSH, are primarily ideological extensions of Emancipation celebrations. Like the older celebrations, these civil-rights organizations annually bestow prestigious awards, such as the NAACP's Spingard Award, upon some courageous champion of freedom and democracy; their delegates are divided into various study committees on issues of vital importance to the Afro-American community; they issue resolutions, letters, and telegrams expressing the Afro-American point of view to elected public officials; and the highlight of these conferences is a keynote address which mirrors in tone and substance traditional Emancipation celebration addresses.

The Emancipation celebrations' successful voter-registration drives and myriad voter-education programs have also contributed to the founding of a raft of Afro-American political organizations in the last two decades. Civil-rights activists, who passed out black and white Juneteenth buttons to symbolize their zeal, fashioned the Black Panther Party and the 1968 National Democratic Party Convention confrontation around the older celebrations' voter-registration drives.[75] The registration of Afro-American voters led to better governmental services, and, finally, to the election of some major Afro-American candidates. The sponsor of the August 1st observance in Windsor, Ontario, remembered the positive impact that his celebration had upon the election of Cleveland Mayor Carl Stokes: "Carl Stokes spoke here in 1966. And he was so shocked and surprised that the whites and blacks could mingle and get along so good that he took movie reel after movie reel. He was a council member of Cleveland at the time. . . . he told me . . . that he was going to show these pictures all over Cleveland. Which everybody [knows] that he was elected mayor of Cleveland in 1967."[76]

The election of such big-city Afro-American mayors as Carl Stokes in Cleveland and Richard Hatcher in Gary, Indiana, was one major factor in the proliferation of several national Afro-American political organizations. In 1972 Mayor Hatcher hosted the historic Black Political Convention. In 1980 more than two thousand Black political activists met in Philadelphia and formed the National Black Independent Political Party.[77] The election of large numbers of Afro-American congressmen and local officials has resulted in the organizing of the National Conference of Black Mayors and the Congressional Black Caucus.[78]

Despite the proliferation of these new groups, Emancipation celebrations have retained their political vigor, and it does not appear that their function as annual political protests will soon end. One celebration speaker maintained that as long as America denies its Afro-American citizens "whatever it is in America that other citizens [have],"[79] Emancipation celebrations will continue to serve as forums of cultural celebration and political protest for Afro-Americans. This January 1st celebrant summed up very well the continued loyalty that masses of Afro-Americans have to traditional political forums, "as a participant . . . in the congregation . . . I've always been interested in the event, the celebration, the emphasis on liberation, Black liberation, deliverance."[80]

[The Emancipation Proclamation] enabled the Negro to play a significant role in his own liberation with the ability to organzie [sic] and struggle, with less of the bestial retaliation his slave status had permitted to his masters.
Dr. Martin Luther King, Jr. [New York]
Amsterdam News (1962)

An Encore of Afro-American Freedom

The passage of the Martin Luther King, Jr., federal holiday bill was almost a historical reenactment of the drama originally played out in Abraham Lincoln's issuance of the Emancipation Proclamation. For the second time in a little more than a century, Washington, D.C., was the center stage upon which this Afro-American morality play of freedom and justice was performed. The initial drama was a one-act play set in the White House, where President Lincoln issued the Emancipation Proclamation on January 1, 1863. The hero of this drama was Lincoln, the first American president to denounce slavery publicly and in an official capacity. Free and enslaved Afro-Americans rejoiced when the Proclamation was released. The second drama was a three-act play that lasted for fourteen years, beginning on April 8, 1968—the year of Martin Luther King's death—when Congressmen John Conyers, Jr. (D-Mich.), introduced a bill in the House of Representatives to make January 15—King's birthdate—a federal holiday. This drama ended on November 2, 1983, when President Ronald Reagan signed a bill making Dr. King's birth date the tenth federal holiday.

The first act of this latter play is set in the streets and among the monuments of our nation's capital. From 1978 to 1982 Afro-Americans from all sections of America commemorated Dr. King's birth date by traveling to Washington, D.C. There they expressed their demands to have this date declared a national holiday by marching to the Lincoln Monument and cheering rousing speeches from such Afro-American spokespersons as Mr. Stevie Wonder, the singer/composer, and Mrs. Coretta Scott King, Dr. King's widow. The second act of the drama moved to the halls and hearingrooms of Congress, where from 1975 to 1983 the American people witnessed the passionate testimonies and spirited debates given in support and opposition to the passage of this holiday bill. Blacks and whites, men and women, Jews and Christians, conservatives and liberals, young and old, northerners and southerners, laborers and executives, Nobel laureates and governmental bureaucrats, racists and integrationists, patriots and Communists stepped upon the congressional stage and shared their opinions with members of the House and Senate.

The third act is set in the Rose Garden of the White House. Americans were bombarded with newspaper pictures and television coverage of President Reagan signing this holiday bill into law while Mrs. King, members of the King family, civil-rights veterans, congressional supporters of the bill from both houses, and a host of reporters and cameramen look on. Ironically, Dr. King, the hero of this Afro-American freedom drama, never appears on stage. However, his presence is felt in pictures of him that the demonstrators carried and in his ringing words of freedom which were quoted by those who testified before the various House and Senate subcommittees.

Afro-Americans and Americans of goodwill have cast Dr. King in the same heroic role that they bestowed upon President Lincoln. Both men are portrayed as symbolizing the best of the American ethos. Black Representative Robert N.C. Nix (R-Pa.) characterized Dr. King's assassination in this manner: "For the first time since the days of Lincoln, America was forced to examine its national guilt, its betrayal of Christian teachings, and its violations of the democratic ethic. The immorality of a way of life that imposed a second-class citizenship on an entire race of people was exposed forcefully by the power of Dr. King's leadership."[1] In the hearings held in the other house of Congress, Senator Edward M. Kennedy (D-Mass.) gave this ringing endorsement of Dr. King's moral impact upon America. In response to a question about whether he would settle for making Dr. King's birthday a commemorative Sunday observance, Senator Kennedy replied:

> We have to ask ourselves if we are serious men and women in this body about recognizing contributions. The fact of the matter is the principal mistake of our Founding Fathers was to fail to address the racial issue.
> . . . And our Founding Fathers bailed out on that issue. It was a magnificent job in the construction of the Constitution of the United States, but they ducked that one.
> And we have had a most important Civil War in this Nation because of that issue and that question. And we have the one person in this country that has done more than all our Founding Fathers to push back the walls of discrimination and prejudice in this country. And that was Martin Luther King, Jr.[2]

Dr. King's personal life and public ministry are closely tied to the earlier Afro-American freedom celebrations triggered by President Lincoln's issuance of the Emancipation Proclamation. On a personal level, Mr. Emanuel C. Wright recalled Dr. King attending a National Freedom Day observance while he was a student at Morehouse College. "Martin Luther King as a boy, as a student, came here. He was at that meeting, that convention, that Dr. Mays spoke. And, after Dr. Mays finished, all the Morehouse students gathered around him, and we had a picture of him [King]. And he was just a young student, you know. And little did you think that out of that group would come Martin Luther King."[3] Meetings like these must have contributed to the development of Dr. King's passion for freedom, justice, and human dignity—three traits that later became the hallmarks of his civil rights ministry.

During his public ministry, Dr. King frequently used the cultural forum of Emancipation celebrations to advocate his message of brotherhood and justice through nonviolent means. On New Year's Day 1957, one year removed from his successful Montgomery Bus Boycott, Dr. King returned home to Atlanta and delivered the keynote Emancipation celebration address. During the course of this speech, Dr. King called upon his overflow audience not to hate their white brothers: "Aim not to defeat the white man—we are out to fight injustices which keep down both black and white alike."[4] He also reminded them that they could not rest in their struggle for freedom.

> . . . there is a danger if you stop fighting at this point. We must hasten the death of old-man-segregation. He is on his death bed; however, an oxygen-tent can keep him alive a long time. . . . [We must] have courage and oppose segregation with all our soul. It might mean going to jail. Then fill it up. Because physical death is the price we must pay to prevent a psychological death. Going to jail or dying is worth it. It is better to be a free pauper than a rich slave.[5]

The next New Year's Day found Dr. King in Newport News, Virginia, delivering an Emancipation celebration keynote address entitled, "Facing the Challenge of the New Age." In this sermon Dr. King challenged his audience to strive for excellence and to embrace nonviolence. Concerning the former goal, Dr. King admonished his listeners not to settle for being "a good Negro anything." Instead, each one of them should strive to "Be the best of whatever you are. If you are a good street sweeper, sweep like Michael Angelo painted pictures, sweep like Beethoven wrote music, sweep like Shakespeare wrote poetry. . . ."[6] Dr. King went on to make his plea for nonviolence: "Stand before the oppressor . . . and say 'I will resist injustice but will not use violence and will not hate you. I will appeal to your heart and conscience and will eventually overthrow your evil system and win your love in the process.' "[7]

Dr. King also received Emancipation celebration awards. He garnered his first award in 1956, the year that the Montgomery Bus Boycott ended.[8] And one year later, at the conclusion of his Atlanta keynote address, Dr. King was given a plaque which recognized his "outstanding contributions to this race, the United States and to the world."[9]

The assassination of Dr. King caused Afro-Americans to add his January 15th birth date to their calendar of freedom observances. One subcommittee witness testified that:

> Every year since the assassination of the Reverend Dr. Martin Luther King, the anniversary of his birth has been marked in communities throughout this country by tributes to his unwavering dedication to the quality of all people. Formal ceremonies recalling his legacy of a single American society have been initiated in churches, community agencies, educational institutions, and the like.[10]

These celebrations of Dr. King's birth date evolved in much the same way that Emancipation observances did. In the first stage the celebrations were primarily spontaneous and mostly informal affairs, such as the one attended by Dr. L. Harold De Wolf, a former teacher of Dr. King at Boston University. He testified: "I was in the congregation of Ebenezer Baptist Church one Sunday morning when, at the close of an evangelistic service, his [Dr. King's] father led in observing the birthday of the martyred leader. Patriotic songs were sung, and the procession to the nearby tomb was led by the bearer of an American flag."[11]

In the second phase the celebrations became quasi-legal holidays in which Afro-American workers did not work and some black community businesses were closed in honor of Dr. King's memory. Congressman John Conyers, Jr., gave this testimony on how the black auto workers in Detroit observe January 15th. "I have been told by people in plant after plant in Detroit that on January 15th, if it is not in the bargaining contract, one does not come to work anyway. It is a holiday already."[12] A Philadelphia business executive noted a similar trend among small businesses in his city. "Recently, [an] increasing number of small businesses in the Philadelphia area where First Pennsylvania Corporation is headquartered have joined in memory of Dr. King by closing their doors on January 15."[13]

In the third stage the celebrations were granted legal sanction by some business or governmental institutions. Black union members have had some success securing Dr. King's birthday as a paid legal holiday. An American Federation of State, County and Municipal Employees official testified that "Since 1968, AFSCME International has established January 15th, Dr. King's birthday, as a paid legal holiday and has encouraged AFSCME local unions and councils to seek inclusion of Dr. King's birthday as a paid holiday in all contract negotiations."[14] Likewise Ms. Pat Brown, an Indianapolis public schoolteacher and chairperson of the NEA Black Caucus, testified: "In our city teachers have negotiated a contract that will allow us to close down schools on Martin Luther King's birthday."[15] Celebrants of Dr. King's birthday, like celebrants of Juneteenth (Texas), Crispus Attucks Day (Massachusetts) and National Freedom Day (Pennsylvania), were also successful in getting an impressive number of state governments to recognize this date in some official way. Mrs. Coretta Scott King testified: "To get a complete appreciation of the official support for the legislation [Dr. King holiday bill], we must take note of the fact that seventeen states, at least seventeen states, as well as the District of Columbia and the Virgin Islands now observe a day for Martin Luther King, Jr., as a legal, public holiday."[16] These state observances include Pennsylvania's "commemorative" day,[17] Virginia's celebrating Dr. King's birthday on New Year's Day,[18] and South Carolina's optional holiday observance. Senator Strom Thurmond (R-S.C.) testified: "In my State of South Carolina Martin Luther King, Jr.'s birthday is not [sic] observed as an optional holiday. The people in the state can observe his birthday, or Robert E. Lee's, whichever they prefer."[19] Senator Thurmond's reluctant observance of Dr. King's birthday contrasts sharply with this enthusiastic remembrance of Mr. David Clarke, chairman of the [Washington] D.C. City Council, who recalled that when the District was granted home rule in 1975, a King holiday bill "was the second bill that we passed, and I think that now we have established a traditional way to celebrate the day that should serve as a model for the rest of the nation."[20]

The fourth stage in the holiday's evolution was the agitation for the passage of a federal holiday bill. The following resolution of the Coalition of Black Trade Unionists (CBTU) is representative of other resolutions sent to Washington by the United Auto Workers (UAW), the AFL-CIO, NEA, and other national labor unions. The CBTU's resolution concludes:

> Whereas: His [Dr. King's] commitment to Black citizens in his struggle for human right [sic], dignity, justice and freedom cost him his life. . . .

Now, Therefore, Be It Resolved:
> That this CBTU convention go on record urging national legislation be passed making Martin Luther King's birthday (January 15) a national holiday.[21]

Because of this impressive groundswell of support, leaders of the Martin Luther King, Jr., holiday movement took the next step and began the long and tedious legislative process to get the bill signed into law. Congressman Conyers, a chief architect of the bill, cited this growing popular support for the King holiday bill during the first hearings held on the subject. He told the subcommittee:

> The support for the notion of making a public legal holiday of his birthday is one that can be measured by the increasing support that it receives every year. May I say to my colleagues on this subcommittee that I have received more mail as the originating sponsor of this bill than on any other legislative proposal. I had intended to bring over the six U.S. mailbags of mail that have come to me in the form of letters and petitions since 1968. It is enormous.
>
> It still comes in. People are still writing, and asking, and I am sure that you and the members of this subcommittee have also received a great deal of mail and encouragement in this matter.[22]

Mrs. King, another major organizer of the holiday-bill movement, mentioned yet another example of popular support from the American people for making her husband's birthday a national holiday. She told the subcommittee: "In the days after my husband's assassination Congress was inundated with petitions calling for a holiday for Martin Luther King, Jr. I know, for example, that one radio station in Newark, New Jersey, collected over 250,000 signatures endorsing a national holiday in honor of Martin's life and work."[23]

Mrs. King, Congressman Conyers, and other supporters of federal recognition of Dr. King's birthday were pursuing a goal that had long been sought by Emancipation celebrants: The King holiday supporters were the latest in a long line of Afro-Americans who have sought to have one day declared a national holiday to commemorate Afro-American freedom. As early as January 1, 1808, these sentiments were expressed. Reverend Absalom Jones told those Afro-Americans gathered to hear him preach a sermon celebrating the end of America's African slave trade that January 1 should "'be set apart in every year, as a day of public thanksgiving' so that the children might remember the crime that dragged their 'fathers from their native country and sold them as bondsmen in the United States of America.' "[24] In 1899 celebrants of New Albany's (Indiana) September 22nd observance expressed an interest in making that date "a national holiday."[25] In 1903 Anderson, Indiana, celebrants of September 22nd proposed a campaign to have either "September 22 or January 1 . . . declared the one holiday of the year for the negro [*sic*] race."[26] And in 1973 I heard Reverend Kelley Williams express these same sentiments during his Juneteenth sermon, when he told his Rockdale, Texas, audience: ". . . many of the Black peoples today feel that we should not celebrate or should not work toward a legal holiday for the deliverance of a Black man from slavery. [But] many of us Black folks today feel that this is wrong . . . we should set aside and work toward a legal holiday."[27]

Given this history, it is not too surprising that the subject of Emancipation celebrations cropped up during the very first congressional hearings on the Martin Luther King, Jr., national holiday bill hearings. Congresswoman Patricia Schroeder (D-Colo.), chairwoman of the subcommittee, broached the subject in the following exchange with Mr. Marc Stepp, Vice President of the UAW.

> *Mrs. Schroeder:* I have one question. I have talked to different members of the Black Caucus about this one. I am interested in your viewpoint.
>
> As a child growing up in the South, we had many people who celebrated Emancipation Day in June, and there were people who have said because we tend to celebrate events rather than people in this country, first Washington and Columbus, that maybe we should look to the Emancipation Proclamation.
>
> I have a very negative opinion of it. I thought it was one day in the South on which we honored the Emancipation Proclamation, one day out of the year.
>
> I think that was my childhood hangup. I wonder if you have any viewpoint on that versus Martin Luther King's birthday.
>
> *Mr. Stepp:* Surely in the whole pageantry of this idea that the Emancipation Proclamation itself, and that which floods to that day, is one that mankind can appreciate where one moves from slavery to freedom.
>
> I guess in the whole history of man, that occurrence is one that is to be appreciated. I would not want to get in the position to debate either/or.
>
> Personally, I can see no reason why we shouldn't have both: Martin Luther King, in terms of the spiritual aspects that I mentioned, and the Emancipation Proclamation for all people who came from slaves to free persons.

I haven't thought about that in terms of either/or, but off the top of the head, if that is not the unwise thing to say, I wouldn't want to get in the debate, because both are extremely important occurrences of man.

Mrs. Schroeder: I am sure it is something we will have to think about when we start making a final decision. It was a negative repression in the South. It would be one day that they would live through segregation.

I tend to lean toward Martin Luther King because it seems to make emancipation more real. It is something we should think about. That will be pointed out as we get closer to deciding.

Mr. Stepp: May I state one slight difference.

The proposal of Martin Luther King, the spirit of what he talked about, can be applied to every man and human dignity. Every individual, irrespective of his or her identity, racial, religion, and whatnot, it can touch every single one. That is the great plus.

Mrs. Schroeder: He stands for a much wider concept. That is true, I agree.

Thank you very much.[28]

This thoughtful exchange over the relative merits of Emancipation Day and Martin Luther King, Jr., Day raised the curtain on eight years of congressional hearings on the Martin Luther King, Jr., Holiday Bill. House and Senate committee chambers were transformed into political stages on which an endless cast of witnesses attacked and defended this piece of legislation with all the acrimony, humor, restrictive reason, effusive eloquence, pathos, and theatrics of an accomplished road company. Heroes (a white Congressman who originally opposed the bill and later becomes one of its staunch defenders) and villians (a black Communist who gives strong testimony against the passage of the bill) that would stretch the credibility of any casting director performed a seemingly endless series of playlets based upon one or more of the following themes: violence, extravagance, history, and patriotism.

Opponents of the legislation, such as E. Stanley Rittenhouse, a legislative aide for the conservative Liberty Lobby, and Congressman Larry P. McDonald (D-Ga.), a right-wing Congressman, constantly launched diatribes based on this convoluted logic: Because his acts of civil disobedience often led to violence, Dr. King was really an advocate of violence and not a man of nonviolence. Mr. Rittenhouse played to the conservative right-wing segment of the drama's audience:

Mr. Chairman [Senator Thurmond], Liberty Lobby believes that S. 25 is a thoroughly bad piece of legislation. It would sanctify and justify a man who deliberately brought violence to American streets, a subversive who was called "the most notorious liar in America" by J. Edgar Hoover—who was in a position to know—It is a very one-sided, racist legislation.[29]

Congressman McDonald stepped from the wings to second this notion that Dr. King was a man of violence. "Mr. Chairman [Senator Kennedy], I submit that Rev. Martin L. King, Jr., was not the caliber of person suitable to be made into a national hero . . . his teaching of contempt for the law and the legal process makes it most unsuitable for his anniversary to be made a national holiday."[30]

Congressman McDonald was challenged by a Mr. Williams, an aide of Senator Birch Bayh (D-Ind.):

> *Mr. Williams:* If there is a law that goes against those principles [life, liberty, and the pursuit of happiness], would you consider that a bad law?
> *Mr. McDonald:* As determined by whom, individual? That would be anarchy.

And later:

> *Mr. Williams:* Well, would you agree that laws that have as their intent segregating the American people on the basis of race, or religion, are bad laws?
> *Mr. McDonald:* Well, I guess there is a great deal of consternation in our society today over the things such as affirmative action on the Bakke Case, and so forth, where one group is selectively penalized to the benefit of another group, and I think that type of thing has created turmoil.[31]

The holiday's $195 million price tag also spawned passionate debate among the drama's players. Liberty Lobbyist E. Stanley Rittenhouse, restating similar lines of such key actors as Senator Thurmond and Congressman McDonald, opposed the holiday bill on the grounds that "it would be very costly to the citizens and taxpayers of America."[32] Senator Bayh replied that the King holiday has a symbolic value which far exceeded its monetary cost.

> The cost? What are the costs of a national holiday? Perhaps more rightly, what are the costs of not having a holiday? What are the costs of second-class citizenship? What are the costs of a little black boy or a little black girl or a little brown boy or a little brown girl not having the opportunity to share in a national holiday of some great leader that happens to look like them, to come from the same heritage that they came from?[33]

Mrs. King's rebuttal was based upon the economic exploitation of slavery.

. . . it would be hard to imagine how American industry could have financed its expansion without the enormous pool of unpaid agricultural labor that was available until the Emancipation Proclamation in 1862. I am not asking for reparations to the black community. No amount of money can compensate for the brutal injustice of slavery in the United States. But, given the hundreds of years of economic sacrifice and involuntary servitude of American blacks, is it too much to ask that one paid holiday per year be set aside to honor the contributions of a black man who gave his life in an historic struggle for social decency?[34]

An attempt to make Dr. King's birth date a commemorative holiday instead of a paid legal holiday was a subplot of these cost debates that drew a wide range of responses. Congressman William Dannemeyer (R-Calif.) and the Speaker of the House, the Honorable Tip O'Neill (D-Mass.) debated this issue:

> *Mr. Dannemeyer:* Mr. Speaker, in December 1979, the House voted to a vote of 207 to 191 to honor the memory of Dr. Martin Luther King by observing the third Sunday in January as a day of prayer and remembrance. . . .
> My question to you is what do you think is the difference between making the day of remembrance a Sunday, which is a non-work day, as opposed to the sense of the proponents of a commemorative resolution is, to hold it on a workday.
> What is the difference really?
> *Mr. O'Neill:* Oh, I think that there is a tremendous difference. You know, we have a Mother's Day, a Father's Day, an Uncle's Day, a Grandmother's Day. It is a day of remembrance.
> *Mr. Dannemeyer:* Mother's Day is on a Sunday, is it not?
> *Mr. O'Neill:* Yes, it is on Sunday. Other than Mother's Day, who adheres to those? Very few. Here is a man whose place is in history. His place is in history, because he changed America. . . .
> I think that a man of beauty, that a man of a minority race of this country—we have honored the great leaders. And he is a great leader that we should honor.
> And I just feel that a Sunday of remembrance. There are so many Sunday remembrances. It is Cap Day in Boston for the Red Sox. That is a remembrance. Let us not put things in categories like that. Let us give this man the homage that is due his greatness. And that would be a national holiday.[35]

The question-and-answer session that followed this conversation produced two divergent responses to Congressman Dannemeyer's question. Congressman Mickey Leland (D-Tex.) improvised this cutting bit of sarcasm off of House Speaker O'Neill's reference to a baseball Cap Day not beginning to approach the significance of Dr. King's holiday. Congressman Leland made the same point with this Super Bowl anecdote, whose bittersweet humor is reminiscent of jokes told by Juneteenth celebrants in his home state of Texas.

> In the last session, one of my more conservative colleagues, who had a thread of sensitivity, I think, particularly for those of us who are black in the Congress, came to me and said:
> "I think that I have the compromise worked out, I think that what we ought to do is put Dr. King's celebration and memorial service on Super Bowl day when the Super Bowl is to be played.
> That way, all Americans would be watching television, and even at the Super Bowl they could have some kind of demonstration to memorialize Dr. King."[36]

But Congressman Louis Stokes (D-Ohio) shunned Leland's technique of comic understatement, and instead delivered a passionate speech of opposition to the establishment of a mere commemorative holiday for Dr. King:

> Various substitutes . . . have been proposed to recognize Dr. King. These substitutes have included the placing of a statue or a bust of Dr. Martin Luther King in the Capital, or designating some Sunday as his day of recognition. But the life that Dr. King gave was not a substitute. It was not a facsimile thereof. It was the genuine thing: his own and his only life. I cannot accept therefore, Madame Chairwoman [Honorable Katie Hall, D-Ind.], a substitute tribute, an ersatz award, for this man who was true to humanity, true to the causes of freedom and justice, true to his commitment to nonviolence, true to his belief in the basic integrity of the American people, true to his dream.[37]

Opponents of the legislation also argued that it was too soon after the death of Dr. King to honor him; they argued that only the test of time would justify such an honor. The testimony of Mr. Clifford J. White, III, the national director of Young Americans for Freedom, is an excellent example of similar testimonies given by Senator Thurmond, Congressman McDonald, and a host of other bit players in this tense American freedom drama. Mr. White said:

> National holidays are important occasions for all Americans. When an individual is recognized—or rather almost canonized—through a national holiday in his honor, it is understood that the individual had a unique and indispensable impact on this Nation's history. So great a recognition is this that only Christopher Columbus and George Washington have in this

way been honored. To so recognize Martin Luther King, a patriotic American to be sure, would be to classify him along with Washington— and above Lincoln, Jefferson and Adams. We would do this without the benefit of being able to put his memory under the test of time.[38]

Proponents of the legislation responded in a variety of ways. Congressman Leland once again drew spirited applause from Afro-American spectators when he lashed out with a justification of Dr. King's greatness shared by many other Afro-Americans.

> . . . I would like to remind the gentleman [Congressman William Dannemeyer, R-Calif.] that Mr. Lincoln advocated the freedom and the liberation of only those slaves that were held within the dissenting States, the Confederate States of this country, and not the liberation of all human beings, as did Dr. Martin Luther King.
> That advocacy puts Dr. King at least one step above Mr. Lincoln in terms of our honoring him.[39]

While Reverend Joseph E. Lowery, president of the Southern Christian Leadership Conference argued that Dr. King was as important an American figure as the Founding Fathers.

> *Dr. Lowery:* While it is regrettably true that in our more than 200-year history, we have not so honored a black American, the designation of Dr. King's birthday as a national holiday would transcend the issue of race and color.
> Martin Luther King's leadership gave all Americans, white, black, yellow, red, and brown, a new sense of worth and purpose. . . .
> His leadership brought together a coalescence of communities and disciplines that demonstrated the unity in diversity that portends a greatness unparalleled in nationhood—under God. If Columbus discovered America, Martin helped America discover itself.
> If Washington established a Nation, Martin led the Nation to understand that there can be no nationhood without brotherhood.
> His leadership personified the spirit of a people whose historic dedication to liberty caused them to tread the unknown, dare to do the dangerous, pioneer into the perilous—knowing that the reward of liberty is more precious than the price the struggle compels us to pay.
> Willing to pay that price Martin Luther King, Jr., sought freedom for all God's children knowing that those who mind the chains that bind [others] are also bound.
> *Senator Kennedy:* You are beginning to preach a little bit here.
> *Dr. Lowery:* Yes. I am about to take an offering. [*Laughter.*]
> His leadership taught us that revolutionary change can occur within the context of nonviolence, when a people inspired and motivated by a sense of justice and the efficacy of love are so determined.

Yes, the designation of Dr. King's birthday as a national holiday will do deserved honor to him, and will likewise honor the Nation and the family of man, and I respectfully urge and support its immediate implementation.[40]

Opponents of the legislation further argued that Dr. King was not the Afro-American who most deserved to be honored with a national holiday. A subcommittee hearing dialogue between Senator Thurmond and Congressman McDonald typifies this line of reasoning:

Senator Thurmond: Congressman McDonald, I just have a few questions to propound to you.

Since you oppose the designation of another Federal legal holiday for Martin Luther King, Jr., do you think there are any other Americans who should be considered for such a legal holiday, if one is going to be named for Martin Luther King?

Mr. McDonald: One would be George Washington Carver; the second would be Booker T. Washington, and I think the man would be shocked at the thought if he were here today—if he could be here today, he would certainly argue against it, but a man who pointed out that he could come from poverty in Florida, whose mother, I believe, ran a school so that he could gain some of the things of life. A family who, as Senator Bayh stated, clawed and worked its way up from poverty, from a poor background, was Gen. Chappy James. Chappy James, as you know, as a member of the Senate Armed Services Committee, passed away perhaps a year ago. I do not think we have had a more dedicated, finer American on the scene than Gen. Chappy James.[41]

Proponents of the legislation were quick to respond to these objections. Mr. Williams leaped to interrogate Congressman McDonald on the issue.

Mr. Williams: . . . I would like to know, what is it that Booker T. Washington did that he could be considered instead of Martin Luther King, what were his characteristics; what was it about that man?

Mr. McDonald: I am glad you asked that question. As you know, he is the author of the book, *Up from Slavery.* He pointed out to the Negro Americans, to black Americans that, "Yes, we have come up from slavery, the bottom level of the ladder, and we should not be, perhaps, so preoccupied with trying to become instant leaders. But we should gain knowledge of two four-letter words." We live in a time when four-letter words are very popular among some segments of our society, but in the case of Booker T. Washington I think they were most apropos because he said the two words "wash"—w-a-s-h—and "work." Intimating that you can be poor, but you can also be clean and work by standards of personal cleanliness, and also work to make yourselves productive citizens in the new land, and gain respect of your fellow members of the community. Out of that respect you will find that your chilren and their children will be able to move up to all levels of American society.[42]

Mrs. King, on the other hand, managed to refute Congressman McDonald's arguments in this straightforward manner.

> It may be argued that throughout American history, there have been many black historical figures other than Martin who deserve to be honored with a holiday in their name—Crispus Attucks to Harriet Tubman to Booker T. Washington—to name just a few. But it should be remembered that previous black leaders necessarily addressed issues that tended to concern blacks exclusively, while Martin Luther King, Jr., spoke to us all.[43]

But opponents of the legislation countered Mrs. King's claim that Dr. King's appeal was universal contending that Dr. King was not a true patriot; in their eyes, he was at best a Communist sympathizer. Mr. Rittenhouse testified: "Enemies, enemies everywhere and not a patriot to be found around Martin Luther King, Jr. The fact is he aided the Communist cause; he abetted it constantly, continuously. Since when does a Nation honor a man who honored its enemy?"[44] Mr. Alan Stang, a "professional journalist and writer," asserted that "Martin Luther King collaborated intimately with the Communists from the very beginning of his career to its end."[45] While Ms. Julia Brown, a black American who was a former member of the Communist Party, told Senator Thurmond: "Mr. Chairman, while I was in the Communist Party as a loyal American Negro, I knew Martin Luther King to be closely connected with the Communist Party. If this measure is passed honoring Martin Luther King, we may as well take down the Stars and Strips that fly over this building and replace it with a Red flag."[46]

Supporters of the legislation did not let these accusations go unchallenged. Mr. Karl Prussion, a former Communist and FBI double agent, was closely cross-examined by Mr. David Boies, chief counsel and staff director of the Senate subcommittee, and Mr. Williams, aide to Senator Birch Bayh, after he had given similar testimony. The former's cross-examination had all the tension of a courtroom drama.

> *Mr. Boies:* Mr. Prussion, I believe you said that you had never been at a Communist meeting with Dr. King; is that correct?
> *Mr. Prussion:* That is correct, sir.
> *Mr. Boies:* Have you ever been at a Communist meeting in which a member of the Communist Party asserted to you that Dr. King was a Communist?

> *Mr. Prussion:* No, sir; but I have been to many meetings where he was referred to as a good leader for Communist-directed activities.

And later:

> *Mr. Boies:* Perhaps my question was not clear. What I was asking was, whether you were ever told by a member of the Communist Party—since you had never talked to Dr. King yourself—but I was asking whether you were ever told by a member of the Communist Party that Dr. King was being directed by the Communist Party.
> *Mr. Prussion:* That was common knowledge in the Communist Party.
> *Mr. Boies:* Were you ever told that, and if so by whom, sir, and under what circumstances and when.
> *Mr. Prussion:* This was common talk within the Communist Party, and I cannot recall by whom. Within the Communist activities there is much conversation, many Communists. It was generally known within the Communist Party, but I have no recollection which particular member told me that.[47]

Mr. Williams's questioning of Mr. Prussion increasingly resembled the style of a detective interrogating a murder suspect in a whodunit:

> *Mr. Williams.* Did you, as an individual, ever attend a Communist meeting when Martin Luther King, Jr., was there?
> *Mr. Prussion:* Never, no. I never attended a meeting where he was there. However, the evidence was presented——
> *Mr. Williams:* No, did you attend a meeting?
> *Mr. Prussion:* Not in his presence ——
> *Mr. Williams:* You never saw Martin Luther King attend Communist meetings. Thank you.[48]

As these subcommittee hearings were about to conclude, some byplay from the theater of the absurd was enacted in the Senate hearing chambers. Just before stiking his gavel and adjourning the hearings, Senator Thurmond noticed a woman in the audience who was trying to get his attention.

> *Senator Thurmond:* All right, thank you, I see a lady raising her hand back there.
> *Ms. Curtis:* I am Mary Lou Curtis. I have kept records on Martin Luther King for 16 years. . . .
> Now, I as a citizen am opposed to the glorification of Martin Luther King on his record. I say anybody to vote on a national holiday based on his color, that this is an act of racism itself.

Ms. Curtis concluded her unscheduled testimony with this "real quick statement."

I thought it was irrelevant when the aide over here was saying, "Do you have proof he was a Communist," that is irrelevant. He was a tool of the Communist, and that is irrefutable; they used him to accomplish their objectives, to get more legislation enacted by the Congress—where we get more growth of Federal Government; Federal regulations over all Americans, all colors, black, yellow, white. Also affirmative action, your busing, et cetera, et cetera.[49]

But the spirit which finally prevailed, allowing this legislation to pass both houses of Congress and be signed into law by President Ronald Reagan in a historic White House, Rose Garden ceremony, was best expressed by Professor George Wald, a 1967 Nobel Laureate.

> The time has come to recognize Martin Luther King as a precious figure in the American tradition. His meaning for us is unique. It comes, not trickling down from the heights, but rising up from the great yearnings of vast numbers of our people to fulfill the American promise, written in the second paragraph of our Declaration of Independence, spoken in Lincoln's Gettysburg address, inscribed on the Statue of Liberty. Its main themes are freedom from discrimination, social justice, human dignity—a widening area of recognition in which one person is as good as another. Those are the things that Martin Luther King stood for. . . .
> That American promise, never fulfilled, needs constantly to be rediscovered and restated, and never more so than now.
> That is what a Martin Luther King Day can do for us.[50]

During the finale of this Afro-American freedom drama a seemingly endless line of Americans stepped upon the congressional stage to spell out the three-part symbolic significance of the Martin Luther King, Jr., national holiday bill. Some portrayed it as a day of recognition of Dr. King's greatness. Others perceived the holiday as a just official recognition of Afro-Americans' contributions to America. While still others saw the day symbolizing democracy and brotherhood, two cornerstones of the American ethos. All of these myriad testimonies are perhaps best expressed by Senator Kennedy's remarks made during the final Senate hearings before the bill was passed and later signed into law.

> . . . it is long time past for our Nation to observe not only the birthday of one of the greatest men in our history, but the contributions of members of an entire race brought here not in hope but in chains, who built so much of this land, and who in their own liberation have lifted the shadow of prejudice from so many of our fellow citizens. Martin Luther King's day must be a day for all Americans, because Martin Luther King's dream is the American dream.

Because he lived, millions of Americans were freed from the oppressive burden of segregation. Because he dreamed, millions more found hope that their own dreams of a better life could be achieved.[51]

Certain cast members of this Afro-American freedom drama deserve curtain calls. Among the supporting actors, Mr. Stevie Wonder's roles as an energetic parade organizer and effective hearings witness must be noted. The Reverends Walter Fauntroy and Andrew Young are two of Dr. King's chief lieutenants whose multiple roles in support of the holiday bill have earned them well-deserved bows. Reverend Fauntroy was a relentless supporter and lobbyist for the holiday bill after his election to Congress. As chairman of the Subcommittee on Historic Preservation and Coinage of the Committee on Banking, Finance and Urban Affairs, he also kept the Martin Luther King, Jr., holiday bill alive by holding hearings on the issue of striking medals in commemoration of the life and ideals of his mentor, Dr. King. Reverend Young literally saw the drama through from beginning to end. He was with Dr. King at the Lorraine Motel shooting and was present at the Rose Garden signing ceremony fourteen years later. Reverend Young played three important roles in assisting the bill's passage. As a Representative from Georgia, he not only annually supported the holiday bill, but it was Congressman Young who also called attention to Dr. King's greatness by introducing legislation to have a Martin Luther King, Jr., commemorative silver dollar minted by the Federal Government, with a percentage of the proceeds going to the Martin Luther King, Jr., Center for Social Change. While serving as America's United Nations Ambassador, Ambassador Young testified for the Carter Administration in favor of the bill. And, finally, as the Mayor of Atlanta, Mayor Young played a major role in defusing the racial tensions caused by the uncomplimentary remarks that President Reagan made about Dr. King, before he signed the bill into law.

There are also some white Americans of goodwill who have earned their places in the spotlight. Edward M. Kennedy, Birch Bayh, and Robert Dole (R-Kans.) called upon their considerable oratorical and political skills to get this bill passed in the Senate. In the House of Representatives special applause was earned by Dan Lungren (R-Calif.), Mickey Edwards (R-Okla.), Newt Gingrich (R-Ga.), Ed Bethune (R-Ark.), and all the other Congressmen who had the courage to shift from opposition to support of the bill.[52]

But Congressman John Conyers, Jr., and Mrs. Coretta Scott King deserve the longest bows and loudest applause. Congressman Conyers introduced the bill in 1968 and annually reintroduced it until its final passage in

1983. Likewise, Mrs. King was with the bill lobby movement from beginning to end. But during this fourteen-year period she also nurtured into reality her dream of the Martin Luther King, Jr., Center for Social Change. I am tempted to compare her to Polly Ann, the widow of John Henry, another slain Afro-American folk hero. In the ballad, when John Henry falls dead, Polly Ann picks up her husband's hammer and "drives steel like a man." So too has Mrs. King picked up her slain husband's primary tool, the philosophy of nonviolence, and continued his work. Thus, the day after her husband's birthday had been signed into law she published a newspaper article which reads in part:

> For me, the overriding importance of the holiday is that it can help America focus on forging a new commitment to nonviolence. With few exceptions, the history book has gloried in the dubious achievement of the generals and warriors who have supposedly "solved" the great conflicts of American history.
> However, in just 13 years of organized nonviolent struggle, black Americans achieved more genuine freedom than the previous four centuries had produced. This is an impressive testament to the power of nonviolence. The efficacy of the philosophy and strategy of nonviolence is the most important lesson we can draw from the life and work of Martin Luther King, Jr.[53]

After this stellar cast made its final curtain call, the house lights were raised and the audience was ready to leave the national theater and struggle anew to make Afro-Americans completely free. Mr. Patrick Ballou, a National Science Foundation clerk, expressed the commitment to this goal: "The holiday represents a milestone for blacks and a reminder that there is reason to continue to think positive and work together. . . . That's how we got this passed, and now we must continue progressing toward new goals like economic and political empowerment."[54] Like Saturday movie serials and weekday television soap operas, the drama of the historical Afro-American struggle toward freedom . . . will be continued.

Notes

ABBREVIATIONS

AN	[New York] *Amsterdam News*
ADW	*Atlanta Daily World*
CD	*Chicago Defender*
CT	*Chicago Tribune*
Cong. Rec.	*Congressional Record*
PT	*Philadelphia Tribune*
PC	*Pittsburgh Courier*

PREFACE

1. "Juneteenth: Texas Carries on Tradition of Emancipation Holiday with Amusement Park Celebration," *Ebony* (June 1951), 27–30. William R. Riddell, "Celebrations of the Anniversary of the Emancipation in Hamilton, Upper Canada," *Journal of Negro History* 22 (April 1928), 192–98. John W. Lyda, "Emancipation Day: Sept. 23, 1888," *The Indiana Negro History Society Bulletin* (Jan. 1944), n.p. Lerone Bennett, Jr., Jubilee: Emancipation of Slaves Marked by Shouting, Weeping and Suffering," *Ebony* (Feb. 1972), 37–40, 42, 44, 46. Roland C. McConnell, "From Preliminary to Final Emancipation Proclamation: The First Hundred Days," *Journal of Negro History* 48 (Oct. 1963), 260–76. Benjamin Quarles, "Historic Afro-American Holidays," *Negro Digest* 16 (Feb. 1967), 14–19.

2. John Hope Franklin, *The Emancipation Proclamation* (Garden City, N.Y.: Doubleday, 1963).

3. J. Mason Brewer, "Juneteenth," *Texas Folk-Lore Society Publications*, no. 10 (1932), 9–54.

4. Letter received from Mr. Haywood Hygh, Jr., n.d.

5. Frederick Douglass, "January First 1863," *Douglass' Monthly*, (Jan. 1863), 769–70.

6. Personal interview with Mrs. Lula Bass, 1 Jan. 1973.

7. Personal interview with Mrs. Mary Morris, 22 Aug. 1972.
8. Personal interview with Dr. Jimmy Williams, 13 July 1972.
9. Postcard from Miss Sue Owings, 20 Jan. 1972.
10. Personal interview with Mr. Jerry Wilson, 5 Nov. 1972.
11. Personal interview with Mr. William H. Ammons, 13 Nov. 1972.
12. Letter from Mrs. Mary B. Wirth, 16 Dec. 1973.
13. Ammons interview.
14. Letter from Mr. Bob Bright, the Texas Legislature Librarian, 6 May 1985.

INTRODUCTION

1. "The Addresses of the 'Emancipators,'" *ADW,* 4 Jan. 1955, p. 5.
2. J.E. Mitchell, "National Freedom Day," in *Twelfth Anniversary Celebration of National Freedom Day,* Souvenir Program, 1 Feb. 1961, p. 5.
3. Letter from Mrs. Elva S. Riggins, 11 April 1972.
4. Personal interview with Mr. Allen Parks, 30 Sept. 1972.
5. Personal interview with Rev. William Holmes Borders, 30 Dec. 1972.
6. Ammons interview.
7. Personal interview with Mr. Robert Lee Perry, 14 Nov. 1973.
8. Personal interview with Mr. Joseph L. Grimes, 14 Nov. 1973.
9. Quarles, "Historic Holidays," 15.
10. "They Discuss 'Freedom Day' Measure," *ADW,* 27 Dec. 1942, p. 1.
11. Jacqueline Bernard, *Journey Toward Freedom: The Story of Sojourner Truth* (New York: Norton, 1967), 81.
12. Quarles, "Historic Holidays," 16.
13. "Celebration of the Abolition of Slavery in the District of Columbia," *Douglass' Monthly,* (Aug. 1862), 694–95.
14. Dickson Preston, *Trappe: The Story of an Old-Fashioned Town* (Easton, Md: Economy Printing Co., 1976), 89.
15. Mark Mayo Boatner, III, *The Civil War Dictionary* (New York: David McKay, 1959), 419. For the text of President Lincoln's rejection see: Archer H. Shaw, comp. and ed., *The Lincoln Encyclopedia: The Spoken and Written Words of Abraham Lincoln Arranged for Ready Reference* (New York: Macmillan, 1950), 115. General John C. Fremont issued a similar order on August 30, 1861, freeing blacks in Missouri (Boatner, 315). And Lincoln overruled him (Shaw, 128). For some unexplained reason, no celebration evolved out of General Fremont's proclamation.
16. Quarles, "Historic Holidays," 17.
17. Ibid.
18. W.C. Nunn, *Texas Under the Carpetbaggers* (Austin: Univ. of Texas Press, 1962), 5.
19. "The Jerry Rescue Celebration," *Douglass' Monthly,* (Dec. 1860), 377.

1. Personal interview with Mr. Johnny Joost, 16 June 1972. For variants of this joke see: James Haskins, *Jokes from Black Folks* (Garden City, N.Y.: Doubleday, 1973), 81; Lawrence W. Levine, *Black Culture and Black Consciousness: Afro-American Folk Thought from Slavery to Freedom* (New York: Oxford Univ. Press, 1977), 342; and Henry D. Spalding, comp. and ed., *Encyclopedia of Black Folklore and Humor* (Middle Village, N.Y.: Jonathan Edwards, 1972), Motif X 1796 "Lies concerning speed," 67.

2. Personal interview with Mrs. A.T. Lewis, 17 June 1972.

3. Personal interview with Mr. Artis Lovelady, 17 June 1972.

4. Transcription: Unknown Juneteenth celebrant, 17 June 1972.

5. Personal interview with Mr. Marvin Smith, 17 June 1972.

6. This and subsequent quotations are from a transcription of services at the Juneteenth celebration in Rockdale, Texas, 17 June 1972.

7. For a recent study of the Afro-American praying tradition, see Harold A. Carter, *The Prayer Tradition of Black People* (Valley Forge, Pa.: Judson Press, 1976).

8. Transcription of services (June 1972).

9. Ibid.

10. Transcription: Rev. C.L. Parks, 18 June 1972. For two printed versions, see Dorothy Scarborough, *On the Trail of Negro Folk-Songs* (Cambridge: Harvard Univ. Press, 1925), 30; and Langston Hughes and Arna Bontemps, eds., *Book of Negro Folklore* (New York: Dodd, Mead, 1958), 504–5.

11. Personal interview with Mrs. Bennie Mae Smith, 9 June 1972.

12. Ibid.

13. Ibid.

14. Ibid.

15. Personal interview with Rev. C.A. Striplin, 6 Aug. 1972.

16. Personal interview with Mr. Claude Snorton, 5 Aug. 1972.

17. Ibid.

18. These and subsequent quotations are taken from a transcription of the Emancipation celebration services held on 1 Jan. 1973 at the New Providence Baptist Church in Columbus, Georgia.

19. Borders interview.

20. Personal interview with Mrs. Agnes Hubert and Mrs. Lula Bass, 1 Jan. 1973. For newspaper accounts of May 28th and May 29th celebrations, see "Citizens Observe Emancipation Day in Thomaston, Ga.," *ADW,* 28 May 1938, p. 1; Mary Merrion, "Washington, Ga.," *ADW,* 31 May 1943, p. 5; Calvin Banks, III, "Thomaston," *ADW,* 26 May 1948, p. 6; "Thomaston," *ADW,* 25 May 1950, p. 4; and "Searcy To Be Emancipation Day Speaker," *ADW,* 29 May 1963, p. 3.

21. Parks interview. For published versions of this folk admonition see: Charles Evers, *Evers* (Cleveland: World Publishing, 1972), 67–68. "White hatemongers all over Mississippi put up signs in all their towns: NEGRO RUN. IF YOU CAN'T READ,

RUN ANYHOW. And if the Negro didn't run, they'd catch him and beat him." Also "But 77-year-old William Mathew Boyd, the grandson of slaves, remembers a sign which he says once decorated the Cullman [Alabama] city limits: 'Nigger, Read and Run. If you Can't Read, Run Anyhow'" (Boyd Lewis, "KKK is back with greater numbers, force," *Indiana Daily Student*, 6 Dec. 1978, p. 9). And see William H. Wiggins, Jr., "The Structure and Dynamics of Folklore in the Novel Form: The Case of John O. Killens," *Keystone Folklore Quarterly* 17 (Fall 1972), 95. John O. Killens's *Youngblood* has this variant: "They gotta great big sign in one uppity section of town, it says—WHITE TRASH READ AND WALK FAST—NIGGER READ AND HAUL ASS." For collected folklore versions of this racial admonition, see J. Mason Brewer, *Worser Days and Better Times: The Folklore of the North Carolina Negro* (Chicago: Quadrangle Books, 1965), 135.

22. Transcription of services (Jan. 1973).

23. Benjamin E. Mays, *PC*, 26 Feb. 1972, p. 6.

24. This and subsequent quotations are from a transcription of the National Freedom Day program held in Philadelphia on 1 Feb. 1972.

25. Ibid.

26. *31st Anniversary Celebration of National Freedom Day*, Souvenir Program, 1 Feb. 1973, n.p.

27. There is some evidence that this is an unrecorded Afro-American folk motif. Charles Evers, civil rights leader and former mayor of Fayette, Mississippi, published this school-day memory. While he and his friends were walking home "in the mud and sloshing rain, white students would drive by in their great big shiny yellow and black school bus. And they'd lean out the windows and shout, 'Let's see you run, niggers!' And the white bus driver could cut at us and make us jump off the road" (*Evers*, 44). The motif also appears in black fiction:

> "Finally, when the bus was less than fifty feet behind us, it veered dangerously close to the right edge of the road where we were running, forcing us to attempt to jump to the bank; but all of us fell short and landed in the slime of the gully.
>
> Little Man, chest-deep in water, scooped up a handful of mud and in an uncontrollable rage scrambled up to the road and ran after the retreating bus. As moronic rolls of laughter and cries of 'Nigger! Mud eater!' wafted from the open windows, Little Man threw his mudball, missing the wheels by several feet. Then totally dismayed by what had happened, he buried his face in his hands and cried" (Mildred D. Taylor, *Roll of Thunder, Hear My Cry* [New York: Dial, 1976], 48).

CHAPTER 2

1. Eugene D. Genovese, *Roll, Jordan, Roll: The World the Slaves Made* (New York: Vintage, 1976), 566–67.

2. Ibid., 577.

3. Ibid., 576.

4. Alice Morse Earle, "Pinkster Day," *Outlook* 46 (1894), 743–44.

5. Mrs. M.B. Richard, "Easter Day on the Plantation," *The Plantation Missionary* 3, no. 2, (1892), 12–14.

6. Lea Marianna Seale, "Easter Rock: A Louisiana Negro Ceremony," *Journal of American Folklore* 55 (1942), 212–18.

7. Genovese, 576.

8. Frederick Douglass, "Narrative of the Life of Frederick Douglass, An American Slave," in *Black Voices: An Anthology of Afro-American Literature,* ed. Abraham Chapman (New York: New American Library, 1968), 253.

9. Ibid., 253–54.

10. Ira De A. Reid, "The John Canoe Festival," *Phylon* 3 (1942), 361.

11. Genovese, 576.

12. Robert Winslow Gordon, "Negro 'Shouts' from Georgia," in *Mother Wit from the Laughing Barrel: Readings in the Interpretation of Afro-American Folklore,* ed. Alan Dundes (Englewood Cliffs, N.J.: Prentice-Hall, 1973), 449–50.

13. Douglass, 254.

14. Ibid., 255.

15. Ibid., 254–55.

16. Personal interview with Reverend J.C. Cook, 2 Jan. 1973.

17. Riggins letter.

18. Hygh letter.

19. Thomas Wentworth Higginson, *Army Life in a Black Regiment* (Boston: Beacon Press, 1962), 36.

20. Ibid., 37.

21. Hubert H.S. Aimes, "African Institutions in America," *Journal of American Folk-Lore* 18 (Jan.–March, 1905), 15.

22. Geraldine R. Pleat and Agnes N. Underwood, "Pinkster Ode, Albany, 1803," *New York Folklore Quarterly* 8 (1952), 31–45. And William S. Walsh, *Curiosities of Popular Customs and Ceremonies* (Philadelphia: J.B. Lippincott, 1898). Carries an account of Pinkster's Toto dance.

23. Reid, 356.

24. Genovese, 572.

25. Ibid., 572–73.

26. B.A. Botkin, ed., *Lay My Burden Down: A Folk History of Slavery* (Chicago: Univ. of Chicago Press, 1945), 56–57.

27. Higginson, 35.

28. Genovese, 233.

29. George Mitchell, *Blow My Blues Away* (Baton Rouge: Louisiana State Univ. Press, 1971), 49–57.

30. Letter received from Mrs. Carrye Bennett, n.d., 1972.

31. Personal interview with Rev. Thomas J. Flanagan, 30 Dec. 1972.

32. Ibid.

33. W.P.A. 36-2, Florida Folklore Book II: Amusements, Contests, Dances, Festivals and Fiestas, TS, Manuscript Room, Library of Congress, 3–4.

34. Personal interview with Mr. Judson Henry, 14 Nov. 1972.

35. "Juneteenth," *Ebony,* (June 1951).

36. Harold W. Thompson, "King Charley of Albany," in *American Negro Folklore,* ed. J. Mason Brewer (New York: Quadrangle/*New York Times* Book, Co., 1968), 33.

37. Aimes, 15.

38. Ibid., 18.

39. Personal interview with Dr. Wesley Lyda, 30 Sept. 1972.

40. Personal interview with Mrs. Katherine Burton, 14 Nov. 1972.

41. David K. Wiggins, "The Play of Slave Children in the Plantation Communities of the Old South, 1820–1860," *Journal of Sport History* 7, no. 2 (Summer 1980), 30.

42. Aimes, 19.

43. "Quoits," *Webster's New Collegiate Dictionary,* 1976 ed.

44. Douglass, 254.

45. David Wiggins, 27.

46. "Rounders," *Webster's New Collegiate Dictionary,* 1976 ed.

47. Thompson, 34.

48. Richard M. Dorson, *American Negro Folktales* (New York: Fawcett World Library, 1970), 133.

49. Ibid., 135.

50. Brewer, *Worser Days,* 109–10.

51. *117th Annual Observance Emancipation Celebration of September 22nd* Program/Flyer, 20–21 Sept. 1980.

52. *19th of June Celebration* Program/Flyer, 19 June 1947.

53. *105th Anniversary of the Emancipation Proclamation of June 19th* Program/Flyer, 19 June 1972.

54. Personal interview with Mr. Overton Smith, 17 Nov. 1972.

55. Personal interview with Mr. J.L. Donaldson, 14 Nov. 1972.

56. Francis M. Williams, Francis Lynn, Martha L. Perkins and Ben E. Boone, III, eds., *The Story of Todd County, Kentucky, 1820–1970* (Nashville: n.p., 1972), 114. Mr. Morton told me: "I never heard too much about it, but the first celebration was in a barn." Personal interview with Mr. Clarence Morton, 5 Aug. 1972.

57. William H. Wiggins, Jr., "January 1: The Afro-American's 'Day of Days,' " *Prospects: An Annual of American Cultural Studies* 4 (1979), 331.

58. Personal interview with Mr. Booker T. Washington Hogan, 5 Nov. 1972.

59. Higginson, 40.

60. Gossie Harold Hudson, " 'Emancipation,' an Unpublished Poem by Paul Laurence Dunbar," *Negro History Bulletin* 36 (Feb. 1973), 41–42.

61. Personal interview with Mr. Charles Morgan, 13 Nov. 1972.

62. Thompson, p. 34.

63. Morton interview.

64. Cook interview.

65. "Duke Ellington To Meet Kiddies at Picnic: Beauty Contest Big Feature of Picnic," *CD,* 1 Aug. 1931, p3. 16; "Bud's Prize Bathing Beauties," *CD,* 20 Aug. 1932, p. 16; Dewey R. Jones, "Rufus Dawes [Pres. of A Century of Progress] Extends Welcome to Queen; Thousands Cheer," *CD,* 5 Aug. 1933, pp. 1 and 4; "Beauties Await 'Miss Bronze America' Contest," *CD,* 24 Aug. 1940, p. 3; "Thugs

Trap Philadelphia Beauties: Inside Story of a Beauty Contest Racket That Leads Young Girls to Life of Vice," *Color*, (March 1953), 20–23.

66. "University of Ala. Elects First Black Queen as Segregation Stumbles," *Jet*, 6 Dec. 1973, pp. 14–16.

67. C. Brown, "New Boom in Black Beauty Pageant Queens," *Jet*, 17 Aug. 1972, pp. 2–24; "Miss Black America '75," *Jet*, 25 Sept. 1975, p. 58; Dorothy Davis, "Positively Black Is the Word for Miss Black America," *Encore* (Sept. 1978). 34–36; "Black College Queens for 1977–78," *Ebony* (April 1979), 144–46+; Lerone Bennett, Jr., "What Is Black Beauty," *Ebony* (Nov. 1980), 159–61; "Gwendelyn Bastiste Crowned Watts Summer Festival Queen," *Los Angeles Times*, Late City Ed., 8 Aug. 1974, Sec. 1, p. 2; "Ex-Watts Beauty Queens Featured," *Los Angeles Times*, Late City Ed., 7 March 1976. Sec. 1, p. 3. Teenage beauty pageants also sprang up among black females during the late 1970s. See: " 'Miss Teenage America' Seeks Black Entrants," *ADW*, 11 Aug. 1977, Sec. 1, p. 3; "Valerie Dunn Crowned 'Miss Black Teenager,' " *Cleveland Call Post*, 13 Aug. 1977, Sec. A. p. 16. And "Miss Black Teenage World Crowned," *AN*, 10 Sept. 1977, Sec. C, p. 11.

68. There was a growing interest in the Miss America Beauty Pageant before Vanessa Williams became the first Afro-American to win the crown in 1984. See: Paul Leorn, "Will There Ever Be a Black Miss America?" *Sepia* (Feb. 1975), 28–30+; Kyle Arnold, "Black Beauty in Other Pageants," *Encore* (Sept. 1978), 36; Kathy Williams, "Miss New York first black Miss America," The *Sunday* [Bloomington, Ind.] *Herald-Telephone*, Late Evening Ed., 18 Sept. 1983, pp. 1, 14; B. Eady, "She's black and Miss America, but Vanessa Williams is most of all her own woman," *People Weekly*, 3 Oct. 1983, pp. 34–36; G. Jaynes, "In New York: The Miss Is a Hit," *Time*, 17 Oct. 1983, pp. 10+; "Movin' on up," *Nation*, 1 Oct. 1983, p. 1. For accounts of Miss Williams's dethroning see: "Beauty contests—the Stakes Are Big," *U.S. News and World Report*, 6 Aug. 1984, p. 14; "Ex-Miss America endures pain, embarrassment sparked by flap over nude pictures," *Jet*, 6 Aug. 1984, pp. 60–62; M. Beck, "For want of a bathing suit," *Newsweek*, 6 Aug. 1984, p. 23; W. Plummer, "Haunted by her past," *People Weekly*, 6 Aug. 1984, pp. 80–82+; "There she goes, Miss America," *Nation*, 4–11 Aug. 1984, p. 65; J. Cocks, "There she goes, Miss America," *Time*, 6 Aug. 1984, p. 61; "Vanessa's story," *People Weekly*, 6 Aug. 1984, pp. 84–87.

69. "*Ebony* Fashion Fair to Tour Country," *Ebony* (Oct. 1959), 132–35+; "Liberated Look: Thirteenth Annual *Ebony* Fashion Fair," *Ebony* (Sept. 1970), 137–41; "Local Chairman paves way for *Ebony* Fashion Fair," *Ebony* (Sept. 1966), 136–37; "Top Styles from Europe in *Ebony's* Fashion Fair," *Ebony* (Nov. 1962), 145–46+; E. W. Johnson, "Twelfth Annual Fashion Fair Theme: Flapper Returns with Soul," *Ebony* (Oct. 1964), 187–88+; "Young Negro Designers Join *Ebony's* Fashion Fair," *Ebony* (Sept. 1961), 108–12.

70. "Washington's [D.C.] 400 Introduces Debs: How Washingtonians present their daughters to society," *Color* (April 1948), 33.

71. Ibid.

72. "1,700 Philadelphians Jam N.Y. Cotillion," *PT*, 7 Jan. 1964, pp. 1 and 7. For critical images of Afro-American cotillions, see John Oliver Killens, *The Cotillion or One Good Bull Is Half the Herd* (New York: Trident Press, 1971), and E.

Franklin Frazier, *Black Bourgeoisie: The Rise of a New Middle Class in the United States* (London: Collier Macmillan Publishers, 1957), 167–68.

73. William H. Wiggins, Jr., "Jack Johnson as Bad Nigger: The Folklore of His Life," in *Contemporary Black Thought: The Best from the Black Scholar,* eds. Robert Chrisman and Nathan Hare (Indianapolis: The Bobbs-Merrill Company, Inc., 1973), 53–70.

74. "Great Athletes Who have Advanced the Negro," *Color* (May 1951), 28.

75. Randy Roberts, *Papa Jack: Jack Johnson and the Era of White Hopes* (New York: The Free Press, 1983), 85–107.

76. Joe Louis, *Joe Louis: My Life,* with Edna and Art Rust, Jr., (New York: Berkley Books, 1981), 125–36.

77. Robert Peterson, *Only the Ball Was White* (Englewood Cliffs N.J.: Prentice-Hall, 1970), 103–15.

78. Henry interview.

79. For a complete record of East-West All-Star Boxscores, see Peterson, 288–310.

80. Jackie Robinson, as told to Alfred Duckett, *I Never Had It Made* (New York: Putman, 1972); Jules Tygiel, *Baseball's Great Experiment: Jackie Robinson and His Legacy* (New York: Oxford Univ. Press, 1983); Jackie Robinson, as told to Wendell Smith, *Jackie Robinson: My Own Story* (New York: Greenberg Publisher, 1948); Jackie Robinson and Charles Dexter, *Baseball Had Done It* (New York: J.B. Lippincott, 1964); Arthur Mann, *The Jackie Robinson Story* (New York: Grosset & Dunlap, 1950); Bill Roeder, *Jackie Robinson* (New York: A.S. Barnes, 1950).

81. See William H. Wiggins, Jr., " 'Did You See Jackie Robinson Hit That Ball?': The Impact of Jackie Robinson's Career on Race Relations in America," paper delivered at a Sports Conference, Univ. of Missouri at St. Louis, 11 April 1983.

82. For some newspaper articles on this awards show that began in the late 1940s, see: Izzy Rowe, "Courier Poll Includes Everything This Time," and "Ballots Simplified for 1951–52 Courier Theatrical Poll Votes," "Some of the Artists Who Always Rank High in Courier Polls," "Attention Voters In Courier Poll," all in *PC,* 12 Jan. 1952, pp. 16–17; "Nominations Rolling in for Theatrical Poll," Isadora Rowe, "Nominations Pouring in for Poll—It's Not Too Late," "Theatrical Poll Nominees," "Courier Theatrical Poll 1951-Musical Favorite-1952, Ballot No. 2" all in *PC,* 19 Jan. 1952, p. 16; and Isadora Smith, "Sarah, Dinah, Lena, Berle Enjoy Top of Ratings This Week," "Duke, Bascomb, Cole, Tharpe, Mr. B. Lead Poll," in *PC,* 26 Jan. 1952, p. 16; and Isadora Rowe, "Ernie Fields, Hamp, Cole, Central State, Ravens, Bascomb Up," *PC,* 2 Feb. 1952, p. 16; Isadora Rowe, "Editor Set to Thin Ranks in Standings as Poll Nears End," "No More Poll Nominations," in *PC,* 9 Feb. 1952, p. 16; Isadora Rowe, "Shaefer, Calvert to Issue Trophies; Duke, Bob White, Cole, Wright Still Leading," "Poll Officially Closes Feb. 23," in *PC,* 16 Feb. 1952, p. 16. Isadora Rowe, "Duke, Wright, Ward, Ravens and Williams on Top," "Why Courier Poll Was Extended," "Final Tabulations in Magazine April 19" all in *PC,* 23 Feb. 1952, p. 16. Isadora Rowe, "Votes Will be Accepted until March 5; Big Names Pulling up in Theatrical Popularity Poll," *PC,* 1 March 1952, p. 16; Isadora Rowe, "Courier Theatrical Poll Officially Closes March 8," *PC,* 8 March 1952, p.

16; Isadora Rowe, "Everything's Over But Concert: April 19 Is Big Day for Courier's Huge Jazz Fete," *PC*, 22 March 1952, p. 16.

83. "American Black Achievement Awards: A Tribute to Black Excellence," *Ebony* (Feb. 1984), 130–32+; "Marilyn McCoo, Robert Guillaime Hosts TV Show of Black Celebrity Achievers," *Jet* 9 Jan. 1984, pp. 30–34+; "A Tribute to Black Excellence," *Ebony* (April 1983), 42–44+.

84. Tony Heilbut, *The Gospel Sound: Good News and Bad Times* (Garden City, N.Y.: Anchor Press, 1975), p. 8.

85. Ibid.

86. WTLC-FM, Indianapolis, Indiana, annually observes this musical month.

87. "A Complicated Affair," *New York Age*, 9 Aug. 1890, p. 1.

88. "300,000 Persons Line Streets to See Elk Parade in Atlantic City," *CD*, 7 Sept. 1929, part 1, p. 3.

89. John Hope Franklin, *From Slavery to Freedom: A History of Negro Americans*, 3rd ed. (New York: Vintage, 1969), p. 490.

90. Louis Stephens, "Railroad Pageant in Bud's Parade: Crowd to See Trains Move Along Route," *CD*, 31 July 1948, p. 21; Louis Stephens, "Joe Louis, Jr. to Greet Throng," *CD*, 7 Aug. 1948, p. 18; "Lens View of the 19th Annual Bud Billiken Parade and Picnic," *CD*, 14 Aug. 1948, p. 12; "Thousands View Bud Billiken Americanism Day Parade and Picnic," *CD*, 17 Aug., 1940, p. 19.

91. "Mardi Gras Parade Ends Program," *AN*, 2 Sept. 1967, p. 32. "Brooklyn West Indian Set Labor Day Festival," *AN*, 28 Aug. 1971, p. D-1; Rhea Calloway, "Hi, There!: A Real West Indian Gala!!!!," *AN*, 11 Sept. 1971, p. D-2; Dick Edwards, "West Indian American Week-end Carnival a Smash Bash in Boro!," *AN*, 11 Sept. 1971, p. D-1; Sadie Feddoes, "West Indian Day Parade: Preparation is Underway," *AN*, 5 Aug. 1972, p. B10; "1M To See West Indian Boro Labor Day Parade," *AN*, 18 Aug. 1973, p. C-1; "Labor Day: Brooklyn A Happy Caribbean Isle!," *AN*, 8 Sept. 1973, p. D-1; "It Looked Like All the World Was West Indian!: Unity Is Theme As Many Groups March Together," *AN*, 8 Sept. 1973, p. C-1; Phyllis Funke, "Getting Ready for the Big Brooklyn Carnival," *New York Times*. Late Evening Ed., 18 Aug. 1974, p. 10B.

92. "The Marching 100," narr. Harry Reasoner, pro. Elliot Erwitt, The Columbia Broadcasting Company/CBS News "Sixty Minutes," 29 March 1981.

93. Carter G. Woodson, "Negro History Week," *Journal of Negro History* XI, no. 2 (April 1926), 239.

94. Alfred Young, "The Historical Origin and Significance of the Afro-American History Month Observance," *Negro History Bulletin*, 45, no. 4, (Oct.–Nov.–Dec. 1982), 101.

95. Alain Locke, "The New Negro," in *The New Negro*, ed. Alain Locke (New York: Athencum, 1970), p. 15.

96. W.E.B. Du Bois, *The Souls of Black Folks* in *Three Negro Classics*, ed. John Hope Franklin (New York: Avon, 1968), 500.

97. Langston Hughes, *The Weary Blues* (New York: Knopf, 1926).

98. James Weldon Johnson, *God's Trombones: Seven Negro Sermons in Verse* (New York: The Murray Printing Company, 1969).

99. Larry Neal, "And Shine Swam On," in *Black Fire: An Anthology of Afro-American Writing*, eds. LeRoi Jones and Larry Neal (New York: William Morrow, 1968), 647.

100. Stephen Henderson, *Understanding the New Black Poetry: Black Speech and Black Music as Poetic References* (New York: William Morrow, 1973), 16.

101. Ibid., 211.

102. Roger D. Abrahams, *Deep Down in the Jungle: Negro Narrative Folklore from the Streets of Philadelphia* (Chicago: Aldine, 1970), 97–172.

103. *The First World Festival of Negro Arts*, UNESCO, 1968. W. Graves, "First World Festival of Negro Arts: An Afro-American View," *Crisis* 73 (June–July 1966), 309–314+.

104. Hoyt W. Fuller, "The Second World Festival of Negro Arts," *Black World* 21 (Nov. 1971), 73; and "Second World Black and African Festival of Arts and Culture," *Black World* 24 (Jan. 1975), 78–82.

105. Thomas Kilgore, Jr., "Christmas from a Black Perspective," *Sepia* (Dec. 1973), 18–19; Omonike Wensi-Purvear, "How I Came to Celebrate Kwanzaa," *Essence* (Dec. 1979), 112–17.

106. "Black Expo Comes of Age—Third Coming Together Brings Joy and Blueprint for Change," *Ebony* (Dec. 1971), 64–68+; J. H. O'Dell, "Black Expo—Matrix of the Design for Unity," *Freedomways* 11, no. 4 (1971), 374–83; "Jesse Jackson Announces PUSH Expo '73," *CT*, Late City, Ed., 31 July 1973, Sec. 1, p. 2; "PUSH Expo '73 Praised," Editorial, *CT*, 17 Sept. 1973, Sec. 1, p. 26; "Jesse Jackson Addresses Opening of Black Expo," *CT*, 20 Sept. 1973, Sec. 1, p. 3; "Jesse Jackson's Wife's Appearance at Expo Discussed," *CT*, 20 Sept. 1973, Sec. 1, p. 3; "Jesse Jackson Calls Expo '73 a Great Success," *CT*, 23 Sept. 1973, Sec. 3, p. 10; "Jesse Jackson Announces the Theme of PUSH Expo," *CT*, 18 July 1974, Sec. 14, p. 14; "Plans for P.U.S.H. Expo '74," *CT*, 26 Sept. 1974, Sec. 2, p. 9; "Speaks at P.U.S.H. Expo Breakfast," CT, 27 Sept. 1974, Sec. 1, p. 2; "Speaks at P.U.S.H. Convention," *CT*, 8 Aug. 1975, Sec. 1, p. 5; "Opens P.U.S.H. Expo in Chicago," *CT*, 25 Sept. 1975, Sec. 2, p. 1; "1st Day of Chicago Operation P.U.S.H. Viewed," *CT*, 28 Sept. 1976, Sec. 3, p. 1.

CHAPTER 3

1. "The Addresses of the 'Emancipators,'" Editorial, *ADW*, 4 Jan. 1955, p. 5.

2. Transcription (June 1972).

3. Wanda Pryor, "Juneteenth Celebration: A Flavor of the 1890's," *Austin* [Texas] *American Statesman*, Late City Ed., 20 June 1976, p. B3.

4. *Seventy Sixth Anniversary of the September 22nd Emancipation Celebration* Souvenir Program, 22 Sept. 1938, n.p.

5. "Brunswick, Ga.," *ADW*, 2 Jan. 1937, p. 8.

6. Rev. D.F. Martinez, "Struggles of Race Depicted: Spectacular Parade, Pageant, Address Add Color to Fête," *ADW*, 13 Jan. 1936, p. 5.

7. William A. Fowlkes, "U.S. Warned to Make Democracy Work at Home," *ADW*, 2 Jan. 1947, p. 6.

8. Joel W. Smith, "Emancipation Event at Wheat Street Church," *ADW*, 28 Dec. 1947, p. 1.

9. Deborah Bowman, "A Bibliographic Essay on Afro-American Folk Drama," *Ohio Folklife: Journal of the Ohio Folklore Society* 79–81 (Spring 1982), 38–39.

10. Roger D. Abrahams, "Folk Drama," in *Folklore and Folklife: An Introduction*. Richard M. Dorson, ed. (Chicago: Univ. of Chicago Press, 1972), 354.

11. Martinez, p. 5.

12. Personal interview with Mr. Mingo Scott, 18 Oct. 1972.

13. "Negro Day To be Gala Affair Here: Pageant Will Be Held in Soldiers Field," *CD*, 12 Aug. 1933, p. 1.

14. Martinex, p. 5.

15. *Color Me Brown,* Souvenir Program, 10 March 1967, n.p.

16. "Historical Pageant: 'The Star of Ethiopia,'" Advertisement, *PT*, 13 May 1916, n.p.

17. Edward J. McCoo, "Ethiopia At the Bar of Justice," in *Plays and Pageants from the Life of the Negro,* ed. Willis Richardson (Washington, D.C.: Associated Publishers, 1924), ix–x.

18. W.E.B. Du Bois, "The National Emancipation Exposition," *The Crisis* (Nov. 1913), 339–41. Also see Du Bois, "The Philadelphia Pageant," *The Crisis* (Aug. 1916), 170–72 and "The Drama Among Black Folk," *The Crisis* (Aug. 1916), 169–73.

19. Du Bois, "Drama," 169.

20. "Historical Pageant," n.p.

21. Du Bois, "Emancipation Exposition," 339.

22. Du Bois, "Philadelphia Pageant." 172.

23. McCoo, 346–47.

24. Ibid., 351.

25. Ibid., 352.

26. Ibid., 358.

27. Ibid., 367.

28. Du Bois, "Emancipation Exposition," 339.

29. "Emancipation Proclamation," Editorial, *ADW*, 30 Dec. 1933, p. 6.

30. Du Bois, "Emancipation Exposition," 339.

31. McCoo, 356.

32. Transcription (Jan. 1973).

33. Transcription (June 1972).

34. McCoo, 356.

35. Du Bois, "Emancipation Exposition," 339.

36. McCoo, 358.

37. "Emancipation Celebration," *ADW*.

38. Donald Bogle, *Toms, Coons, Mulattoes, Mammies, Bucks: An Interpretative History of Blacks in American Films* (New York: Viking, 1973), 236.

39. "Shaft in Africa," *Ebony* (March 1973), 147–51.

40. E.B. "There Really Is A Timbuktu," *Ebony* (Feb. 1972), 76–82+, and R. Broder, "The Glory that Was Timbuktu," *Sepia* (March 1972), 39–45. For articles on the play's star, Eartha Kitt, see: Albert Ebert, "Eartha!," *Essence* (June 1978),

68–71+; C. David, "Eartha Kitt Out Cattin' Again," *Encore*, 21 Feb. 1978, pp. 20–22+; and "Kitt Sizzles on Broadway," *Jet*, 31 Aug. 1978, pp. 22–24. For reviews of the play, see: "Timbuktu," *Encore*, 3 April 1978, pp. 26–7; "Timbuktu," *New Yorker*, 20 March 1978, pp. 89–90; "Timbuktu," *New Leader*, 27 March 1978, p. 28; "Timbuktu," *Newsweek*, 13 March 1978, p. 95; "Timbuktu," *Saturday Review*, 29 April 1978, p. 26; "Timbuktu," *Theatre Crafts*, May 1978, pp. 13–15+; and "Timbuktu," *Time*, 13 March 1978, p. 75.

41. Milton Jordan, "African Kingdom in South Carolina," *Sepia* (April 1975), 17–25; and "Coming of Age: A Baptist Minister Borrows African Tradition to Devise Ritual for Son's 16th Birthday," *Ebony* (Dec. 1974), 83–84+.

42. E.U. Essien-Udom, *Black Nationalism: A Search for an Identity in America* (New York: Dell, 1969).

43. Ibid., 48–51, 52, 57–58, 60, 72–73, 74, 76.

44. Randy Whitestone, "Dozens of houses burn after attack on radical group," [Louisville, Ky.] *Courier-Journal*, 14 May 1985, pp. 1A and 8A.

45. McCoo, 359.

46. For printed references to Dr. Borders's poem, see: J.P. Reynolds, "Auburn Avenue Says: Rev. Borders Says 'I Am Somebody' Over the Radio," *ADW*, 13 Jan. 1943, p. 6, Rep; "National Negro History: Extension of Remarks of Hon. Charles C. Diggs of Michigan," *Cong. Rec.*, 5 Jan. 1955 to 2 Aug. 1955, p. 4972. Congressman Diggs later recited the poem at Atlanta's January 1st celebration and acknowledged Reverend Borders as the author. See: Reverend Taschereau Arnold, "NAACP Emancipation Day Sidelights at Wheat Street," *ADW*. 3 Jan. 1956, p. 2. In the 1970s Reverend Jesse Jackson composed a poem with a similar title and refrain. See: Barbara A. Reynolds, *Jesse Jackson: The Man, the Myth, the Movement* (Chicago: Nelson-Hall, 1975), 7–8, 18, 41, 158, 162, 287. Booker T. Washington echoed this folk view in his autobiography. See: Booker T. Washington, *Up From Slavery* in *Three Negro Classics*, ed. John Hope Franklin (New York: Avon, 1965), 38–39.

47. Arnold, 2.

48. McCoo, 358.

49. Personal interview with Mr. Richard Jones in *Life Under the "Peculiar Institution: Selections from the Slave Narrative Collection*, ed. Norman R. Yetman (New York: Holt, Rinehart and Winston, 1970), 192.

For variants of this red-cloth etiological tale, see: "How Blacks Got to America," in *Shuckin' and Jivin': Folklore from Contemporary Black Americans*, ed. Daryl Cumber Dance, (Bloomington: Indiana Univ. Press, 1978), 10, and Lawrence W. Levine, *Black Culture and Black Consciousness*, 86–87.

50. Zora Neale Hurston, "Cudjo's Own Story of the Last African Slaver," *Journal of Negro History* 12 (Oct. 1927), 648–63.

51. Carolyn Yette, "Charlie Smith, 130, was the star of the annual centenarian reunion," [Louisville, Ky.] *Courier-Journal*, Late City Ed., 21 May 1973, p. A14.

52. Yetman, 198.

53. Yetman, 290.

54. McCoo, 354.

55. Transcription (Jan. 1973).

56. Personal interview with Mr. Jerry Wilson, 15 Nov. 1972.

57. Washington, 37. There is some evidence that this belief was held by some white Americans also. William Hay Williamson, editor of the *Chicago Herald and Examiner,* has been quoted as saying: "The world would not have seen the likes of Booker T. Washington and Dr. Morton, 'if years ago Dutch traders had not brought their ancestors from the wilderness of Africa. . . .' Slavery 'is a curse with a silver lining. . . .'" See: Zita Louis Bakes, "Was Slavery a Curse or a Blessing?," *CD,* 7 Sept. 1929, pp. 1, 2.

58. "The First One Hundred Years," Editorial, *ADW,* Jan. 1963, p. 4.

59. "Can Negroes Free America?—A Story Showing How the Negro's Battle for Freedom Will Help Free the World," *Color* (April 1951), 40–42.

60. Transcription (Feb. 1973).

61. Benjamin E. Mays, *The Negro's God as Reflected in His Literature* (New York: Atheneum, 1969), 183.

62. Transcription (Jan. 1973).

63. Du Bois, "Emancipation Exposition," 340.

64. Transcription: Reverend Williams.

65. Du Bois, "Emancipation Exposition," 341.

66. Charlotte K. Brooks, "Firm Foundations: A Radio Skit for Negro History Week," *Negro History Bulletin* 17, no. 6 (March 1954), 130.

67. Franklin, 210–11.

68. Ibid., 188 and 212.

69. Franklin, 161.

70. Ibid., 212–13, 243.

71. Du Bois, "Emancipation Exposition," 340.

72. Brooks, 129.

73. Du Bois, "Emancipation Exposition," 341.

74. McCoo, 365–66.

75. The popular abolitionist medallion bearing this credo was struck off by Josiah Wedgwood, the famous English pottery industrialist, in the late 18th century. One is located in the Smithsonian Institution, Division of Ceramics and Glass, Lloyd E. Hawes Collection. See: Roger Burns, ed., *Am I Not A Man and A Brother: The Anti-Slavery Crusade of Revolutionary America, 1688–1788* (New York: Chelsea House, 1977), xxvi–xxvii.

76. Mays, 411–12.

77. Benjamin Quarles, ed., *Great Lives Observed: Frederick Douglass* (Englewood Cliffs, N.J.: Prentice-Hall, 1968), 48.

78. Transcription (Feb. 1973).

79. Transcription (June 1973).

80. McCoo, 366.

81. Ibid., 358–59.

82. Ibid., 360.

83. Ibid., 359.

84. Yetman, 172.

85. Ibid., 236.

86. Ibid., 296.

87. Ibid., 289.

88. Botkin, ed., *Lay My Burden Down,* 16.

89. John Lovell, Jr., *Black Song: The Forge and the Flame. The Story of How the Afro-American Spiritual Was Hammered Out* (New York: Macmillan, 1972), 122, 282, 376, 526.

90. Botkin, 19.

91. Ibid., 16.

92. Ibid., 18–19.

93. Ibid., 16.

94. Yetman, 289.

95. Botkin, 18.

96. Yetman, 73. For further Lincoln lore see: David Donald, *Lincoln Reconsidered: Essays on the Civil War Era* (New York: Vintage Books, 1961), 144–65; and Ray B. Browne, ed., *Lincoln-Lore: Lincoln in the Popular Mind* (Bowling Green, Ohio: Popular Press, 1974).

97. Transcription (June 1972).

98. Rev. E.J. Echols, "Negro Slavery, Freedom, Education," *ADW,* 29 Dec. 1939, p. 6.

99. Botkin, 17.

100. Class assignment: Mr. David A. Haney, n.d. June 1978.

101. Personal interview with Mr. L. Williams, 16 June 1972.

102. Yetman, 289.

103. Botkin, 18.

104. Ibid., 17.

105. Personal interview with Mrs. Juanita Ballard, 15 June 1972.

106. "Juneteenth," *Ebony* (June 1951), 30.

107. Personal interview with Mr. Robert E. Felder, 14 Nov. 1972.

108. Hon. Alan Wheat, "Juneteenth Celebration," *Cong. Rec.*—Extension of Remarks, 15 June 1983, p. E2936.

109. "The Speeches Went 'Round an' 'Round," Editorial, *ADW,* 8 Jan. 1941, p. 6.

110. Personal interview with Mrs. Lillian Crisp, 19 June 1972.

111. "'Juneteenth': Elizabeth Burham honors the day," [Bloomington, Ind.] *Herald-Telephone,* Late City Ed., 21 June 1984, p. 9.

112. Hygh letter, n.d.

113. "Rev. C. K. Steele Asks Albanians to Complete the Job of Freedom," *ADW,* 1 Jan. 1966, p. 5.

114. Transcription (Jan. 1973).

115. "The Spirit of Booker T. Washington," Editorial, *ADW,* 31 Dec. 1933, p. 4.

116. Washington, 56–57.

117. Elizabeth Ross Haynes, *The Black Boy of Atlanta* (Boston: The House of Edinboro, 1952), 14–15. For a copy of the poem inspired by this remark see: John Greenleaf Whittier, *Anti-Slavery Poems: Songs of Labor and Reform* (Boston: Houghton, Mifflin, 1837), 64–65. For additional biographical sketches of Major Wright see: Webb Waldon, "'Massa, Tell 'Em We're Rising!,'" *Reader's Digest* 46

(April 1945), 53–56 and " 'Massa, Tell 'em We're Rising!' " *The Progressive* 9, 12 March 1945, pp. 9–10; also "Milestones: Dead," *Time*, 14 July 1947, p. 76; "Transition: Died," *Newsweek*, 14 July 1947, p. 44; "The Talk of the Town: Banker," *The New Yorker*, 5 July 1947, pp. 16–17.

118. Transcription (Feb. 1973).

119. McCoo, 362.

120. Du Bois, "Emancipation Exposition," 341.

121. McCoo, 362.

122. Abrahams, *Deep Down in the Jungle*, 126.

123. Ibid., 128.

124. Ibid.

125. Albert B. Friedman, ed., *The Viking Book of Folk Ballads of the English-Speaking World* (New York: Viking, 1971), 388.

126. Ibid., 389.

127. Transcription (June 1972).

128. McCoo, 364.

129. "26 Negro Rallies Back Roosevelt: Meeting Throughout the East Join 14,000 in Garden Here for New Deal Drive," *The New York Times*, 23 Sept. 1936, p. 41.

130. George M. Coleman, "Increase Vote Strength to Stop Bias Says Rep. Diggs to Atlanta: Emancipation Day Speaker Deplores Low Registration," *ADW*, 3 Jan. 1956, pp. 1 and 4.

131. Dick Gregory, *From the Back of the Bus* (New York: Avon Books, 1966).

132. Haskins, *Jokes from Black Folks*, 62–63; Henry D. Spalding, ed., *Encyclopedia of Black Folklore and Humor* (Middle Village, N.Y.: Jonathan David Publishers, 1972), 486–87; Brewer, 88–89.

133. William H. Wiggins, Jr., "Black Folktales in the Novels of John O. Killens," *The Black Scholar* 3, no. 3 (1971), 56; Haskins, p. 93.

134. V.W. Hodges, "Judge Delaney Raps Official Silence . . . Urges Negroes to Join Fight for Freedom Now," *ADW*, 2 Jan. 1952, pp. 1 and 4.

135. Larry Wilde, *The Official White Folks Joke Book* (New York: Pinnacle Books, 1975), 52.

136. Langston Hughes and Arna Bontemps, eds. *Book of Negro Folklore* (New York: Dodd, Mead 1958), 505.

137. Alan Dundes, ed., *Mother Wit from the Laughing Barrel: Readings in the Interpretation of Afro-American Folklore* (Englewood Cliffs, N.J.: Prentice-Hall, 1973), xiii–xiv.

138. Hughes and Bontemps, 510–11.

139. Haskins, 82. Norine Dresser, "The Metamorphosis of the Humor of the Black American," *New York Folklore Quarterly* 26 (1970), 216–28. And Daryl C. Dance, ed., *Shuckin' and Jivin'*, 172.

140. Personal interview with Reverend William Holmes Borders. A published variant reads: "The Indian fought and fought until he died, the Negro laughed and laughed and multiplied." See: "Photo-Editorial: Are Negroes Losing Their Humor," *Ebony* (Jan. 1951), 80.

CHAPTER 4

1. *117th Annual Emancipation Celebration of September 22nd* Program/Flyer.

2. *106th Annual Emancipation Homecoming of August 8th* Flyer.

3. Jeff Todd Titon, *Early Downhome Blues: A Musical and Cultural Analysis* (Urbana: Univ. of Illinois Press, 1977), xiii.

4. Millicent R. Ayoug, "The Family Reunion," *Ethnology* 5 (1966), 428.

5. Hyman Rodman, *Lower-Class Families: The Poverty in Negro Trinidad* (New York: Oxford Univ. Press, 1971), 147.

6. E. Franklin Frazier, *The Negro Church in America* (New York: Schocken Books, 1974), 49.

7. Personal interview with Mr. Paul Darby, 17 Nov. 1972.

8. Personal interview with Mrs. Bennie Mae Smith.

9. Kathleen Zobel, "Hog Heaven: Barbecue in the South," *Southern Exposure* (Summer–Fall 1977), 58–61.

10. Personal interview with Mr. Artis Lovelady.

11. Higginson, *Army Life,* 36.

12. "This Is No Rib—It's Hot," *Windsor* [Ontario, Canada] *Star,* Late City Ed., 3 Aug. 1957, p. 3.

13. Dorson, *American Negro Folktales,* 156.

14. Personal interview with Mrs. Rosie Parks, 16 June 1972.

15. "Atlantan In Emancipation Address to Albany Group," *ADW,* 3 Jan. 1959, p. 1.

16. C. Eric Lincoln, *The Black Muslims in America* (Boston: Beacon Press, 1961).

17. Ibid., 81.

18. Eldridge Cleaver, *Soul On Ice* (New York: Dell Press, 1970).

19. "Black Nutritionist Finds Soul Food Unhealthy—Black Students Demand It," *Jet,* 8 April 1971, p. 23.

20. For a variant of this saying, see Melville J. Herskovits, *The Myth of the Negro Past* (Boston: Beacon Press, 1941), 208: "Southerntowners say that if a Negro is not a Baptist someone has been tampering with him."

21. Mrs. Bennie Mae Smith interview. One published variant read: "Congregation of one church sings: 'Will there be any stars, any stars in my crown?' Choir of the church next door sings, 'No, not one! No, not one!' " See Haskins, *Jokes from Black Folks,* 22. Another version appears as a family memorat: "I remember a little story he [i.e. Henry Clay Hughes] used to tell. He used to tell about being out in the field plowing, and while he was plowing he was singing the song, 'Will there be an-y stars, an-y stars in my crown?' and seems that as he paused a moment, he heard somebody say across the field singing, 'No, not one. No, not one!' " See: Helen H. Sewell, "Folktales from a Georgia Family: An Annotated Field Collection," (M. A. Thesis, Indiana University, 1963), 34.

22. Lovell, Jr., *Black Song: The Forge and the Flame,* 278. And John W. Work, ed., *American Negro Songs and Spirituals* (New York: Bonanza Books, 1940), 219.

23. Howard Thurman, *With Head and Heart: The Autobiography of Howard Thurman* (New York: Harcourt Brace Jovanovich, 1979), 10.

24. Ibid.

25. Richard R. Wright, Jr., *87 Years Behind the Black Curtain: An Autobiography* (Philadelphia: Rare Book Co., 1965), 80. Bishop Wright gives a detailed discussion of the cultural importance of the baptism ritual, 78–81.

26. Clifton H. Johnson, ed., *God Struck Me Dead: Religious Conversion Experiences and Autobiographies of Ex-Slaves*. Foreword by Paul Radin (Philadelphia: Pilgrim Press, 1969).

27. Personal interview with Rev. William Holmes Borders.

28. Anne Moody, *Coming of Age in Mississippi* (New York: Dial Press, 1969), 71.

29. Borders interview.

30. James Weldon Johnson, *God's Trombones: Seven Sermons in Verse* (New York: Penguin Books, 1972), 6.

31. Levine, *Black Culture and Black Consciousness*, 32.

32. Frederick Douglass, *My Bondage and My Freedom* (New York: Arno Press and *The New York Times*, 1968), 220.

33. Du Bois, *Souls of Black Folks* in *Three Negro Classics*, ed. Franklin, 294. This same image appears in this Afro-American work song lyric: "I say wake up ol' dead man,/Help me carry my row, help me carry my row." See: Bruce Jackson, ed., *Wake Up Dead Man: Afro-American Worksongs from Texas Prisons* (Cambridge, Mass.: Harvard Univ. Press, 1972), p. 80.

34. *Messenger from Violet Drive* (film), 1964.

35. "Emam Muhammad Calls for 'genuine patriotism,'" *Bilalian News* 22 (July 1977) 4.

36. Work, *Songs and Spirituals*, 125.

37. Ibid., 55.

38. Ibid., 163.

39. Ibid., 80.

40. Work, 161.

41. Lovell, 317.

42. This image of the persistent prayer crops up in such spirituals as "I Went Down in the Valley." See: Work, 69.

43. This spiritual cropped up in a celebration recitation. Transcription: Choir, 1 February 1973. "Hold on!"

44. Work, p. 94.

45. Ibid., 1975.

46. Ibid., 152.

47. Ibid., 188.

48. See Tony Heilbut, *The Gospel Sound: Good News and Bad Times* (Garden City, N.J.: Anchor Press/Doubleday, 1975), 30, for lyrics of "Precious Lord."

49. Frederick Douglass, "Fourth of July Celebration at Himrods," *Douglass' Monthly* (Aug. 1862), 594.

50. Higginson, 40–41.

51. Guy Carawan and Candie Carawan, eds., *We Shall Overcome!: Songs of the Southern Freedom Movement* (New York: Oak Publications, 1963), 11.

52. Ibid., for lyrics.

53. James Weldon Johnson, *Along This Way: The Autobiography of James Weldon Johnson* (New York: Viking Press, 1968), 154.

54. Johnson, *Autobiography,* 155.

55. Ibid.

56. Work, 129.

57. Frederick Douglass, *Bondage and Freedom,* 220.

58. Toni Morrison, *Song of Solomon* (New York: Knopf, 1977), 3–9, 321–24, 328–29.

59. John McCluskey, *Look What They Done to My Song* (New York: Random House, 1974), 5 and 6.

60. C.L. Franklin, "The Eagle Stirreth Her Nest," Chess, 9310-A, 9310-B, n.d. This sermon has also been associated with the black Kentucky preacher, Peter Vinegar, who lived in Lexington and died in 1905. See: Tristram Potter Coffin and Hennig Cohen, eds., *Folklore: From the Working Folk of America* (Garden City, N.Y.: Anchor Press, 1974), 387.

61. Paul Laurence Dunbar, "Sympathy," in *The Life and Complete Works of Paul Laurence Dunbar* (New York: Kraus Reprint Co., 1971), 207.

62. Maya Angelou, *I Know Why the Caged Bird Sings* (New York: Random House, 1969).

63. Du Bois, *Souls of Black Folks,* 258.

64. Kelly Miller, "Frederick Douglass," in *Black American Literature: Essays, Poetry, Fiction, Dramas* (Columbus, Ohio: Charles E. Merrill Publishing Co., 1970), 69.

65. William H. Wiggins, Jr., "*In the Rapture:* The Black Aesthetic and Folk Drama," *Callaloo,* no. 2 (February 1978) 103–11.

66. Work, 148–49.

67. Personal interview with Mrs. Leila Blakey, 9 June 1972.

68. Bobby "Blue" Bland, "Stormy Monday Blues," Duke, 355, 1962.

69. Hughes and Bontemps, *Negro Folklore,* 509. Richard M. Dorson, *American Negro Folktales,* 185–86.

70. Personal interview with Mr. Willie Hygh, 16 June 1972.

71. Personal interview with Mr. Orangie Smith, 30 Sept. 1972.

72. The theme of the 1972 African-American Day Parade was: "Salute to Black History." See: John Thomas, "Fitting end to marvelous Parade Day," *AN,* 16 Sept. 1972, pp. A1; "350,000 expected at Afro-American fete," *AN,* 9 Sept. 1972, pp. A1 and A3; "Join African-American Day Parade (Largest Black Parade in America) A Day of Black Unity Sunday, Sept. 10, 1972, in Harlem, 1 p.m.," *AN,* adv., 26 Aug. 1972, p. A2.

73. Michael Edgerton, "Mas'—Just Like Carnival Day in Trinidad," *Tuesday: At Home* 4 (Jan. 1975), 10. Similar tar figures have been observed in West African funeral processions. A Black missionary has noted: "A number of women had their faces, hair and loin clothes smeared over with a black preparation which trickled all down their legs. . . . It was their mode of mourning for the deceased." See William H. Sheppard, *Pioneers in the Congo* (Louisville: Pentecostal Publishing Co., n.d.), 31.

74. William Renwick Riddell, "Celebrations of the Anniversary of the Eman-

cipation in Hamilton, Upper Canada, 1859," *Journal of Negro History* 22 (April 1928), 196.

75. "Brunswick [Ga.] Church Site of Colorful January 1 Exercise," *ADW*, 8 Jan. 1940, p. 2.

76. "Emancipation Celebration," *Terre Haute Evening Gazette*, 24 Sept. 1888, p. 1.

77. Genovese, *Roll, Jordan, Roll*, 559.

78. John Hope Franklin, *From Slavery to Freedom*, 226.

79. Mary Boykin Chestnut, *A Diary from Dixie*, ed. Ben Ames Williams (Cambridge, Mass.: Riverside Press, 1949), 539.

80. Ibid., 536.

81. Ibid., 544.

82. Gary B. Nash, *Class and Society in Early America* (Englewood Cliffs, N.J.: Prentice-Hall, 1970), 6.

83. Hylan Lewis, *Blackways of Kent* (Chapel Hill: Univ. of North Carolina Press, 1955), 54.

84. Jack Schwartz, "Men's Clothing and the Negro," *Phylon* 26 (Fall 1963), 224–31. For a rebuttal of "fly" male fashion see: Judith Rollins, "Do Clothes Unmake the Man," *Black World* 23 (May 1974), 8–9.

85. Paul Darby interview.

86. Don L. Lee, "African Liberation Day: Thousands of black Americans march to support African freedom fighters," *Ebony* (July 1973), 41–44; 46.

87. Ibid., 46. The clenched fist was the official logo of Chicago's Black Expo '71. See: "Black Expo Comes of Age; Third 'coming together' brings joy and blueprint for change," *Ebony* (Dec. 1971), 64–68, 70–72. A special issue of the *Negro Digest* (Nov. 1966) entitled, "The Meaning and Message of Black Power," carried a cover shot of a clenched fist.

88. "James Brown Goes 'Natural,'" *Tan* (Dec. 1968), 62–63, For other "natural" hair-style articles, see "Natural Look: Is It Here to Stay?" *Ebony* (Jan. 1969), 104–106+. And "Natural Look," *Ebony* (June 1966), 142–44+.

89. "Al Young" in *Interviews With Black Writers*, ed., John O'Brien (New York: Lineright, 1973), 259.

90. For a study of this group's grooming habits and beliefs see: G. Llewellyn Watson, "Patterns of Black Protest in Jamaica: The Case of the Ras-Tafarians." *Journal of Black Studies* 4 (March 1974), 329–43. For a discussion of hair grooming and racial identity, see J. Spencer Condie and James W. Christiansen, "Indirect Technique for the Measurement of Changes in Black Identity," *Phylon* 38 (March 1977), 46–54. Also see Hazel Reed, "Bob Marley: Up From Babylon," *Freedomways* 21, no. 3 (1981), 171–79.

91. Lee, 41–44.

92. Ibid.

93. WPA 36-2 Florida Folklore Book II.

94. Hortense J. Spillers, "Martin Luther King and the Style of the Black Sermon," *The Black Scholar* 3, no. 1 (Sept. 1971), 21.

95. William H. Wiggins, Jr., "Jack Johnson as Bad Nigger" *Black Scholar*, 41. A related joke has a black man dreaming of returning to Georgia with "a white

woman, a white Cadillac, and a white suit." However, his dream is shattered by a friend who promises to "get a black woman, in a black Cadillac, a black suit" and see his friend's "black ass hanging." See Dance, 107–108.

96. Paulette Cross, "Jokes and Black Consciousness: A Collection with Interviews," in *Mother Wit From the Laughing Barrel*, 650–51.

97. CME Bishop Luther Stewart often chided his Kentucky Conference delegates with this saying.

98. Black comedian Jackie "Moms" Mabley used this saying in her comic routine.

99. "Arnold Pleases Audience with Emancipation Day Address Here," *ADW*, 3 Jan. 1953, p. 3.

100. Personal interview with Mr. Judson Henry.

101. "Sports world coming out of the closet," [Bloomington, Indiana] *Herald-Telephone*, Late City Ed., 20 March 1978, p. 9.

102. Albert G. Spalding, *America's National Game: Historic Facts Concerning the Beginning, Evolution, Development and Popularity of Baseball, with Personal Reminiscences of Its Vicissitudes, Its Victories and Its Votaries* (New York: American Sports Publishing Co., 1911), 361.

103. Ibid.

104. "Taft's pitch was the first," [Louisville, Kentucky] *Courier-Journal*, Late City Ed., 10 July 1978, p. B8.

105. Personal interviews with Mr. Judson Henry and Mrs. Bennie Mae Smith.

106. " 'Segregation Is Out!' Borders Tells Stamford," *ADW*, 5 Jan. 1965, p. 2.

107. Questionnaire: Mrs. Bennie Mae Johnson, Spring, 1973.

108. Albert Murray, *Stomping the Blues* (New York: McGraw-Hill, 1976), 189.

109. Titon, xiv.

110. Ibid., 28.

111. Murray, 139.

112. Paul Oliver, *The Meaning of the Blues* (New York: Collier-Macmillan, 1969), 187.

113. Ibid.

114. Richard M. Dorson, *American Negro Folktales*, 149.

115. For a computerized version of this joke see: Dance, ed., *Shuckin' and Jivin'*, 88.

116. Washington, *Up from Slavery* in Franklin, ed., *Three Negro Classics*, 91.

117. See Hughes, Bontemps, eds., *Negro Folklore*, 514, for this variant: "Mule die—Buy another one/Negro die—Hire another one."

118. Chester Himes, *The Quality of Hurt: The Autobiography of Chester Himes* (Garden City, N.Y.: Doubleday, 1972), 18.

119. Personal interview with Mr. Claude Snorton.

120. For a photograph of Dr. King's funeral procession, see David L. Lewis, *King: A Critical Biography* (New York: Praeger, 1970), 148a. These mule-drawn wagons have become a civil rights funeral tradition. See: "500 Gather to send Ben Owens to Final Reward," *Jet*, 24 Feb. 1977, p. 15. Mr. Owens's casket was also carried by a mule wagon.

121. Murray, 12.

122. Ibid., 254.

CHAPTER 5

1. Personal interview with Rev. William Holmes Borders.

2. Personal interview with Dr. Wesley Lyda.

3. Personal interview with Rev. Thomas Flanagan, 30 Dec. 1972.

4. Personal interview with Mr. Herman Guy, 12 Nov. 1972.

5. Personal interview with Mrs. Leila Blakey.

6. Personal interview with Mr. Andrew Powers, 12 Nov. 1972.

7. Personal interview with Rev. Nathaniel Lindsey, 29 Dec. 1972.

8. Lyda interview.

9. Ibid.

10. "Parade to Precede Emancipation Meeting," *ADW*, 1 Jan. 1944, p. 1. "Thousands See Colorful Parade," *ADW*, 2 Jan. 1944, pp. 1, 2.

11. Wendy Watriss, "Celebrate Freedom: Juneteenth," *Southern Exposure* 5, no. 1 (1977), 80–87.

12. "Mr. Cleveland . . . ," *Washington* [D.C.] *Bee*, 24 April 1886, p. 1.

13. "Honorable Grover Cleveland, Pres. U.S.," *Washington* [D.C.] *Bee*, 16 April 1887, p. 1.

14. "Two Cities to Celebrate Emancipation," *ADW*, 28 Dec. 1947, p. 2.

15. "Prizes Will Be Given Monday," *ADW*, 29 Dec. 1933, p. 1.

16. V.W. Hodges, "Negroes Want Normal American Privileges—Carey," *ADW*, 2 Jan. 1945, pp. 1, 6.

17. "Ribbins Makes Eloquent Emancipation Day Speech," *ADW*, 8 Jan. 1946, p. 6.

18. Hodges, pp. 1, 6.

19. "Borders Delivers Emancipation Day Address in Indiana," *ADW*, 5 Jan. 1950, p. 2.

20. "Over 3,000 to Hear 'Mr. Civil Rights,' Miss Mattiwilda Dobbs," *ADW*, 1 Jan. 1955, pp. 1 and 4.

21. "Leaders Urged to Resist Segregation by NAACP," *ADW*, 3 Jan. 1956, p. 3.

22. "Borders Delivers Address."

23. "Leaders Urged to Resist."

24. "Miles Prexy Is Emancipation Day Speaker, Jan. 1st," *ADW*, 27 Dec. 1944, p. 5. For other celebration references to ex-slaves see: "Ex-Slaves to Also Receive Honor at Program This Afternoon. Hon. Ben J. Davis Is Principal Speaker," *ADW*, 1 Jan. 1932, p. 2. "Brunswick Church Site of Colorful January 1 Exercises," *ADW*, 8 Jan. 1940, p. 2. And "Rev. Hurley to Be Emancipation Speaker," *ADW*, 30 Dec. 1940, p. 1.

25. "Expect Throng at NAACP Mass Meet Saturday," *ADW*, 29 Dec. 1937, p. 1.

26. Personal interview with Mr. Emanuel C. Wright, 2 Feb. 1973.

27. Guy interview.

28. William Gordon, "Ballot Is Road To Economic Freedom, Says Mrs. Bethune," *ADW,* 3 Jan. 1950, p. 1.

29. George M. Coleman, "Emancipation Day Speaker Deplores Low Registration," *ADW,* 3 Jan. 1956, pp. 1 and 4.

30. *Power and Prejudice in America,* narr. Judy Woodruff, pro. and dir. Karen Thomas, The Film Company/PBS News Special, 25 June 1984.

31. Ibid.

32. Personal interview with Mrs. A.T. Lewis, 17 June 1972.

33. Lyda interview.

34. Emancipation Celebration: The Way Politics Was Dragged into It . . . An Apology," *Terre Haute Evening Gazette,* 24 Sept. 1888, p. 1. For another case, see "Ends in Politics: Emancipation Meeting Taken Advantage of. Colored People Very Indignant," *Indianapolis Recorder,* 26 Sept. 903 [sic], p. 1.

35. "Negro Clergymen Plan Landon Drive: Bishop Sims Says his People Belong to Republican Party by History and Tradition," *New York Times,* n.d. Sept. 1936, p. 18L.

36. "Demos in Giant Rally at Gary," *Indianapolis Recorder,* 26 Sept. 1936, p. 1.

37. "Emancipation Day Anniversary. How It Will Be Celebrated," *Washington* [D.C.] *Bee,* n.d. April 1888, p. 1.

38. Blakey interview.

39. "Celebration At North Elba," *Douglass' Monthly,* (Sept. 1860), 331.

40. Frederick Douglass, "Celebration of the Twenty-First Anniversary of West India Emancipation at Geneva," *Douglass' Monthly,* (August 1859), 113.

41. Personal interview with Mrs. E.B. Tollette, 12 Nov. 1972.

42. Personal interview with Mr. Mingo Scott, 18 Oct. 1972.

43. Charles R. Hunter, "Emancipation Day Proclamation," *Terre Haute Tribune,* 22 Sept. 1918, p. 4.

44. Wright interview.

45. *31st Anniversary Celebration of National Freedom Day* Souvenir Program.

46. *22nd Anniversary Celebration of National Freedom Day* Souvenir Program.

47. Striplin interview.

48. Tollette interview.

49. Personal interview with Mrs. Lillian Crisp, 19 June 1972.

50. Personal interview with Mr. Marzee Douglass, 19 June 1972.

51. "Progress of Race Lauded by President," *ADW,* 9 Jan. 1936, p. 1.

52. "26 Negro Rallies Back Roosevelt: Meetings Throughout the East Join 14,000 in Garden Here for New Deal Drive," *New York Times,* Late City Ed., 23 Sept. 1936, p. 4L.

53. Tollette interview.

54. Striplin interview.

55. Blakey interview.

56. Ibid.

57. Ibid.

58. Striplin interview.

59. Transcription (Jan. 1973).

60. "Arnold Pleases Audience With Emancipation Day Address Here," *ADW,* 3

Jan. 1953, p. 3. I also collected an oral variant of this joke from Rev. J.C. Cook, 2 Jan. 1973. For a printed version of this joke, see Levine, *Black Culture and Black Consciousness*, 330.

61. "Borders Calls on Race to Unite Save Gains," *ADW*, 3 Jan. 1946, p. 1.

62. George M. Coleman, "Increase Vote Strength to Stop Bias Says Rep. Diggs to Atlanta: Emancipation Day Speaker Deplores Low Registration," *ADW*, 3 Jan. 1956, p. 1.

63. Transcription (Feb. 1973).

64. Personal interview with Mrs. J.C. Cook, 2 Jan. 1973.

65. Personal interview with Mr. Ted Powell, 29 July 1972.

66. Transcription (Feb. 1973). Goode.

67. Blakey interview.

68. Lindsey interview.

69. Personal interview with Dr. David Johnson, 14 Nov. 1972.

70. Tollette interview.

71. Blakey interview.

72. Transcription (Feb. 1973).

73. Ibid.

74. Milton Meltzer, ed., *In Their Own Words: A History of the American Negro—1865–1916* (New York: Thomas Y. Crowell, 1965), 150.

75. Franklin, *From Slavery to Freedom*, 498–99.

76. Powell interview.

77. Franklin, *From Slavery to Freedom*, 502–3.

78. For discussions of these two organizations, see "CBS Legislative Weekend Caucus Readies for Assault on 'Reaganomics' in 1982," *Jet*, 15 Oct. 1981, pp. 5–6; "Congressional Black Caucus," *Crisis* (April 1981), 116–131; Isaiah J. Poole, "The Congressional Black Caucus Struggles to Find a New Way," *Black Enterprise* (Dec. 1981), 37; "Afro-American Patrolmen Honor Black Mayors in Chicago," *Jet*, 1 Nov. 1973, pp. 24–26; "Southern Black Mayors Conference," *Jet*, 1 March 1973, pp. 24–34; "Other Black Caucus," *Black Enterprise* (Jan. 1972), 28–33.

79. Transcription (Jan. 1973).

80. Lindsey interview.

CHAPTER 6

1. *Cong. Rec.*, 8 April 1968, p. 9249.

2. U.S. Cong., House, Subcommittee on Census and Statistics of the Committee on Post Office and Civil Service, *Martin Luther King, Jr., Holiday Bill*, 98th Cong. 1st sess., H.R. 800 (Washington, D.C.: GPO, 1983), 23–24.

3. Wright interview.

4. "A New Apostle of a New Day Comes to Judgment," *ADW*, 3 Jan. 1957, p. 3.

5. Thaddeus T. Stokes, "Rev. King Calls on All Federal Branches to Oppose Segregation," *ADW*, 2 Jan. 1957, p. 4.

6. J.H. Knight, "Montgomery's Rev. King in Newport News: 'Two Worlds: The Dying Old, The Emerging New.' " *Norfork Journal and Guide*, 11 Jan. 1958, p. 2.

7. Ibid.

8. Martin Luther King, Jr., Center for Social Change Archive.

9. Stokes, p. 4.

10. U.S. Cong., House, Subcommittee on Census and Population of the Committee on Post Office and Civil Service, *Designate the Birthday of Martin Luther King, Jr., as a Legal Public Holiday,* 94th Cong. 1st sess., H.R. 1810 (Washington, D.C.: GPO, 1975), 26.

11. Ibid., 21.

12. House Subcommittee on Census and Statistics, 42.

13. House subcommittee on Census and Population, 26.

14. House Subcommittee on Census and Statistics, 73.

15. U.S. Cong., Senate, Committee on the Judiciary, and House, Committee on Post Office and Civil Service, *Martin Luther King, Jr., Holiday Bill,* 96th Cong., 1st sess., S. 25 (Washington, D.C.: GPO, 1979), 31.

16. House Subcommittee on Census and Statistics, 9.

17. House Subcommittee on Census and Population, 26.

18. Senate Committee on the Judiciary, and House Committee on Post Office and Civil Service, 81.

19. Ibid, 72.

20. Edward D. Sargent, "100 Give Thanks for Passage of Holiday Measure," *Washington Post,* 20 Oct. 1983, p. A17.

21. House Subcommittee on Census and Statistics, 77.

22. House Subcommittee on Census and Population, 4–5.

23. Senate Committee on the Judiciary, and House Committee on Post Office and Civil Service, 19.

24. I am indebted to Peter Wood for this quotation. He copied it from the caption of a Raphaelle Peale portrait of Absalom Jones, part of an art exhibition on "The Black Presence in the Era of the American Revolution 1770–1800," which hung in the Smithsonian Institution's National Portrait Gallery. Letter received from Peter Wood, 6 Aug. 1973.

25. "New Albany Notes," *Indianapolis Recorder,* 30 Sept. 1899, p. 1.

26. "Will Ask a National Holiday for Negroes," *Terre Haute Daily Tribune,* 22 Sept. 1903, p. 1.

27. Transcription (June 1972).

28. House Subcommittee on Census and Population, 17.

29. Senate Committee on the Judiciary, and House Committee on Post Office and Civil Service, 34.

30. Ibid., 59.

31. Ibid., 67.

32. Ibid., 34.

33. Ibid., 7.

34. Ibid., 19.

35. House Subcommittee on Census and Statistics, 21.

36. Ibid.

37. Ibid., 67.

38. Senate Committee on the Judiciary; and House Committee on Post Office and Civil Service, 75.

39. House Subcommittee on Census and Statistics, 24.

40. Senate Committee on the Judiciary, and House Committee on Post Office and Civil Service, 27–28.

41. Ibid., 72.

42. Ibid., 73.

43. Ibid., 21.

44. Ibid., 36.

45. Ibid., 41.

46. Ibid., 43.

47. Ibid., 49.

48. Ibid., 48.

49. Ibid., 86.

50. House Subcommittee on Census and Statistics, 79.

51. Ibid., 18.

52. David S. Broder, "The King Holiday: More Than Politics," *Washington Post,* 17 Aug. 1983, p. A23.

53. Coretta Scott King, "How We Can Observe This Holiday," *Washington Post,* 23 Oct. 1983, p. C8a.

54. Sargent, p. A17.

Bibliography

BOOKS

Abrahams, Roger D. *Deep Down in the Jungle: Negro Narrative Folklore from the Streets of Philadelphia*. Chicago: Aldine, 1970.

Angelou, Maya. *I Know Why the Caged Bird Sings*. New York: Random House, 1969.

Baker, Houston A., Jr., ed. *Black Literature in America*. New York: McGraw-Hill, 1971.

Bernard, Jacqueline. *Journey Toward Freedom: The Story of Sojourner Truth*. New York: Norton, 1967.

Boatner, Mark Mayo, III. *The Civil War Dictionary*. New York: David McKay, 1959.

Bogle, Donald. *Toms, Coons, Mulattoes, Mammies, & Bucks: An Interpretive History of Blacks in American Film*. New York: Viking Press, 1973.

Botkin, B. A., ed. *Lay My Burden Down: A Folk History of Slavery*. Chicago: Univ. of Chicago Press, 1969.

Brewer, J. Mason. *Worser Days and Better Times: The Folklore of the North Carolina Negro*. Chicago: Quadrangle Books, 1965.

Brown, William Wells. *The Escape; Or A Leap for Freedom*. Philadelphia: Historic Publications, 1969.

Browne, Ray B., ed. *Lincoln-Lore: Lincoln in the Popular Mind*. Bowling Green, Ohio: Popular Press, 1974.

Buckmaster, Henrietta. *Let My People Go: The Story of the Underground Railroad and the Growth of the Abolition Movement*. Boston: Beacon Press, 1959.

Burns, Roger, ed. *Am I Not A Man and A Brother: The Anti-slavery Crusade of Revolutionary America, 1688–1788*. New York: Chelsea House, 1977.

Carawan, Guy, and Candie Carawan, eds. *We Shall Overcome!: Songs of the Southern Freedom Movement*. New York: Oak Publications, 1963.

Carter, Harold A. *The Prayer Tradition of Black People*. Valley Forge, Pa.: Judson Press, 1976.

Chapman, Abraham, ed. *Black Voices: An Anthology of Afro-American Literature*. New York: New American Library, 1968.

Chestnut, Mary Boykin. *A Diary from Dixie*. Ed. Ben Ames Williams, Cambridge, Mass.: Riverside Press, 1949.

Cleaver, Eldridge. *Soul On Ice*. New York: Dell, 1970.

Coffin, Tristram Potter, and Hennig Cohen, eds. *Folklore: From the Working Folk of America*. Garden City, N.Y.: Anchor Press, 1974.

Dance, Daryl C. *Shuckin' and Jivin': Contemporary Folklore from Black Americans*. Bloomington: Indiana Univ. Press, 1978.

Donald, David. *Lincoln Reconsidered: Essays on the Civil War Era*. New York: Vintage, 1961.

Dorson, Richard M. *American Negro Folktales*. New York: Fawcett World Library, 1970.

Douglass, Frederick. *My Bondage and My Freedom*. New York: Arno Press and *The New York Times*, 1968.

———. *Narrative of the Life of Frederick Douglass: An American Slave*. New York: New American Library, 1968.

Du Bois, W.E.B. *The Souls of Black Folks*. In *Three Negro Classics*, ed. John Hope Franklin. New York: Avon, 1965.

Dunbar, Paul Laurence. *The Life and Complete Works of Paul Laurence Dunbar*. New York: Kraus Reprint Co., 1971.

Dundes, Alan, ed. *Mother Wit from the Laughing Barrel: Reading in the Interpretation of Afro-American Folklore*. Englewood Cliffs, N.J.: Prentice-Hall, 1973.

Essien-Udom, E.U. *Black Nationalism: A Search for an Identity in America*. New York: Dell, 1969.

Evers, Charles. *Evers*. Cleveland: World, 1971.

Franklin, John Hope. *From Slavery to Freedom: A History of Negro Americans*. New York: Vintage, 1969.

Frazier, E. Franklin. *Black Bourgeoisie: The Rise of a New Middle Class in the United States*. London: Collier/Macmillan, 1957.

———. *The Negro Church in America*. New York: Schocken, 1974.

Friedman, Albert B., ed. *The Viking Book of Folk Ballads of the English-Speaking World*. New York: Viking Press, 1971.

Genovese, Eugene. *Roll, Jordan, Roll: The World the Slaves Made*. New York: Vintage, 1976.

Gregory, Dick. *From the Back of the Bus*. New York: Avon, 1966.

Haley, Alex. *Roots: The Saga of an American Family*. Garden City, N.Y.: Doubleday, 1976.

Haskins, James. *Jokes from Black Folks*. Garden City, N.Y.: Doubleday, 1973.

Haynes, Elizabeth Ross. *The Black Boy of Atlanta*. Boston: The House of Edinboro, 1952.

Heilbut, Tony. *The Gospel Sound: Good News and Bad Times*. Garden City, N.J.: Anchor/Doubleday, 1975.

Henderson, Stephen. *Understanding the New Black Poetry: Black Speech and Black Music as Poetic References*. New York: William Morrow, 1973.

Herskovits, Melville J. *The Myth of the Negro Past*. Boston: Beacon Press, 1941.

Higginson, Thomas Wentworth. *Army Life in a Black Regiment*. Boston: Beacon Press, 1962.

Himes, Chester. *The Quality of Hurt: The Autobiography of Chester Himes*. Garden City, N.Y.: Doubleday, 1972.

Hughes, Langston. *The Weary Blues*. New York: Knopf, 1926.

———, and Arna Bontemps, eds. *Book of Negro Folklore*. New York: Dodd, Mead, 1958.

Jackson, Bruce, ed. *Wake up Dead Man: Afro-American Worksongs from Texas Prisons*. Cambridge, Mass.: Harvard Univ. Press, 1972.

Johnson, Clifton H., ed. *God Struck Me Dead: Religious Conversion Experiences and Autobiographies of Ex-Slaves*. Philadelphia: Pilgrim Press, 1969.

Johnson, Guy B. *John Henry: Tracking Down a Negro Legend*. Chapel Hill: Univ. of North Carolina Press, 1929.

Johnson, James Weldon. *Along This Way: The Autobiography of James Weldon Johnson*. New York: Viking Press, 1968.

———. *God's Trombones: Seven Negro Sermons in Verse*. New York: Penguin, 1972.

Jones, LeRoi, and Larry Neal, eds. *Black Fire: An Anthology of Afro-American Writing*. New York: William Morrow, 1968.

Killens, John Oliver. *The Cotillion, or One Good Bull Is Half the Herd*. New York: Trident, 1971.

Kochman, Thomas, comp. *Rappin' and Stylin' Out: Communication in Urban Black America*. Urbana: Univ. of Illinois Press, 1972.

Levine, Lawrence W. *Black Culture and Black Consciousness: Afro-American Folk Thought from Slavery to Freedom*. New York: Oxford Univ. Press, 1977.

Lewis, David L. *King: A Critical Biography*. New York: Praeger, 1970.

Lewis, Hylan. *Blackways of Kent*. Chapel Hill: Univ. of North Carolina Press, 1955.

Lincoln, C. Eric. *The Black Church Since Frazier*. New York: Schocken, 1975.

———. *The Black Muslims in America*. Boston: Beacon Press, 1961.

Locke, Alain, ed. *The New Negro*. New York: Atheneum, 1970.

Long, Richard A., and Eugenia W. Collier, eds. *Afro-American Writing: An Anthology of Prose and Poetry*. New York: New York Univ. Press, 1972.

Louis, Joe. *Joe Louis: My Life*, with Edna and Art Rust, Jr. New York: Berkley Books, 1981.

Lovell, John, Jr. *Black Song: The Forge and the Flame; the Story of How the Afro-American Spiritual Was Hammered Out*. New York: Macmillan, 1972.

Mann, Arthur. *The Jackie Robinson Story*. New York: Grosset & Dunlap, 1950.

Mays, Benjamin E. *The Negro's God as Reflected in His Literature*. New York: Atheneum, 1969.

McCluskey, John. *Look What They Done to My Song*. New York: Random House, 1974.

Mitchell, George. *Blow My Blues Away.* Baton Rouge: Louisiana State Univ. Press, 1971.

Moody, Anne. *Coming of Age in Mississippi.* New York: Dial Press, 1969.

Morgan, Kathryn L. *Children of Strangers: The Stories of a Black Family.* Philadelphia: Temple Univ. Press, 1980.

Morrson, Toni. *Song of Solomon.* New York: Knopf, 1977.

Murray, Albert. *Stomping the Blues.* New York: McGraw-Hill, 1976.

Nash, Gary B. *Class and Society in Early America.* Englewood Cliffs, N.J.: Prentice-Hall, 1970.

The New York Times Film Reviews, 1973–1974. New York: *New York Times* & Arno Press, 1975.

Nicholas, A. X., ed. *Woke Up This Mornin': Poetry of the Blues.* New York: Bantam, 1973.

Nunn, W. C. *Texas Under the Carpetbaggers.* Austin: Univ. of Texas Press, 1962.

O'Brien, John, ed. *Interviews With Black Writers.* New York: Lineright, 1973.

Oliver, Paul. *The Meaning of the Blues.* New York: Collier/Macmillan, 1969.

Peterson, Robert. *Only the Ball Was White.* Englewood Cliffs, N.J.: Prentice-Hall, 1970.

Preston, Dickson. *Trappe: The Story of an Old-Fashioned Town.* Easton, Md: Economy Printing Co., 1976.

Quarles, Benjamin, ed. *Great Lives Observed: Frederick Douglass.* Englewood Cliffs, N.J.: Prentice-Hall, 1968.

Reynolds, Barbara A. *Jesse Jackson: The Man, the Movement, the Myth.* Chicago: Nelson-Hall, 1975.

Richardson, Willis, ed. *Plays and Pageants from the Life of the Negro,* Washington, D.C.: Associated Publishers, 1924.

Roberts, Randy. *Papa Jack: Jack Johnson and the Era of White Hopes.* New York: Free Press, 1983.

Robinson, Jackie. *I Never Had It Made,* as told to Alfred Duckett. New York: Putnam, 1972.

———. *Jackie Robinson: My Own Story,* as told to Wendell Smith. New York: Greenberg Publisher, 1948.

Rodman, Hyman. *Lower-Class Families: The Poverty in Negro Trinidad.* New York: Oxford Univ. Press, 1971.

Roeder, Bill. *Jackie Robinson.* New York: A.S. Barnes, 1950.

Scarborough, Dorothy. *On the Trail of Negro Folk-Songs.* Cambridge: Harvard Univ. Press, 1925.

Schuyler, George S. *Black No More.* College Park, Md.: McGrath, 1969.

Shaw, Archer H., comp. and ed. *The Lincoln Encyclopedia: The Spoken and Written Words of Abraham Lincoln Arranged for Ready Reference.* New York: Macmillan, 1950.

Sheppard, William H. *Pioneers in the Congo.* Louisville: Pentecostal Publishing Co., n.d.

Spalding, Albert G. *America's National Game: Historic Facts Concerning the Beginning, Evolution, Development and Popularity of Baseball, with*

Personal Reminiscences of Its Vicissitudes, Its Victories and Its Votaries. New
  York: American Sports, 1911.
Spalding, Henry D., comp. and ed. *Encyclopedia of Black Folklore and Humor.*
  Middle Village, N.Y.: Jonathan Edwards, 1972.
Taylor, Mildred D. *Roll of Thunder, Hear My Cry.* New York: Dial, 1976.
Thurman, Howard. *With Head and Heart: The Autobiography of Howard
  Thurman.* New York: Harcourt, Brace, Jovanovich, 1979.
Titon, Jeff Todd. *Early Downhome Blues: A Musical and Cultural Analysis.*
  Urbana: Univ. of Illinois Press, 1977.
Turner, Darwin T. *Black American Literature: Essays, Poetry, Fiction, Dramas.*
  Columbus, Ohio: Charles E. Merrill, 1970.
Tygiel, Jules. *Baseball's Great Experiment: Jackie Robinson and His Legacy.*
  New York: Oxford Univ. Press, 1983.
Walsh, William S. *Curiosities of Popular Customs and Ceremonies.*
  Philadelphia: Lippincott, 1898.
Washington, Booker T. *Up From Slavery.* In *Three Negro Classics,* ed. John
  Hope Franklin. New York: Avon, 1965.
White, Walter. *Rope and Faggot: A Biography of Judge Lynch.* New York:
  Knopf, 1929.
Whittier, John Greenlead. *Anti-Slavery Poems: Songs of Labor and Reform.*
  Boston: Houghton Mifflin, 1888.
Williams, Francis M., Francis Lynn, Martha L. Perkins, and Ben E. Boone, III,
  eds. *The Story of Todd County, 1820–1970.* Nashville, N.P., 1972.
Work, John W., ed. *American Negro Songs and Spirituals.* New York: Bonanza,
  1940.
Wright, Jr., Richard R. *Eighty-Seven Years Behind the Black Curtain: An
  Autobiography.* Philadelphia: Rare Book Co., 1965.
Yetman, Norman R., ed. *Life Under the "Peculiar Institution": Selections from
  the Slave Narrative Collection.* New York: Holt, Rinehart and Winston, 1970.

ANTHOLOGY ARTICLES

Cleaver, Eldridge. "As Crinkly as Yours." In *Mother Wit from the Laughing
  Barrel: Readings in the Interpretation of Afro-American Folklore,* ed. Alan
  Dundes, 9–21. Englewood Cliffs, N.J.: Prentice-Hall, 1973.
Cross, Paulette. "Jokes and Black Consciousness: A Collection with Interviews."
  In *Mother Wit From the Laughing Barrel: Readings in the Interpretation of
  Afro-American Folklore,* ed. Alan Dundes, 649–69. Englewood Cliffs, N.J.:
  Prentice-Hall, 1973.
Cullen, Countee. "Heritage." In *Black Literature in America,* ed. Houston A.
  Baker, Jr., 154. New York: McGraw-Hill, 1971.
Garnett, Henry Highland. "An Address to the Slaves of the United States of
  America." In *Afro-American Writing: An Anthology Prose and Poetry,* eds.
  Richard A. Long and Eugenia W. Collier, 39. New York; New York Univ.
  Press, 1972.

Gordon, Robert Winslow. "Negro 'Shouts' from Georgia." In *Mother Wit from the Laughing Barrel: Readings in the Interpretation of Afro-American Folklore,* ed. Alan Dundes, 445–51. Englewood Cliffs, N.J.: Prentice-Hall, 1973.

Grant, Caesar. "All God's Children Had Wings." *In Book of Negro Folklore,* eds. Langston Hughes and Arna Bontemps, 62–65. New York: Dodd, Mead, 1958.

Horton, John. "Time and Cool People." In *Rappin' and Stylin' Out: Communication in Urban Black America,* comp. Thomas Kochman, 19–31. Urbana: Univ. of Illinois Press, 1972.

King, B. B. "Why I Sing the Blues." In *Woke Up This Mornin': Poetry of the Blues,* ed. A. X. Nicholas, 116–18. New York: Bantam, 1973.

Locke, Alain. "The New Negro." In *The New Negro* ed. Alain Locke, 44–55. New York: Atheneum, 1970.

McCoo, Edward J. "Ethiopia At the Bar of Justice." In *Plays and Pageants from the Life of the Negro,* ed. Willis Richardson. Washington, D.C.: Associated Publishers, 1924.

Neal, Larry, "And Shine Swam On." In *Black Fire: An Anthology of Afro-American Writing,* eds. LeRoi Jones and Larry Neal, 638–56. New York: Morrow, 1968.

Thompson, Harold W. "King Charley of Albany." In *American Negro Folklore,* ed. J. Mason Brewer, 32–34. New York: Quadrangle/*New York Times* Book Co., 1968.

Wiggins, William H., Jr. "Jack Johnson as Bad Nigger: The Folklore of His Life." In *Contemporary Black Thought: The Best from the Black Scholar,* eds. Robert Chrisman and Nathan Hare, 53–70. Indianapolis: Bobbs-Merrill, 1973.

MAGAZINE AND JOURNAL ARTICLES

Black Enterprise

"The Congressional Black Caucus Struggles to Find a New Way," (Dec. 1981), 37.
"The Other Black Caucus," (Jan. 1972), 28–33.

Black Scholar

"Black Folktales in the Novels of John O. Killens," (Nov. 1971).
"Jack Johnson as Bad Nigger: The Folklore of His Life" (Jan. 1971).
"Martin Luther King and the Style of the Black Sermon" (Sept. 1971).

Black World

"African Liberation Day" (May 1973).
"African Liberation Day: An Assessment" (Oct. 1974).
"African Liberation Month" (May 1974).

"Do Clothes Unmake the Man?" (May 1974).
"Second World Black and African Festival of Arts and Culture" (Jan. 1975).
"The Second World Festival of Negro Arts" (Nov. 1971).
"Washington's [D.C.] 400 Introduces Debs" (April 1948).

Crisis

"Congressional Black Caucus" (April 1981).
"The Drama Among Black Folk" (Aug. 1916).
"First World Festival of Negro Arts: An Afro-American View" (June–July 1966).
"The National Emancipation Exposition" (Nov. 1913).
"The Philadelphia Pageant" (Aug. 1916).
"The Waco Horror" (July 1916).

Douglass' Monthly

"Celebration at North Elba" (Sept. 1860).
"Celebration at Ithaca" (July 1862).
"Celebration of the Twenty-First Anniversary of West India Emancipation at Geneva" (Aug. 1859).
"First of August at Myricks" (Sept. 1862).
"Fourth of July Celebration at Himrods" (Aug. 1862).
"January First 1863" (Jan. 1963).
"Jerry Rescue Celebration" (Nov. 1860).
"The Jerry Rescue Celebration" (Dec. 1860).
"The Slaveholders Rebellion" (Aug. 1862).
"Speech of Frederick Douglass" (Sept. 1860).

Ebony

"African Liberation Day" (July 1973).
"American Black Achievement Awards: A Tribute to Black Excellence" (Feb. 1984).
"Black College Queens for 1977–78" (April 1979).
"Black Expo Comes of Age" (Dec. 1971).
"Coming of Age: A Baptist Minister Borrows African Tradition to Devise Ritual for Son's 16th Birthday" (Dec. 1974).
"*Ebony* Fashion Fair to Tour Country" (Oct. 1959).
"Juneteenth: Texas Carries on tradition of emancipation holiday with amusement park celebration" (June 1951).
"Liberation Look: Thirteenth Annual *Ebony* Fashion Fair" (Sept. 1970).
"Local Chairman paves way for *Ebony* Fashion Fair" (Sept. 1966).
"Natural Look" (June 1966).
"Natural Look: Is It Here to Stay?" (Jan. 1969).
"Photo-Editorial: Are Negroes Losing Their Humor?" (Jan. 1951).
"Shaft in Africa" (March 1973).
"There Really Is a Timbuktu" (Feb. 1972).

"Top Styles from Europe in *Ebony's Fashion Fair*" *(Nov. 1982)*.
"*A Tribute to Black Excellence*" *(April 1983)*.
"*Twelfth Annual Fashion Fair Theme: Flapper Returns with Soul*" *(Oct. 1964)*.
"*We Still Have a Dream*" *(Nov. 1983)*.
"*What Is Black Beauty?*" *(Nov. 1980)*.
"*Young Negro Designers Join Ebony's* Fashion Fair" (Sept. 1961).

Encore

"African Liberation Day, 1977: Supporting Southern Africa," 23 May 1977.
"Black Beauty in Other Pageants" (Sept. 1978).
"Eartha Kitt out cattin' again," 21 Feb. 1978.
"Postively Black Is the Word for Miss Black America" (Sept. 1978).
"Timbuktu," 3 April 1978.

Essence

"Eartha!" (June 1978).
"How I Came to Celebrate Kwanzaa" (Dec. 1979).

Freedomways

"Black Expo—Matrix of the Design for Unity" (1971).
"Bob Marley: Up From Babylon" (1981).

Jet

"African Liberation Day Is Success," 14 June 1973.
"Afro-American Patrolmen Honor Black Mayors in Chicago," 1 Nov. 1973.
"Black Nutritionist Finds Soul Food Unhealthy—Black Students Demand It," 8 April 1971.
"Black Stars Boost Black Expo 1971," 23 Sept. 1971.
"CBC Legislative Weekend Caucus Readies for Assault on 'Reaganomics' in 1982," 15 Oct. 1981.
"Ebony Fashion Fair to Tour Country," 14 Oct. 1959.
"Ex-Miss America Endures Pain, Embarrassment Sparked by Flap over Nude Pictures," 6 Aug. 1984.
"15,000 Gather for African Liberation Day," 15 June 1972.
"500 Gather to Send Ben Owens to Final Reward," 24 Feb. 1977.
"July 4th Speech of Fred Douglass Haunts U.S. Today," 8 July 1976.
"'Juneteenth' Day Becomes State Holiday in Texas," June 1979.
"Kitt Sizzles on Broadway," 31 Aug. 1978.
"Marilyn McCoo, Robert Guillaime Host TV Show of Black Celebrity Achievers," 9 Jan. 1984.
"Miss Black America '75," 25 Sept. 1975.
"New Boom in Black Beauty Pageant Queens," 17 Aug. 1972.
"PUSH Expo '76 Sparks New Direction: Stars Abound," 21 Oct. 1976.
"Southern Black Mayors Conference," 1 March 1973.

"Stevie Wonder: Uses Fame in Campaign for King Holiday" (Dec. 1980).
"University of Alabama Elects First Black Queen as Segregation Stumbles" (Dec. 1973).

Journal of American Folklore

"African Institutions in America" (Jan.–March 1905).
"Easter Rock: A Louisiana Negro Ceremony" (1942).

Journal of Negro History

"Celebrations of the Anniversary of the Emancipation in Hamilton, Upper Canada, 1859" (April 1928).
"Cudjo's Own Story of the Last African Slaves," 12 Oct. 1927.
"Martin R. Delaney and Robert Campbell: Black Americans in Search of an African Colony" (April 1926).
"Negro History Week" (April 1926).

Nation

"Movin' on up," 1 Oct. 1983.
"There she goes, Miss America," 4–11 Aug. 1984.

Negro Digest

"Chitterlings: Culinary Orphan" (Nov. 1946).
"Historic Afro-American Holidays" (Feb. 1967).
"The Meaning and Message of Black Power" (Nov. 1966).

Negro History Bulletin

" 'Emancipation,' an Unpublished Poem by Paul Laurence Dunbar" (Feb. 1973).
"Firm Foundations" (March 1954).
"The Historical Origin and Significance of the Afro-American History Month Observance" (Oct.–Nov.–Dec. 1982).

Newsweek

"For want of a bathing suit," 6 Aug. 1984.
"Timbuktu," 13 March 1978.
"Transition: Died," 14 July 1947.

New Yorker

"The Talk of the Town: Banker," 5 July 1947.
"Timbuktu," 20 March 1978.

New York Folklore Quarterly

"The Metamorphosis of the Humor of the Black American" (1970).
"Pinkster Ode, Albany, 1803" (1952).

People Weekly

"Haunted by her past," 6 Aug. 1984.
"She's black and Miss America, but Vanessa Williams is most of all her own woman," 3 Oct. 1983.
"Vanessa's story," 6 Aug. 1984.

Phylon

"Indirect Technique for the Measurement of Changes in Black Identity" (March 1977).
"The John Canoe Festival" (1942).

Sepia

"African Kingdom in South Carolina" (April 1975).
"Christmas from a Black Perspective" (Dec. 1973).
"The Glory That Was Timbuktu" (March 1972).
"Stevie Wonder Tells Why Nation Needs MLK Holiday" (Dec. 1980).
"Will There Ever Be a Black Miss America?" (Feb. 1975).

Southern Exposure

"Celebrate Freedom: Juneteenth" (1977).
"Hog Heaven: Barbecue in the South" (Summer–Fall 1977).

Time

"In New York: The Miss Is a Hit," 17 Oct. 1983.
"Milestones: Dead," 14 July, 1947.
"Timbuktu," 13 March 1978.
"There she goes, Miss America," 6 Aug. 1984.

Miscellaneous Magazines and Journals

Ayoung, Millicent R. "The Family Reunion," *Ethnology* 5 (1966).
"Beauty Contests—the Stakes are Big." *U.S. News and World Report,* 6 Aug. 1984.
Chon, William. "A National Celebration: The Fourth of July in American History." *Cultures* 3, no. 2 (1976), 141–56.
Earle, Alice Morse. "Pinkster Day." *Outlook* 46 (1894), 743–44.
Edgerton, Michael. "Mas'—Just Like Carnival Day in Trinidad." *Tuesday: At Home* 4 (Jan. 1975), 10.
Garvey, Marcus. "Centenary of Negro Emancipation." *The Blackman* 5 (May–June 1934), 11–12.
"James Brown Goes 'Natural.'" *Tan* (Dec. 1968).
Julian, Bea. "7 Kwanzaa Principles Help Build Ivory Coast." *Ebony, Jr.* 7, no. 8 (Dec. 1979), 112–17.
Kilgore, Thomas, Jr. "Christmas from a Black Perspective." *Sepia* 27, no. 3 (Dec. 1973), 18–19.

Richard, M. B. "Easter Day on the Plantation." *The Plantation Missionary* 3, no. 2 (1892), 12–14.

Schlicher, Raymond J. "Commemorating Emancipation." *The Palempsest* 28, no. 5 (May 1947), 150–57.

"Timbuktu." *New Leader*, 27 March 1978, p. 28.

"Timbuktu." *Saturday Review*, 29 April 1978, p. 26.

"Timbuktu." *Theatre Crafts* (May 1978), 13–15.

Waldron, Webb. " 'Massa, Tell 'Em We're Rising!' " *The Progressive*, 12 March 1945, pp. 9–10.

———. " 'Massa, Tell 'Em We're Rising!' " *Reader's Digest* 46 (April 1945), 53–56.

Watson, G. Llewellyn. "Patterns of Black Protest in Jamaica: The Case of the Ras-Tafarians." *Journal of Black Studies* 4 (March 1974), 329–43.

Wiggins, David K. "The Play of Slave Children in the Plantation Communities of the Old South, 1820–1860." *Journal of Sport History* 7, no. 2 (Summer 1980).

Wiggins, William H., Jr. "*In the Rapture:* The Black Aesthetic and Folk Drama." *Callaloo*, no. 2 (Feb. 1978), 103–11.

———. "January 1: The Afro-American's 'Days of Days.' " *Prospects: An Annual of American Cultural Studies* 4 (1979), 331–53.

———. "The Structure and Dynamics of Folklore in the Novel Form: The Case of John O. Killens." *Keystone Folklore Quarterly* 17, no. 3 (Fall 1972), 92–118.

NEWSPAPER ARTICLES

[New York] Amsterdam News

"Brooklyn West Indians set Labor Day festival," 28 Aug. 1971, p. D-1.

"Fitting end to marvelous Parade Day," 16 Sept. 1972, p. A1.

"Hi, There!: A Real West Indian Gala!!!!," 11 Sept. 1971, p. D-2.

"It Looked Like All the World was West Indian!; Unity Is Theme as Many Groups March Together," 8 Sept. 1973, p. C-1.

"Join African-American Day Parade (Largest Black Parade in America) a Day of Black Unity Sunday, September 10, 9172, in Harlem, 1 p.m.," 26 Aug. 1972, p. A2.

"Labor Day: Brooklyn a Happy Caribbean Isle!," 8 Sept. 1973, p. D-1.

"Mardi Gras Parade Ends Program," 2 Sept. 1967, p. 32.

"Miss Black Teenage World Crowned," 10 Sept. 1977, p. 11.

"1M To See West India Boro Labor Day Parades," 18 Aug. 1973, p. C-1.

"350,000 expected at Afro-American fete," 9 Sept. 1972, pp. A1, A3.

"West Indian-American weekend carnival a smash bash in Boro!" 11 Sept. 1971, p. D-1.

"West Indian Day Parade: Preparation Is Underway," 5 Aug. 1972, p. B10.

Atlanta Daily World

"The Addresses of the 'Emancipators,' " 4 Jan. 1955, p. 5.

"Albany College Choir Sings Emancipation Day," 31 Dec. 1947, p. 1.

"Arnold Pleases Audience with Emancipation Day Address Here," 3 Jan. 1953, p. 3.

"Atlantan In Emancipation Address to Albany Group,"3 Jan. 1959, p. 1.

"Atlantans Set for Emancipation Day," 31 Dec. 1941, p. 1.

Auburn Avenue Says: Rev. Borders Says 'I Am Somebody' Over the Radio," 13 Jan. 1943, p. 6.

"Ballot Is Road to Economic Freedom, Says Mrs. Bethune," 3 Jan. 1950, p. 1.

"Borders Delivers Emancipation Day Address in Indiana," 5 Jan. 1950, p. 2.

"Brunswick, Ga.," 2 Jan. 1937, p. 8.

"Brunswick Church Site of Colorful January 1 Exercise," 8 Jan. 1940, p. 2.

"Citizens Observe Emancipation Day in Thomaston, Ga.," 28 May 1938, p. 1.

"Congressman Diggs to Give Emancipation Address," 1 Jan. 1956, p. 1.

"Covington, Ga." 6 Jan. 1949, p. 2.

"De Priest Speaks In Goldsboro January 1st," 4 Jan. 1934, p. 1.

"Dobbs Delivers Brilliant Emancipation Day Address," 4 Jan. 1952, p. 2.

"Dramatic Presentation to Feature Emancipation Day: Star-Studded Cast Has Been Selected For NAACP Drama," 30 Dec. 1947, p. 1.

"Emancipation Celebration," 30 Dec. 1933, p. 6.

"Emancipation Day Program at Wheat St. Features Rep. Diggs," 31 Dec. 1955, p. 1.

"Emancipation Event at Wheat Street Church," 28 Dec. 1947, p. 1.

"Expect Throng at NAACP Meet Saturday," 29 Dec. 1937, p. 1.

"Ex-Slaves to Also Receive Honor at Program this Afternoon. Hon. Ben J. Davis Is Principal Speaker," 1 Jan. 1932, p. 2.

"The First One Hundred Years," 6 Jan. 1963, p. 4.

"Increase Vote Strength to Stop Bias Says Rep. Diggs to Atlanta: Emancipation Day Speaker Deplores Low Registration," 3 Jan. 1956, p. 1.

"Judge Delaney Raps Official Silence . . . urges Negroes to Join Fight for Freedom Now," 2 Jan. 1952, pp. 1, 4.

"Judge J. Earl Dearing, Emancipation Proclamation Speaker, Today," 1 Jan. 1964, p. 4.

"Leaders Urged to Resist Segregation by NAACP," 3 Jan. 1956, p. 3.

"Miles Prexy Is Emancipation Day Speaker, January 1st," 27 Dec. 1944, p. 5.

" 'Miss Teenage America' Seeks Black Entrants," 11 Aug. 1977, p. 3.

"NAACP Emancipation Day Sidelights at Wheat Street," 3 Jan. 1956, p. 2.

"NAACP to Observe 80th Anniversary of Emancipation," 28 Dec. 1948, p. 4.

"Negro Slavery, Freedom, Education," 29 Dec. 1939, p. 6.

"Negroes Want Normal American Privileges—Carey," 2 Jan. 1945, pp. 1, 6.

"Noted NAACP Figure Is In City: Walter White Gives Emancipation Day Address Here," 11 Dec. 1934, pp. 1, 5.

"Over 3,000 to Hear 'Mr. Civil Rights,' Miss Mattiwilda Dobbs," 1 Jan. 1955, pp. 1, 4.

"Parade to Precede Emancipation Meeting," 1 Jan. 1944, p. 1.

"Pinkston Speaks at NAACP Meeting," 27 Dec. 1942, p. 1.

"Progress of Race Lauded by President," 9 Jan. 1936, p. 1.

"Rev. C.K. Steele Asks Albanians to Complete the Job of Freedom," 1 Jan. 1966, p. 5.

"Rev. Hurley to Be Emancipation Speaker," 30 Dec. 1940, p. 1.

"Ribbins Makes Eloquent Emancipation Day Speech," 9 Jan. 1946, p. 6.

"Searcy to Be Emancipation Day Speaker," 29 May 1963, p. 3.

" 'Segregation Is Out!' Borders Tells Stamford," 5 Jan. 1965, p. 2.

"Sound Advice from Congressman Diggs," 3 Jan. 1956, p. 6.

"The Speeches Went 'Round an' 'Round," 8 Jan. 1941, p. 6.

"The Spirit of Booker T. Washington," 31 Dec. 1933, p. 4.

"Struggles of Race Depicted: Spectacular Parade, Pageant, Address Add Color to Fête," 13 Jan. 1936, p. 5.

"They Discuss 'Freedom Day' Measure," 27 Dec. 1942, p. 1.

"Thomaston," 26 May 1948, p. 6.

"Thomaston," 25 May 1950, p. 4.

"Thousands See Colorful Parade," 2 Jan. 1944, pp. 1, 2.

"Two Cities To Celebrate Emancipation," 28 Dec. 1947, p. 2.

"U.S. Warned to Make Democracy Work at Home," 2 Jan. 1947, p. 6.

"Walter White Thrills Large Audience," 1 Jan. 1935, pp. 1, 4.

"Washington, Ga.," 31 May 1943, p. 5.

"Wheat Street Baptist Ready for Emancipation Day Throng," 1 Jan. 1952, p. 1.

Bloomington Herald-Telephone

" 'Juneteenth': Elizabeth Burham Honors the Day," 21 June 1984, p. 9.

"Sports World Coming out of the Closet," 20 May 1978, p. 9.

Williams, Kathy. "Miss New York First Black Miss America." *Sunday Bloomington Herald-Telephone, 18 Sept. 1983, pp. 1, 5.*

Chicago Defender

"Beauties Await 'Miss Bronz America' Contest," 24 Aug. 1940, p. 3.

"Bud's Prize Bathing Beauties," 20 Aug. 1932, p. 16.

"Duke Ellington to Meet Kiddies at Picnic: Beauty Contest Big Feature of Picnic," 1 Aug. 1931, p. 16.

"Joe Louis, Jr., to Greet Throng," 7 Aug. 1948, p. 18.

"Lens View of the 19th Annual Bud Billiken Parade and Picnic," 14 Aug. 1948, p. 12.

" 'Negro Day' to Be Gala Affair Here: Pageant Will Be Held in Soldiers Field," 12 Aug. 1933, pp. 1, 4.

"Railroad Pageant in Bud's Parade: Crowd to See Trains Move Along Route," 31 July 1948, p. 21.

"Rufus Dawes [Pres. of A Century of Progress] Extends Welcome to Queen; Thousands Cheer," 5 Aug. 1983, pp. 1, 4.

"Thousands View Bud Billiken Americanism Day Parade and Picnic," 17 Aug. 1940, p. 19.
"Was Slavery a Curse or a Blessing?," 7 Sept. 1929, pp. 1, 2.

Chicago Tribune

"First Day of Chicago Operation P.U.S.H. Viewed," 28 Sept. 1976, p. 1.
"Jesse Jackson Addresses Opening of Black Expo," 20 Sept. 1973, p. 3.
"Jesse Jackson Announces PUSH Expo '73," 31 July 1973, p. 2.
"Jesse Jackson Announces the Theme of PUSH Expo," 18 July 1974, p. 14.
"Jesse Jackson's Wife's Appearance at Expo Discussed," 20 Sept. 1973, p. 3.
"Opens P.U.S.H. Expo in Chicago," 25 Sept. 1975, p. 1.
"Plans for P.U.S.H. Expo '74," 26 Sept. 1974, p. 9.
"PUSH Expo '73 Praised," 17 Sept. 1973, p. 26.
"Speaks at P.U.S.H. Expo Breakfast," 27 Sept. 1974, p. 2.

Christian Science Monitor

"Black Americans: A Recognition," 19 Oct. 1983, p. 19.
"Efforts Renewed to Establish US Holiday Honoring Martin Luther King," 14 Jan. 1982, p. 4.

[Louisville] Courier-Journal

"Charlie Smith, 130, was the star of the annual centenarian reunion," 21 May 1973, p. A14.
"Taft's pitch was the first," 10 July 1978, p. B8.
"Your Turn: In a Time of Celebration in the South, American Blacks Face an Unfinished Task," 23 Aug. 1985, p. A13.

Indianapolis Recorder

"Demos in Giant Rally at Gary," 26 Sept. 1936, p. 1.
"8th Annual Emancipation and Carnival," 29 July 1905, p. 4.
"Emancipation Celebration," 21 Sept. 1901, p. 1.
"Emancipation Celebration Day!," 17 Sept. 1904, p. 1.
"Emancipation Celebration Day!," 24 Sept. 1904, p. 1.
"Emancipation Celebration! Monday Aug. 6," 4 Aug. 1906, p. 4.
"Emancipation Day," 26 Sept. 1908, p. 2.
"Emancipation Day," 14 Sept. 1912, p. 2.
"Emancipation Day Celebration!," 27 Aug. 1904, p. 4.
"Emancipation Day. The Grandest Celebration Ever Held in this Country," 5 Oct. 1889, p. 1.
"Ends in Politics: Emancipation Meeting Taken Advantage of. Colored People Very Indignant," 26 Sept. 1903, p. 1.
"Great Emancipation Affair," 29 July 1905, p. 4.
"Great Emancipation Day!," 30 July 1904, p. 4.
"Lest You Forget! Emancipation Day Celebration," 19 Sept. 1908, p. 4.

"New Albany Notes," 30 Sept. 1899, p. 1.
"On August 4,"25 July 1908, p. 1.

Los Angeles Times

"Director of Watts Summer Festival, Tommy Jacquette Interviewed," 18 Aug. 1973, p. 6.
"Disruptions Mar Watts Summer Music Concerts," 21 Aug. 1973, p. 3.
"8th Annual Watts Festival Parade Highlighted," 20 Aug. 1973, p. 3.
"8th Annual Watts Summer Festival Opens," 16 Aug. 1973, p. 1.
"8th Annual Watts Summer Festival Viewed," 14 Aug. 1973, p. 6.
"Ex-Watts Beauty Queens Featured," 7 March 1976, p. 3.
"Gwendelyn Bastiste Crowned Watts Summer Festival Queen," 8 Aug. 1974, p. 2.
"King holiday signed by Reagan: stirred our nation to its soul," 3 Nov. 1983, p. 4.
"7th Annual Watts Summer Festival Ends," 21 Aug. 1972, p. 3.

New York Times

"Congessional memorial to Dr. King stirs debate," 15 Sept. 1981, p. 14.
"Getting Ready for the Big Brooklyn Carnival," 18 Aug. 1974, p. 10B.
"Mondale endorsed by Vernon Jordan," 31 July 1984, p. A14.
"Negro Clergymen Plan Landon Drive: Bishop Sims Says His People Belong to Republican Party by History and Tradition," (Sept. 1936), 18L.
"President [Reagan] says he's sympathetic, but cautious on a King Holiday," 11 May 1982, p. B13.
"26 Negro Rallics Back Roosevelt: Meetings throughout the East Join 14,000 i Garden Here for New Deal Drive," 23 Sept. 1936, p. 41.41.

Philadelphia Tribune

"Historical Pageant: 'The Star of Ethiopia,' " 13, May 1916, n.p.
"1,700 Philadelphians Jam N.Y. Cotillion," 7 Jan. 1964, pp. 1, 7.
"To-Night, Saturday, 'The Star of Ethiopia,' " 20 May 1916, n.p.

Pittsburgh Courier

"Attention Voters in Courier Poll," 12 Jan. 1952, p. 17.
"Ballots Simplified for 1951–52 Courier Theatrical Poll Votes," 12 Jan. 1952, p. 16.
"Courier Poll Includes Everything this Time," 12 Jan. 1952, p. 16.
"Courier Theatrical Poll 1951—Musical Favorite—1952 Ballot No. 2," 19 Jan. 1952, p. 16.
"Courier Theatrical Poll Officially Closes March 8," 8 March 1952, p. 16.
"Duke, Bascomb, Cole, Tharpe, Mr. B. Lead Poll," 26 Jan. 1952, p. 16.
"Duke, Wright, Ward, Ravens and Williams on Top," 23 Feb. 1952, p. 16.
"Editor Set to Thin Ranks in Standings as Poll Nears End," 9 Feb. 1952, p. 16.

"Ernie Fields, Hamp, Cole, Central State, Ravens, Bascomb Up," 2 Feb. 1952, p. 16.
"Everything's Over But Concert: April 19 Is Big Day for Courier's Huge Jazz Fête," 22 March 1952, p. 16.
"Final Tabulations in Magazine April 19," 23 Feb. 1952, p. 16.
"My View: Emancipation was it January 1 or February 1," 26 Feb. 1972, p. 6.
"No More Poll Nominations," 9 Feb. 1952, p. 16.
"Nominations Pouring in for Poll—It's Not Too Late," 19 Jan. 1952, p. 16.
"Nominations Rolling in for Theatrical Poll," 19 Jan. 1952, p. 16.
"Poll Officially Closes February 23," 16 Feb. 1952, p. 16.
"Sarah, Dinah, Lena, Berle Enjoy Top of Ratings this Week," 26 Jan. 1952, p. 16.
"Shaefer, Calvert to Issue Trophies; Duke, Bob White, Cole, Wright Still Leading," 16 Feb. 1952, p. 16.
"Some of the Artists Who Always Rank High in Courier Polls," 12 Jan. 1952, p. 17.
"Theatrical Poll Nominees," 19 Jan. 1952, p. 16.
"Votes Will Be Accepted until March 5; Big Names Pulling up in Theatrical Popularity Poll," 1 March 1952, p. 16.
"Why Courier Poll Was Extended," 23 Feb. 1952, p. 16.

Terre Haute Evening Gazette

"Emancipation Celebration," 24 Sept. 1888, p. 1.
"Emancipation Celebration: The Way politics Was Dragged Into It . . . An Apology," 24 Sept. 1888, p. 1.

Terre Haute Tribune

"Colored Folk Have Elaborate Parade," 22 Sept. 1920, p. 8.
"Emancipation Day Proclamation," 22 Sept. 1918, p. 4.
"Honor Day of Emancipation: Colored People of the City Turn Out to Keep Anniversary Day of Freedom," 23 Sept. 1907, p. 2.
"Rival Parades held by Colored People," 22 Sept. 1921, p. 1.
"Will Ask a National Holiday for Negroes," 22 Sept. 1903, p. 1.

Wall Street Journal

"Martin Luther King Day brings scattered closings," 15 Jan. 1980, p. 10.
"Reagan signs bill to make King's birthday a holiday," 3 Nov. 1983, p. 22.

Washington Bee

"Eman, Ex-Comm," 2 May 1885, p. 3.
"Emancipation Day Anniversary. How It Will Be Celebrated," (April 1888), 1.
"Honorable Grover Cleveland, Pres. U.S.," 16 April 1887, p. 1.
"Mr. Cleveland . . . " 24 April 1886, p. 1."

Washington Post

"How we can observe this holiday," 23 Oct. 1983, p. C8.
"The King holiday: more than politics," 17 Aug. 1983, p. A23.
"King is saluted as President signs holiday into law," 3 Nov. 1983. p. A1.
"100 give thanks for passage of holiday measure," 20 Oct. 1983, p. A17.

Miscellaneous Newspapers

"A complicated Affair," *New York Age*, 9 Aug. 1980, p. 1.
Ashby, Lynn. "Juneteenth," *Houston Post*, 23 May 1980, n.p.
"Emam Muhammad Calls for 'genuine patriotism,'" *Bilalian News*, 22 July
    1977, p. 4.
"Emancipation rally a success despite Jackson's absence," *Indianapolis Star*,
    Late City Ed., 3 Jan. 1984, p. 26.
Fly, Richard. "Juneteenth holiday bill signed into law," *Houston Chronicle*, 14
    June 1979, n.p.
Knight, J.H. "Montgomery's Rev. King in Newport News: 'Two Worlds: The
    Dying Old, The Emerging News,'" *Norfork Journal and Guide*, 11 Jan.
    1958, p. 2.
Lewis, Boyd. "KKK is back with greater numbers, force," *Indiana Daily
    Student*, 6 Dec. 1978, p. 9.
"Segregation Still Target of NAACP," *Chattanooga News-Free Press*, Late City
    Ed., 2 Jan. 1973, Sec. 1, pp. 1, 2.
"This Is No Rib—It's Hot," *Windsor* [Ontario, Canada] *Star*, Late City Ed., 3
    Aug. 1957, p. 3.
"Valerie Dunn Crowned 'Miss Black Teenager,'" *Cleveland Call & Post*, 13
    Aug. 1977, Sec. A, p. 16.
Woolley, Bryan. "Juneteenth, Texas and Clay Smothers," *Dallas Times-Herald*,
    17 June 1979, n.p.

U.S. GOVERNMENT PUBLICATIONS AND RESOURCES

"Juneteenth Celebration: Extension of Remarks of Alan Wheat." *Congressional
    Record*. (15 June 1983), p. E2936.
"National Freedom Day." *Congressional Record*. 80th Cong., 2nd sess. (19
    June–31 Dec., 1948), Appendix, Vol. 94, part 12, pp. A4175–A5384 and
    A5175–A5177.
"National Freedom Day." Chapter 755-Public Law 842. *United States Code
    Congressional Service*. 80th Cong., 2nd Sess. (6 Jan.–7 Aug. 1948), Vol. 1
    (St. Paul, Minn., 1948), p. 838.
"National Negro History: Extension of Remarks of Hon. Charles C. Diggs of
    Michigan." *Congressional Record*. 84th Cong., 1st sess. (5 Jan.–2 Aug.,
    1955), Appendix, Vol. 101, part 2, p. 4972.
"Requesting the President to Proclaim February 1 as National Freedom Day."

Senate. 80th Cong., 1st sess. (3 Jan.–19 Dec., 1947), Misc., Vol. 4. Report on 761-Calendar No. 818.

U.S. Congress. House. Subcommittee on Census and Statistics of the Committee on Post Office and Civil Service. *Martin Luther King, Jr., Holiday Bill.* 98th Cong., 1st sess., H.R. 800 (Washington, D.C.: GPO, 1983).

U.S. Congress. House. Subcommittee on Census and Population of the Committee on Post Office and Civil Service. *Designate the Birthday of Martin Luther King, Jr., as a Legal Holiday.* 94th Cong., 1st sess., H.R. 1810 (Washington, D.C.: GPO, 1975).

U.S. Congress. Senate Committee on the Judiciary, House Committee on Post Office and Civil Service. *Martin Luther King, Jr., Holiday Bill.* 96th Cong., 1st sess., S. 25 (Washington, D.C.: GPO, 1979).

WPA 36-2 Florida Folklore Book II: Amusements, Contests, Dances, Festivals, Fiestas. WPA Folklore Papers. Manuscript Room, Library of Congress, Washington, D.C., n.d.

UNPUBLISHED SOURCES

Gravely, William B. "The Dialect of Double-Consciousness in Black Freedom Celebrations, 1808–1863." Paper presented at the annual meeting of the American Academy of Religion, Chicago, 10 Nov. 1973.

Wiggins, William H., Jr. " 'Did You See Jackie Robinson Hit that Ball?': The Impact of Jackie Robinson's Career on Race Relations in America." Paper given at Conference on Sports, St. Louis. 11 April 1983.

Sewell, Helen H. "Folktales from a Georgia Family: An Annotated Field Collection." M.A. Thesis, Indiana University, 1963.

CELEBRATION FLYERS AND PROGRAMS

Color Me Brown, Souvenir Program, 10 March 1967.

Nineteenth of June Celebration, Program/Flyer, 19 June 1947.

105th Anniversary of the Emancipation Proclamation of June 19th, Program/Flyer, 19 June 1972.

117th Annual Observance Emancipation Celebration of September 22nd, Program/Flyer, 20–21 Sept. 1980.

106th Annual Emancipation Homecoming of August 8th, Flyer, 8 Aug. 1975.

Recruitment Flyer:National Black Independent Party (NBIPP).

Seventy-Sixth Anniversary of the September 22nd Emancipation Celebration, Souvenir Program, 22 Sept. 1938.

31st Anniversary Celebration of National Freedom Day, Souvenir Program, 1 Feb. 1973.

Twelfth Anniversary Celebration of National Freedom Day, Souvenir Program, 1 Feb. 1961.

Twenty-Second Anniversary Celebration of National Freedom Day, Souvenir Program, 1 Feb. 1963.

FILMS AND VIDEO TAPES

The First World Festival of Negro Arts, UNESCO (1968).
Messenger from Violet Drive (1964).
Power and Prejudice in America, narr. Judy Woodruff, prod. and dir. Karen Thomas, The Film Company/PBS News Special, 25 June 1984.

RECORDS

Bland, Bobby "Blue." *Stormy Monday Blues.* Duke, 355, 1962.
Franklin, C.L. *The Eagle Stirreth Her Nest.* Chess, 9210-A, 9310-B, n.d.

INTERVIEWS AND CORRESPONDENCE

Ammons, Mr. William H. 13 Nov. 1972.
Ballad, Mrs. Juanita. 15 June 1972.
Bass, Mrs. Lula. 1 Jan. 1973.
Bennett, Mrs. Carrye. Letter to author. n.d. 1972.
Blakey, Mrs. Leila. 9 June 1972.
Borders, Dr. William Holmes. 30 Dec. 1972.
Burton, Mrs. Katherine. 14 Nov. 1972.
Cloud, Rev. C.C. 1 Jan. 1973.
Cook, Rev. J.C. 2 Jan. 1973.
Crisp, Mrs. Lillian. 19 June 1972.
Darby, Mr. Paul. 17 Nov. 1972.
Davis, Dr. John W. 1 Feb. 1973.
Donaldson, Mr. J. L. 17 Nov. 1972.
Edison, Miss Bon Ella. 14 Nov. 1972.
Felder, Mr. Robert E. 14 Nov. 1972.
Flanagan, Reverend Thomas J. 30 Dec. 1972.
Goode, Mr. Mal. 1 Feb. 1973.
Haney, Mr. David A. n.d. June 1978.
Henry, Mr. Judson. 14 Nov. 1972.
Hickman, Bishop Ernest L. 1 Feb. 1973.
Hogan, Booker T. Washington. 5 Nov. 1972.
Howell, Mr. William B. 1 Jan. 1973.
Hubert, Mrs. Agnes. 1 Jan. 1973.
Hygh, Mr. Haywood. Letter to author. 4 March 1972.
Hygh, Haywood, Jr. Letter to author. n.d.
Hygh, Mr. Willie. 16 June 1972.

Johnson, Mrs. Bennie Mae. Spring, 1973.
Joost, Johnny. 16 June 1972.
Kirby, Mrs. Ethyln. 1 Jan. 1973.
Lewis, Mrs. A.T. 17 June 1972.
Lomax-Hawes, Bess. Letter to author. n.d.
Lovelady, Mr. Artis. 17 June 1972.
Lyda, Dr. Wesley. 30 Sept. 1972.
Morgan, Mr. Charles. 13 Nov. 1972.
Morris, Mrs. Mary. 22 Aug. 1972.
Morton, Mr. Clarence. 5 Aug. 1972.
Parks, Mr. Allen. 30 Sept. 1972.
Parks, Reverend C.L. 18 June 1972.
Parks, Mrs. Ida L. 16 June 1972.
Perry, Mr. Robert Lee. 14 Nov. 1973.
Riggins, Mrs. Elva S. Letter to author. 11 April 1972.
Scott, Dr. Mingo. 18 Oct. 1972.
Smith, Mrs. Bennie Mae. 9 June 1972.
Smith, Rev. Marvin. 17 June 1972.
Smith, Mr. Orangie. 30 Sept. 1972.
Smith, Mr. Overton. 17 Nov. 1972.
Snorton, Mr. Claude. 5 Aug. 1972.
Stevenson, Mr. Robert Louis. Summer 1971.
Stevenson, Reverend William E. 1 Feb. 1973.
Striplin, Rev. C.A. 6 Aug. 1972.
Thomas, Dr. George B. 1 Jan. 1973.
Walker, Mrs. Rosie. 1 Jan. 1973.
Williams, Dr. Jimmie. 13 July 1972.
Williams, Rev. Kelly. 17 June 1972.
Williams, Mr. L. 16 June 1972.
Wilson, Mr. Jerry. 5 Nov. 1972.
Wood, Peter. Letter to author. 6 Aug. 1973.
Wright, Mr. Emanuel C. 2 Feb. 1973.
Wirth, Mrs. Mary Bolton. Letter to author. 16 Dec. 1973.

Index

O *Freedom!* was designed by Dariel Mayer; composed by The Composing Room of Michigan, Inc., Grand Rapids, Michigan; printed by Thomson-Shore, Inc., Dexter, Michigan; and bound by John H. Dekker & Sons, Grand Rapids, Michigan. The book is set in 10/13 Sabon with Sabon display and is printed on 60-lb. Glatfelter.